# THE LAST
# BLUE WATER LINERS

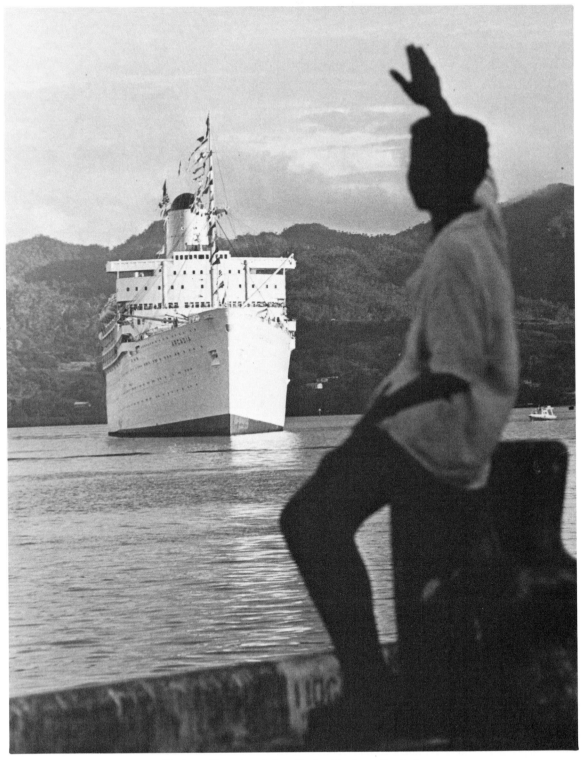

*During a 'line voyage', from England to Australia via the Suez and homeward via the Pacific, North America and the Caribbean, P&O-Orient's* Arcadia *calls at Suva in Fiji.*

# THE LAST
# BLUE WATER LINERS

## William H. Miller

THE LAST BLUE WATER LINERS Copyright © 1986 by
William H. Miller. All rights reserved. Printed in Great
Britain. No part of this book may be used or reproduced in
any manner whatsoever without written permission except
in the case of brief quotations embodied in critical articles or
reviews. For information, address St. Martin's Press,
175 Fifth Avenue, N.Y., 10010.

Design by Tony Garrett

First published by Conway Maritime Press Limited, 24 Bride
Lane, Fleet Street, London EC4Y 8DR.

CIP DATA TK
Miller, William H., 1948–
   The last blue water liners.

   1. Ocean liners – History.    I. Title.
VM381.M449  1986     387.2'432     86–3934

ISBN 0-312-46980–2

First U.S. Edition

10  9  8  7  6  5  4  3  2  1

## AUTHOR'S NOTE

Nearly forty passenger ship firms are included in this
book; had it not been for the limitations imposed by
its size, there might have been an even greater
number. Certainly, firms such as the Booth Line and
Pacific Steam Navigation, the Compagnie Paquet and
Nouvelle Paquebots, Naviera Aznar, the Grace and
Moore-McCormack lines and the Cogedar, Matson,
American President and Orient Overseas lines had a
perfect right to be included. In most cases, they and
their ships will appear in a sequel – a contemporary
history of ocean cruising and round-trip sailings. I
have included in this book, however, what might be
considered some of the more important and interesting liners – the last fleet to offer 'line voyages'.

The tonnage figures used are those most commonly
quoted during the passenger ships' final years. All
tonnages listed are for gross tonnage. Accommodation figures are also variable; those used are the most
accepted configurations.

# CONTENTS

## 8: THE LAST LINE VOYAGES

## APPENDIX:

## BIBLIOGRAPHY

## INDEX

# INTRODUCTION

For my summer travels in 1973 I made something of a sentimental journey – a round-trip crossing of the North Atlantic by liner, a trade then almost in its final twilight. For years and years, I had watched the big Atlantic liners at New York – the 'Queens' and other Cunarders, the record-breaking *United States* and so many more. However, by the early seventies, they had all but disappeared completely, decisively pushed from their trades and their economic well-being by the aggressive, merciless jet. I sailed eastbound in the stunning *France*, the last of the grand French liners, but even she was running short on time. Two-thirds full and struggling against insurmountable operating costs, she would – much to our surprise – last little more than another fourteen months (until September 1974). After a five-day passage, we steamed up the Solent and into Southampton's Ocean Terminal, a rather imposing postwar creation which now, too, has gone. Although Southampton Docks had seen busier days, there were at least a few visible reminders of 'other' liners from 'other' trades: P&O's *Orsova* and Union-Castle's *Windsor Castle* in the Western Docks, Elder Dempster's *Aureol* on the outer side of the old Empress Dock and Sitmar's *Fairsky* laid-up at the inner bulkhead of the Ocean Dock. Homebound, aboard the Italian Line's *Raffaello*, from Naples to New York, I came across another Italian, the *Donizetti*, at Genoa; Spain's *Satrustegui* also lying idle at Barcelona and Companhia Colonial's *Imperio* at Lisbon. Each of these passenger ships ran 'line voyages', those great port-to-port sailings out to such areas as Australia, South and East Africa, the west coast of South America and the Caribbean. If their lives were not already over, they were nearing their final days.

In earlier years, during my summer afternoon visits to the great steamship company offices of Lower Manhattan, I recall seeing special selections of brochures of evocative foreign firms like Blue Star, Bibby, British India, Lloyd Triestino, Ybarra and Royal Mail. There seemed to be dozens of these firms, which together ran hundreds of passenger liners. On long voyages, they travelled to Buenos Aires and Bombay, Mombasa and Melbourne, Singapore and Santos.

In the early seventies, the unstoppable intrusion of the jet-aircraft would finish off almost all of the last of these 'line voyages'. Those long-established runs to Latin America, Africa, the Far East and elsewhere would soon be the exclusive domain of a new fraternity with corporate names such as British Airways, Lufthansa, Alitalia and Qantas.

The shipping firms and their liners would also face other problems: the huge transition to containerized cargo services, escalating operational costs, more frequent strikes and other disruptions, and even stiff new maritime regulations and codes that ageing passenger ships were unable to pass, at least not without costly refits and modernizations. When the cost of fuel oil skyrocketed from $35 to $95 per ton in 1973–74, it was impossible thereafter for many ships to earn even the smallest profit, even if filled to the very last upper berth. Thus the fate of many liners, about whose future only the slightest doubts had been held, was sealed.

In solemn boardroom decisions, the shipowners were faced with the harsh realities: close their long-established passenger services and sell off their ships. Most of them, such as the aforementioned *Orsova*, would steam off – partially stripped, rusting and lonely, and manned by a small crew – on a final journey to the scrappers. Almost invariably, this final destination was Kaohsiung on Taiwan, home of the most voracious ship-breakers on earth. Over eighty per cent of the ships listed in these pages finished their careers in that Eastern port. Once there, near lifeless ships might wait at a desolate harbour anchorage, possibly surrounded by other forlorn and out-of-work freighters, tankers and even another liner, before being brought to an inner berth. Often, these ships would be run aground deliberately. The last crew would then go ashore, the master as company representative would sign the final legal documents and then, without ceremony or notice of any sort, the ship-breakers would take possession. A cruel task followed: men with hammers, axes and acetylene torches would rip away at the wheelhouses and empty officers' mess rooms, the musty smoking rooms and barren little first class bars, the stripped staterooms and the long, quiet but odour-filled kitchens. Piece by piece, the remains would be brought ashore, and then taken away, mostly for some form of recycling. In a matter of a few months, all that would remain would be the rusted, scarred hulk that would be gradually hauled ashore and cut-up as well. Hardly anyone but a small crew of workers even noticed these last rites. Certainly, there are very few photographic records available. How lonely it must have been for the final days of such once glorious and majestic liners as the *Himalaya* and *Arcadia*, the *Athlone Castle*, the *Vera Cruz*, the *Giulio Cesare* and the *Libertad*.

Some other liners did, however, find new life. A fortunate few were converted and re-adapted for that most profitable venture of passenger shipping – pleasure cruising. Former African colonial liners might now ply the lazy waters of the Aegean, others are among the Caribbean islands or in the South Pacific. Some former liners went to less recognizable second and even third owners, who have had them rebuilt as car carriers, sheep carriers and stationary accommodation and recreation centres. About a fifth of the ships listed herein still survive, but mostly in non-passenger roles.

Except for just a very few companies mentioned rather briefly in the final chapter, the era of the 'line voyage' is gone forever. This book has been created for a nostalgic recollection of these extinct trades.

William H Miller,
Jersey City, New Jersey, Summer 1985.

## ACKNOWLEDGEMENTS

This book was sparked off to a large extent by its predecessor, *The Last Atlantic Liners*, published at the end of 1984. Just as there had to be more of a record for those final transatlantic ships, so too for those ships which were the last to make the famed 'line voyages' – to Latin America, Australia, Africa, the Middle East and the Orient. I dedicate this book to a man who knew some of these ships and their trading conditions in superb detail. John Havers had some fifteen years with the illustrious Union-Castle Line and most generously, in the quiet comfort of his garden in Winchester, he shared many of his most detailed memories of his 'life with the liners'. I am deeply indebted to him.

Very special gratitude also goes to C M Squarey, for his writings on the postwar liners, particularly with reference to their interiors; to Luis Miguel Correia, a wonderfully skilled photographer at Lisbon; to Dr David Kirkham, who shared his many recollections of Southeast Asian passenger shipping while we were aboard the cruise ship *Princess Mahsuri*, out of Singapore in the summer of 1984; and to two excellent dockside photographers, F Leonard Jackson and Stanley Rawlings.

Important and enlightening anecdotes, conversations, memories and specially requested materials were provided by Captain Bob Ellingham, Captain Philip Jackson, Captain Terry Russell, David Llewhellin and John Smith at P&O; Len Wilton at Safmarine Lines; David Carr, formerly with P&O and now serving with Cunard; the noted maritime journalist James L Shaw; veteran traveller Leslie Shaw; Captain Elvio Arimondo and Emile Girault at Costa Line; Jeremy Gray and Jan Lee at Blue Funnel Cruises in Singapore; J Goossens and C Vermuyten at Compagnie Maritime Belge in Antwerp; Andrew Bell at Curnow Shipping Limited at Porthleven in Cornwall; Bob Cummins, who has served with a great number of British passenger firms; John Draffin, formerly with New Zealand Shipping Co; Eric Brown, formerly with the Anchor Line and now serving with Cunard; Neville Gordon, formerly with British India; Peter Eisele, editor of the very fine *Steamboat Bill*, the journal of the Steamship Historical Society of America; Frank Duffy, public relations director at Moran Towing & Transportation Co in New York and Richard K Morse, who has graciously offered his extraordinary ocean liner photo collection.

Photographs, especially new and exciting ones, mean something special to passenger ship enthusiasts and historians. To provide a new set of views, I have had the most valuable assistance of Stephen Rabson and John Steele at P&O; and Jeff Blinn, J K Byass, Michael Cassar, Alex Duncan, Jim Fost, Fred Hawks, Michael Lennon, Vincent Messina, Hisashi Noma, Antonio Scrimali, Sal Scannella, Victor Scrivens, James Sesta, Roger Sherlock, Captain Cornelius van Herk, Everett Viez and H J Wood. Firms and other organizations which assisted include the Argentine State Line, Companhia Portugesa de Transportes Maritimas, Elder Dempster Lines, French Line, Holland-Africa Line, Italian Line Cruises International, Leif Hoegh & Co, Shaw Savill & Albion Line, Sitmar Cruises, Skyfotos, Spanish Line, Union-Castle Line and the World Ship Society's Photo Library.

Other much appreciated material and recollections were supplied by Frank Andrews, Pam Cunningham, E Drummond, Roland Hasell, David Hutchings, Neil McCart, M H Pryce and Leonard Weir. Special thanks to Conway Maritime Press for acccepting the project.

*The* Strathaird, *flying her 'paying-off' penant, leaves Tilbury for the last time, on 24 June 1961. She is bound for scrapyards in the Far East.*

Richard K Morse Collection

# CHAPTER ONE

# AROUND THE WORLD WITH P&O

In 1960, one of the final years of a very extensive worldwide passenger ship network, two of Britain's best-known and busiest passenger shipping firms, the famed P&O Line (the Peninsular & Oriental Steam Navigation Company Limited) and the Orient Line, merged their services. Since both companies primarily traded to Australia, it seemed a sensible decision. Futhermore, the combination of their ships would allow for a very important extension of their trade into the vast Pacific, the 'last frontier of passenger shipping', according to one P&O director. The combination of these two companies to form P&O–Orient Line, (a name adopted in 1960 and then discontinued, reverting solely to P&O six years later) created the largest deep-sea passenger ship fleet then in existence. P&O contributed the greater number of ships: the four 'Straths' – *Strathaird, Strathnaver, Strathmore* and *Stratheden*, three other prewar ships: the *Carthage, Corfu* and *Canton*, and then a sizeable postwar generation of successively larger or improved ships: the *Himalaya, Chusan, Arcadia, Iberia* and the biggest of all, in fact the largest ocean liner yet built for a service other than the North Atlantic, the 45,700-ton flagship *Canberra*, which was still at the builder's yard at Belfast and due for delivery in spring 1961. The Orient Line added a string of their famed 'O Boats' — the prewar *Orontes* and *Orion* and then the postwar *Orcades, Oronsay, Orsova* and a slightly smaller yet faster companion to the aforementioned new P&O flagship, the *Oriana*, which was nearing completion at Barrow-in-Furness. Also, soon after the merger, as the combined companies recognized that some of the older, prewar ships were soon destined for the scrap-heap, two Belgian combination passenger-cargo liners were acquired especially for the auxiliary run to the Far East. These became the *Cathay* and *Chitral* by the spring of 1961.

P&O-Orient was said to offer more 'line voyages' than any other firm, British or otherwise, at the time, with schedules listing voyages that touched at over a hundred ports on five continents. As an example of their expectionally wide range, in a sample day, the *Orontes* was at London, the *Chusan* at Southampton, the *Orcades* at Gibraltar, the *Stratheden* at Naples, the *Carthage* at Port Said, the *Himalaya* at sea off Ceylon, the *Oronsay* at Melbourne, the *Arcadia* at Kobe, the *Orsova* at Los Angeles and the *Iberia* homeward bound from Port Everglades and Bermuda to London. P&O-Orient employed a sea-going staff of over 6000, serving aboard over 300,000 tons of passenger ships.

While this fleet was later to feel the full effects of airliner competition, containerized freight services (all of the P&O liners relied to a considerable extent on their cargo capacities) and even new, strict regulations for older ships flying the British flag, it remained unchanged for the most part until as late as the early seventies. This was long after shipping companies on the transatlantic run, such as the once mighty Cunard Line, had been hard-hit by a losing battle with the jet. By the mid-sixties Cunard had begun something of a wholesale reduction of its fleet, which included retirement of the two 'Queens', *Queen Mary* and *Queen Elizabeth*. Initially, the P&O-Orient Lines were concerned only with retiring their older, less efficient passenger ships.

The ORONTES

The Orient Line's *Orontes* was the last two-funnelled, black-hulled passenger liner in the P&O-Orient fleet. Commissioned in July 1929, from the Vickers-Armstrongs yard at Barrow-in-Furness, she was one of five near-sisters that were the biggest, fastest and finest Orient Line ships yet. They were the arch-rivals to the P&O liners on the same Australian run, from London via the Mediterranean and the Suez, out to Brisbane, Fremantle, Melbourne and Sydney. The *Orama*, the first of the group, was delivered in the autumn of 1924 and was followed by the *Oronsay* in February 1925, the *Otranto* in the following December, the *Orford* in October 1928 and finally, almost as something of an after-thought, the *Orontes*.

*P&O's* Strathaird *at the London Docks. She and the* Strathnaver *were known as the 'white sisters'.*

Being just short of 20,000 tons, the *Orontes* had accommodation for 500 in first class, which was easily convertible for high-standard cruise quarters as well, and for 1112 in third class, the most lucrative on the Australian trade, just as steerage class had been in earlier years on the North Atlantic. Similar to P&O and others, the Orient Line was supported by a steady flow of outbound migrants, mostly British, who were seeking a 'new life' in Australia. On their outward voyages these liners were often filled to the very last bunk.

Costing some £950,000 to build, the accommodation aboard the *Orontes* and her sisters made them highly popular summer-time cruise ships as well. Initially the *Orontes* travelled to the Norwegian fjords for thirteen-day periods, with rates beginning at £10, and to the Atlantic Isles (the Canaries and Madeira) for a fortnight, with fares from £11.

Requisitioned by the Government for trooping soon after the Second World War started, the *Orontes* remained in military service until as late as 1947. She was one of two of the original class that survived the hostilities. The *Orama* was sunk in the North Sea in June 1940, the *Orford* bombed off Marseilles in the same month and the *Oronsay* was torpedoed off West Africa in October 1942. The fourth ship and other survivor, the *Otranto*, was returned to the Orient Line in 1948, but then rebuilt solely for the migrant trade with 1412 all-tourist class berths only. She was never again used in the normal luxury trade and endured until scrapped in Scotland in 1957.

Once decommissioned, the *Orontes* underwent a million pound refit and overhaul by Thornycroft at Southampton. Postwar ship repair and construction costs had reached such a high level that the ship's restoration amounted to more than her actual building costs nearly two decades earlier. Repainted and looking as handsome as in her prewar guise, the *Orontes* – with modified accommodation for 502 in first class and 610 in tourist class – left the Tilbury Docks at London, on 17 June 1948, bound for Fremantle, Melbourne and Sydney via the Suez Canal. This was to be her employment for the remainder ot her sea-going career.

At first, she was matched with the brand-new *Orcades* of 1948, then the fastest ship on the Australia run (which cut the passage time from five to four weeks), and another prewar ship, the *Orion* of 1935. The *Otranto* ran the all-migrant sailings along with another veteran, the *Ormonde* of 1918. Later, when ships were planned, namely the *Oronsay* of 1951 and the *Orsova* of 1954, the *Orontes* replaced the migrant-class *Ormonde* on low-fare sailings. In 1953, her two-class quarters were converted to one-class only, giving a total of 1410 berths.

The *Orontes* had six passenger decks, a series of public rooms, two dining rooms and cabins with two, three, four, and six berths. Very few of these cabins had private bathroom facilities. The ship had punkah-louvre ventilation throughout. In her final years, her voyages were routed as London, Gibraltar, Naples, Port Said, Aden, Colombo, Fremantle, occasionally Adelaide, Melbourne and Sydney and then homeward in reverse order, but with an added call at Marseilles. Her final years were not without incident, however. Captain Bob Ellingham served aboard her and recalled a visit to Marseilles. 'In 1961, we were swept at 100 mph by the infamous mistral [a notorious wind] from the breakwater to the dock, dragging the tugs and anchors as well. We rammed the dock, finishing with a big hole in the stern. Fortunately, there were no casualties. We kept the passengers onboard for the night and then sent them by train to Paris and then to London. Temporary repairs were made after which we took the empty *Orontes* home to England for a thorough patching. Rather ironically, I also met my future wife on this trip.'

Soon after the P&O-Orient Line merger, the *Orontes*, at nearly thirty-three years of age, was among the first candidates selected for disposal. Shortly after completing her final homeward voyage to London, she was sold for breaking-up to Ordaz & Company, of Valencia in Spain. In the winter of 1962, Captain Ellingham was again aboard the 'old girl', as she was then called in the fleet, and among the fifty-odd crew that took her to the scrapyard. 'We crept along, taking sixteen days from Tilbury. At sea, we were advised that we could have any keepsakes we wished. With no time for shipping arrangements from Spain, this was rather disappointing as the ship was still fully fitted: bedding, linen, silverware, furniture and even the old grand piano.'

### The STRATHNAVER and STRATHAIRD

In the fifties, Captain Philip Jackson served aboard the famed P&O 'Straths', the twins *Strathnaver* and *Strathaird* of 1931–32, the *Strathmore* of 1935 and then the *Stratheden* from 1937. 'At the time, the P&O procedure was fairly well established. A third mate's position on a freighter [Captain Jackson had then most recently served aboard the cargo liner *Somali* on the Far Eastern run] led to a third mate's role on a passenger ship. My first assignments were on the earliest of the very well known 'Strath' liners, the *Strathnaver* and *Strathaird*. They were then still two-class ships [573 in first class and 496 in tourist class].

The passengers in first class seemed to rattle around in very spacious quarters. These were mostly service and commercial people, the equivalent of today's airline first and club classes. In the tourist-class section, we had mostly migrants, who were travelling under a special fare of £10. The Australian Government wanted to increase its population, and especially to expand its competitive technological force. These low fares were offered for outward resettlement passages. Homebound, we would carry many Australian families, who would be on three to six month cultural or family visits to Britain and continental Europe.'

During the fifties, the four 'Straths' worked a balanced schedule between London, Gibraltar, Aden, Bombay, Colombo, Adelaide, Fremantle, Melbourne and Sydney. Captain Jackson recalled, 'We had 2½ weeks at the Tilbury Docks near London for loading and unloading of cargo, which was then very much a part of our liner operation. For the passengers, tugs would later move these liners [and all other P&O-Orient passenger ships] to the Tilbury Landing Stage for four to five hours, and meet the special 'boat trains' that were down from Fenchurch Street Station. Of course, physically, the 'Straths' and all subsequent 9 liners were different from the rest of the fleet in that they had white hulls and yellow funnels. Our freighters and earlier passenger steamers had black hulls and black funnels. The white passenger ships were made to appear light and tropical looking, they were easier to maintain and they were, in fact, ten degrees cooler inside. There was very limited air-conditioning on the 'Straths' or any other P&O liners until the late fifties.'

When designed and built by Vickers-Armstrongs at Barrow-in-Furness, in 1931–32, the *Strathnaver* and *Strathaird* were a radical departure from all previous P&O liners. Most noticeably and importantly, they adopted the white hull and yellow funnel for the first time and were known for all of their lives as the 'white sisters'. Built as a response to the Orient Line's new generation of 'O Boats', which included the 20,000-ton *Orontes*, the 'Straths', which even adopted a new naming scheme (previous P&O passenger ships had mostly geographical names of overseas origin), were planned to be the finest and fastest ships yet on the Australian run. They were, in fact, the first P&O liners to have running water in all passenger cabins regardless of class.

As expected, the first class accommodation was superb. All of A Deck was the first class sun and sports area. The public rooms consisted of a main lounge, verandah lounge, smoking room, a reading-writing room, a dance hall, twin corridor lounges and a verandah café. There was also a large dining room, a children's nursery and playground, and an open-air swimming pool. Many cabins, most of which were either single or double berth, had private bathrooms.

The *Strathnaver* was handed over to P&O in September 1931, after completing a series of highly successful trials, including a run at over 23 knots (17½ knots was the intended operating speed). The *Strathaird* followed in January 1932. Similar to other large P&O and Orient liners of the time, these ships divided their work between Australian voyages and holiday cruises. Two classes were used even for the latter voyages; in the mid-thirties a two-week Mediterranean cruise cost £15 in first class and £12 in tourist class. Despite the harsh economic conditions of the Depression, these 'Strath' sisters were among the very first and most popular liners to introduce ocean cruising to the general British public. At approximately 'a pound a day', many were able to escape, at least briefly, the hard times at home.

Although the new sisters were revolutionary and innovative in many ways, two of the design decisions were based on experiences with earlier company passenger ships. P&O directors felt that three funnels were a symbol of size and might and had used them rather successfully once before, aboard the sisters *Naldera* and *Narkunda* of 1918–20. Furthermore, three- and especially four-funnel liners on the prestigious North Atlantic run were among the most successful ships of all time. Therefore, the three-funnel design was selected for the new 'Straths'. In reality, only the middle funnel was functional; the first and third were dummies and placed aboard only for effect. However, the idea was less than successful in that it seemed to destroy the ships' modern image. It was not used for subsequent liners, namely the *Strathmore* of 1935, as she was designed from the start with a single 'working stack'. During their extensive postwar refits, the *Strathnaver* and *Strathaird* had their dummy stacks removed and thereafter looked very similar to their near-sisters *Strathmore* and *Stratheden*.

In selecting machinery for their propulsion, the company had been quite pleased with the *Viceroy of India*, the London-to-Bombay express liner of 1929, which had turbo-electric drive. Several other shipping firms were experimenting with this as well and, most notable of all, the French planned to use it in their giant, record-breaking *Normandie* of 1935. P&O felt confident and installed steam turbo-electric machinery in the *Strathnaver* and *Strathaird*. Once again, however, the choice was less than satisfactory. When the *Strathmore* was commissioned in 1935, she had the more customary steam geared turbines.

Both the *Strathnaver* and *Strathaird* gave heroic service during the war. Stripped, painted over in grey and recertified to carry as many as 5000 troops under emergency conditions (the *Strathaird* evacuated over 6000 desperate French citizens from Brest in June 1940), they sailed out to Australia and New Zealand, helped to reinforce the Middle East and North Africa, carried thousands of Indian troops and even crossed the North Atlantic out of American ports. Both took part in one of the war's most impressive convoys of troop transports, sailing from Australia and New Zealand for the Middle East in January 1940. The cruiser HMS *Kent* led Canadian Pacific's *Empress of Japan* and *Empress of Canada*, Orient Line's *Orcades* and New Zealand Shipping Company's *Rangitata*. The battleship HMS *Ramillies* led the Orient Line's *Orion* and *Orford*, and British India's *Dunera*. Finally, the French carrier *Suffren* led both the *Strathaird* and *Strathnaver* along with the Orient Line's *Otranto* and the Polish Ocean Lines' *Sobieski*.

The *Strathnaver* nearly became a wartime casualty when, on 11 November 1942, steaming into the port of Algiers, she was caught in a sudden enemy air attack. After several near hits, she set off for Bougie, also in Algeria, and arrived during very heavy torpedo and minelaying attacks. P&O's *Cathay* and British India's *Karanja* were ablaze nearby. Once again, the *Strathnaver* was very fortunate to have escaped without damages or casualties.

The *Strathaird*, after completing her Government duties in late 1946, went back to her builder's yard at Barrow-in-Furness for a thorough restoration. She resumed commercial service in January 1948. The *Strathnaver* was not released from military service until November 1948, and was then sent to the Harland & Wolff yards at Belfast for conversion. She returned to the P&O schedules in January 1950. Both of these older 'Straths', along with the *Strathmore* and *Stratheden*, assisted the brand-new *Himalaya* on the Australian run. The veteran sisters *Maloja* and *Mooltan* from the early twenties worked the migrant service, carrying one-class passengers only. Several years later, in 1954, as the brand-new near-sisters *Arcadia* and *Iberia* were about to come into service, the older migrant ships were sold for scrapping and the *Strathaird* and *Strathnaver*, once the pride of the P&O fleet, were relegated to one-class, low-fare sailings only. Their postwar accommodation, listed as 573 berths in first class and 496 in tourist class, were combined to create 1252 all-tourist class berths.

Author Neil McCart, in his article 'The Two White Sisters', wrote that the *Strathaird* had two further incidents of note in her distinguished career in the late fifties. On 15 February 1958, she made an emergency call at Djakarta to evacuate Dutch nationals from politically troubled Indonesia. A year later, on 24 June, while off Singapore, she valiantly rescued two airmen from a downed Tiger Moth.

The *Strathaird* was also among the first casualities of the P&O-Orient merger in 1960. Shortly afterward, the company announced from its London headquarters that this ship, the eldest of the surviving 'Strath' quartet, was to be retired at Tilbury on 18 June 1961. She was to be replaced by none other than the brand-new superliner *Canberra*. The two ships met off Port Said on 8 June. The elder ship radioed to the new P&O flagship: 'You look magnificent and all in *Strathaird* wish you a happy and successful maiden voyage, and from the old to the new, *Strathaird* bids you farewell'. The *Canberra* responded: 'You too look magnificent with your paying-off penant flying gaily. You look a gracious and not too elderly lady. All well here.'

On 24 June the *Strathaird* left Tilbury for the last time and reached Hong Kong, where she would be scrapped, on 27 July. She had been sold to the Shung Fung Ironworks for £382,500. By the end of the year, with demolition well underway, it was announced that her steel was being recycled for use in the construction of a new Hong Kong housing complex. The *Strathnaver*, which was to continue sailing well into 1962, had her schedule abruptly shortened following a change in plans with the Australian Government's migrant contract. She finished her P&O service on 23 February 1962, and arrived at Hong Kong on 2 April for breaking-up. Also sold to the Shung Fung Ironworks, she fetched a slightly lower price of £325,000. The first of the 'Straths' had finished exactly thirty years of very popular and profitable service.

### The Corfu and Carthage

In addition to its far better known run to Australia, P&O ran a secondary passenger and cargo service out to the Far East. The routing was from London to Port Said, Aden, Bombay, Colombo, Penang, Singapore, Hong Kong and then in reverse order on the return journey (in later years, this would be extended to include Japanese ports as well). The two largest ships for this service yet built were created at the same time as the *Strathnaver* and *Strathaird*. They were ordered from the Clyde, however, from Alexander Stephen & Sons Limited at Glasgow. It was intended they should be named *Chefoo* and *Canton*, but they were completed instead as the *Corfu* and *Carthage* respectively.

Stanley W Rawlings

At 14,300 tons each, they had appropriate accommodation for the Far Eastern trade: some 175 berths in first class and 200 in second class. There were no extensive quarters for tourist class or third class accommodation for migrants. The *Corfu* was delivered in October 1931, the *Carthage* a month later. Although used almost continuously on their intended route, the *Corfu* did make three special round-trip voyages to Melbourne and Sydney in 1932.

Both ships had rather traditional P&O looks: two rather widely spaced black funnels, two masts, light stone-coloured superstructures and black hulls. While the P&O management were very pleased with the white hulls and yellow funnels on the new 'Straths', this look was not extended to rest of the passenger fleet until after the Second World War. In fact, some passenger ships, such as the vintage *Maloja* and *Mooltan*, which sailed until the early fifties, retained their black hulls and black funnels until the very end. Among other possible reasons, the company

*Seen through the lattice steel leg of a crane in the London Docks in the fifties is* Carthage, *offloading cargo from Eastern ports. In the foreground, Glen Line's* Denbighshire, *which carried eighteen passengers and freight on the Far Eastern route as well.*

evidently felt that the lighter colouring would not enhance some of the older ships.

Both the *Corfu* and *Cathage* were called to war duty soon after the German invasion of Poland. They were refitted as armed merchant cruisers and sailed for the Royal Navy. In 1943, the *Carthage* was outfitted as a troop ship and the *Corfu* followed suit a year later. Both were decommissioned in 1947 and sent to the Clyde for their postwar refits. It was the ideal opportunity for some modernization work: the original second 'dummy' funnels were removed, the remaining single stack painted in yellow, the hulls were done in more tropical white and the passenger quarters modified slightly to 181 berths in first class

Stanley W Rawlings

*P&O Group*

*Shielded from harsh sea breezes, the first class pool aboard the* Orion *was positioned just forward of the ship's aft cargo hatches.*

and 213 in tourist. By the end of 1948, both ships had returned to the Far East run. They were teamed with the 16,000-ton *Canton*, an improved and larger version of the same design that had been finished in 1938. The trio rotated their sailings from London and Southampton.

Like the other prewar P&O liners, the P&O-Orient merger spelled these ships' end. Early in 1961, they were sold to the Mitsui Company of Osaka for scrapping. Upon completing their final homeward P&O voyages, they were prepared for the final delivery trips, carrying a mere forty members each, as the *Carthage Maru* and the *Corfu Maru*. The *Carthage Maru* reached Osaka in May; the *Corfu Maru* went to Niihama in August.

### The ORION

Frank Andrews, then a youngster fascinated by the great liners docking at his native Melbourne, recalled the first appearance of the Orient Line's *Orion* of 1935. 'She was the first ship on the Australian run that could seriously rival, in fact surpass, some ships on the more famous North Atlantic run. Everything about her was new and fresh: the first large liner to have just a single

*With the bow of the* Himalaya *just to the left the* Orion *is seen in the Tilbury Docks in the mid-fifties; her boats being lowered in a Board of Trade inspection.*

mast, her corn-coloured hull and her exceptionally modern passenger accommodation. She introduced art deco to the Pacific: the light woods, bright public spaces and a total feeling of exceptional spaciousness. To all of us who watched ships on the Australian run, the *Orion* was a very radical departure from the traditional. She was, of course, the Orient Line's answer to P&O's 'Strath' ships. By far, she was the superior ship.'

The *Orion*, ordered as was typical of the Orient Line from the Vickers-Armstrongs yard at Barrow-in-Furness, was the first of a pair of sisters. The slightly different *Orcades* followed two years later, in 1937, with a noticeably taller stack. Launched on 7 December 1934, the *Orion* was commissioned in the following summer, being introduced with a special cruise to the Mediterranean. During the return of this trip, on 5–6 December, she performed an heroic mission. Mr Leslie Shaw of Rainham in Kent was aboard the 16,400-ton Cunard-White Star liner *Doric*, which was also returning from a late summer cruise. 'We were about forty miles off Oporto, in the thickest fog, when we collided with the French steamer *Formigny*. I had gone to bed after the cinema, at 10 o'clock, but was awakened at three in the morning. We were told of the collision and that we must prepare to leave the *Doric*. She was already listing about seven or eight degrees. Women and then some blind ex-soldiers were put in the lifeboats first. I was among those transferred at eight in the morning, carrying our own bags into the lifeboats, and sent off on a dead flat sea. Two lifeboats were towed by one motorized lifeboat. Just before we left the *Doric*, we were asked which rescue ship we preferred: P&O's *Viceroy of India* or the brand-new Orient liner *Orion*. The 800 passengers from the *Doric* were to be divided evenly, 400 to each ship. I went to the *Viceroy of India* and recall being served a cold breakfast soon after we went aboard. We then sailed home to Tilbury. It was the first of dozens of subsequent voyages for me aboard P&O-Orient liners.'

The *Orion* finally entered the Australian trade, leaving London on 29 September, for Gibraltar, Naples, Port Said, Aden, Colombo, Fremantle, Adelaide, Melbourne and Sydney. As was the custom with most major P&O and Orient liners, there was a homeward call at Marseilles. Many passengers found this convenient, either wanting a fast return to Britain by taking a train across France and then one of the Channel ferries or simply wanting to avoid the notorious Bay of Biscay. Mr Shaw recalled one of his frequent short holidays in the thirties. 'We would take the night train out of London to Paris and then to the south of France. At Marseilles, I remember boarding the P&O *Narkunda* for the five-day homeward run to London. It was the ideal fortnight and cost about £10.'

The *Orion* was called to duty almost immediately after the German invasion of Poland, in September 1939. Converted to a troop transport, she was listed as having a wartime capacity of 5449, a dramatic increase from her peacetime figure of 1139. The only mishaps seems to have been a collision during an Indian Ocean convoy with the battleship HMS *Revenge* on 15 September 1941. While both ships suffered damage, repairs were quickly made. Her sistership was far less fortunate, however. Also converted to a trooper in the autumn of 1939, the *Orcades* was bound from Capetown to England, on 10 October 1942, when she was hit by two torpedoes from the German submarine *U 172*. At sea, some 300 miles west of the Cape of Good Hope, her 1000 passengers and troops took to the lifeboats. In all, there were forty-eight casualties. While an attempt was made to sail her to port with a small, but very loyal crew, she was, in fact, too badly damaged and had to be abandoned and allowed to sink.

The *Orion* returned to her builder's yard in 1946 and was restored, with accommodation for 546 first class and 706 tourist class passengers. She resumed her Australian sailings, leaving London for the first time on 25 February 1947. She was soon joined by the new *Orcades*, delivered at the end of 1948. Thereafter, while the sailings of both the P&O and Orient lines became more and more integrated, there were definite differences between the two firms. Captain Ellingham recounted, 'The Orient Line differed from their P&O counterpart in that Orient had all-European crews. The P&O line had British officers

*The idea of painting the 'Strath' liners with all-white hulls, which it was hoped would reduce onboard temperatures, was a great success. After the Second World War, all P&O's new liners were treated similarly. The Strathmore, completed in 1935, had the classic good looks that were a trademark of the company for several decades.*

and some European crew, but mostly Goanese and Lascars from India. The Orient liners were each quite superb in their overall design and decoration, possibly the best on the "Aussie" run at the time. First class accommodation was situated forward on the upper deck; tourist class was aft. The tourist sections were almost always fully booked by the British Government for outward migrants. It was quite rare to have available space. At times, this presented a problem. For example, we often put into Navarino Bay in Greece to load Greek migrants, whose passage was being underwritten by one of the big tanker tycoons. We simply had to put them in first class. It was rather difficult since they travelled with one set of clothes and ninety-five per cent of their baggage was olive oil. Of course, we returned with reverse immigrants – those souls, who after a year of two, did not find Australian life to their liking. Other homeward passengers included near-endless numbers of Australian tourists bound for Britain and continental Europe.'

Captain Ellingham continued his remembrances of the Orion. 'In the mid fifties, the P&O and Orient lines began to spread their range across the Pacific to North America [to Vancouver, San Francisco and Los Angeles] and thereby becoming the most diverse liner operation in the world. However, this initial expansion was not without its problems. I can remember steaming into San Francisco [in 1954] in the Orion with ten first class passengers aboard. We simply weren't known in America and the few who had heard of us thought we were a Japanese company'.

While the Orion made only three trips to the North American West Coast, she continued in regular 'line voyage' service to Australia. In 1958, her accommodation was altered to 342 berths in cabin class and 722 in

P&O Group

*The Stratheden and her near-sisters retained their 1930s style décor to the very end of their P&O careers. The Stratheden's main lounge, above, is quite typical of the art deco period.*

tourist class. Two years later, after the P&O-Orient merger, she was mostly used as a low-fare, one-class migrant ship with a capacity for 1691 passengers. David Carr was a young cadet officer when he joined the ship, then the eldest in the fleet, in 1963. 'I was aboard for her final sailings out to Australia. After London, we put into Piraeus for a large group of Greek immigrants. Homeward, we carried lots of young Australian girls who were bound either for a grand tour of Europe or temporary jobs in Britain. Being non air-conditioned [except in two dining rooms], the *Orion* was among the last P&O liners without such a feature. I can recall the captain sometimes turning the ship around for ten minutes or so just to catch a Red Sea breeze.'

In the end, rather than going directly to the scrap-heap (at Tamise in Belgium), the *Orion* was chartered for several months to serve as a floating hotel at Hamburg for the International Gardening Exhibition. Prior to her arrival at the German port [in

*The first class dance floor aboard the Stratheden of 1937. The windows along each side could be opened for ventilation.*

James Sesta Collection

*This suite aboard the* Stratheden *included a bedroom, sitting area and separate verandah with large windows that overlooked the sea. Notice the innovation of the telephone, which is elevated on a special shelf.*

May 1963], special preparations were made at the Overseas Landing Stage. David Carr recalled, 'As we arrived, the special walkways to the ship that were pre-constructed were mismeasured and didn't fit. They had to be redone. After a busy summer, she was handed over to the breakers in October.'

### The STRATHMORE and STRATHEDEN

So successful were the *Strathnaver* and *Strathaird* of 1931–32 that the P&O Company ordered a third, modified near-sister of these ships in 1934 from the same Vickers-Armstrongs at Barrow-in-Furness. She was launched a year later, on 4 April, by the very popular Duchess of York, who became Her Majesty Queen Elizabeth and later Her Majesty the Queen Mother. The Duchess's father was the Earl of Strathmore – the ship was commissioned in September as the *Strathmore*.

Looking quite modern, with a single funnel instead of the three fitted on the earlier pair of 'Straths', the new ship's steam turbines were powerful. She soon broke the existing speed record between London and Bombay, then held by an earlier P&O liner, the *Viceroy of India*. She even surpassed the 'crack ship' on

James Sesta Collection

the Indian run, Italy's 13,000-ton *Victoria* of Lloyd Triestino.

Soon afterwards, in 1936, further orders were placed with the Vickers yard for a final pair of 'Strath' liners. They were to be almost exact duplicates of the highly successful *Strathmore*. The first ship, named the *Stratheden*, was launched on 10 June 1937, with the ceremony being performed by the Duchess of Buccleuch & Queensferry. She was delivered that December. The second ship, the *Strathallan*, was launched on 23 September 1937, with the Countess of Cromer acting as sponsor. She entered service in March 1938. Their accommodation was very similar, including the novelty of air-conditioning in their first class restaurants. The *Strathmore*'s berthing was arranged as 525 in first class and 500 in tourist class whereas the *Stratheden* and *Strathallan* took 530 in first and 450 in tourist class. The trio, scheduled with the earlier *Strathnaver* and *Strathaird*, ran Australian sailings as well as cruises, mostly of a fortnight's duration, from both London and Sydney.

Both the *Strathmore* and *Stratheden* came out of the Second World War unharmed, but the *Strathallan*, while sailing into the Mediterranean from the Clyde in December 1942 with over 4000 troops onboard, was torpedoed by U-boat *U 562*. She was the fourth P&O liner to be lost within six weeks during the North African campaign. The *Stratheden* was released by the Government in 1946 and was sent to her builders' yard for restoration. Her accommodation was revised slightly, to provide 527 berths in first class and 453 in tourist class. She resumed her Australian sailings in June 1947. The *Strathmore* was reconditioned during 1948–49, with her figures being revised as 497 in first and 487 in tourist class. She left London on her first postwar sailing to Melbourne and Sydney, on 27 October 1949. When the *Strathnaver* resumed commercial sailings three months later, all four 'Straths' had been restored. Soon, however, they were to become the oldest and slowest liners on the P&O Australian run. First, they were overshadowed by the new *Himalaya* of 1949, and then by the near-sisters *Arcadia* and *Iberia* of 1954.

In 1961, soon after the P&O-Orient merger, when the older *Strathnaver* and *Strathaird* were earmarked for retirement, the *Strathmore* and the *Stratheden* were demoted to migrant ships, carrying all-tourist class passengers at bargain fares. Both were used periodi-

cally for cruises, including charter voyages for the Travel Savings Association, a discount cruise organization that used aged or unprofitable British liners. By 1963, however, their P&O days were numbered. Both ships were sold to John S Latsis, a Greek owner with a considerable background in the tramp and tanker trades and further interests in the Mediterranean passenger and Muslim pilgrim trades. The *Strathmore* was handed over in November 1963, the *Stratheden* in the following February. Renamed the *Marianna Latsi* and *Henrietta Latsi* respectively, they were to be used as hotel-ships in Mediterranean waters, as pilgrim ships and to sit out periodic slack seasons in lay-up. Little became known of their whereabouts and sailing patterns except that the former *Stratheden* was once reported to be passing through the Suez Canal from Libya to Jeddah with 4000 pilgrims onboard. In 1966, for no obvious reason, the two ships exchanged names: the *Strathmore*, ex-*Marianna Latsi*, was now the *Henrietta Latsi* and the *Stratheden*, the former *Henrietta Latsi*, became the *Marianna Latsi*. Soon afterward, they seemed to be laid-up permanently at Perama Bay, near Piraeus in Greece. In 1969, with little future in sight, they were

sold to Italian breakers. The ex-*Stratheden* arrived at La Spezia on 19 May, the ex-*Strathmore* followed eight days later. It was the end of the 'Straths', among the most famous, popular and profitable liners ever owned by the P&O Company.

### The CANTON

Built especially for the Far Eastern trade (and periodic cruising) and as an improved, larger version of the *Corfu* and *Carthage* of 1931–32, the *Canton* also came from the Clyde, from the Alexander Stephen & Sons yards at Govan, Glasgow. Launched on 14 April 1938 and commissioned in September, she was, in fact, the last P&O liner to be constructed prior to the Second World War and the last to be built with the once customary colours of black hull, light stone superstructure and black funnel. After the war, in the late forties, almost all of the company's passenger ships resumed sailings with the all-white livery and yellow stack colouring.

Placed on the run from London as far as Yokohama and Kobe, with important calls at Singapore and Hong Kong, the *Canton* was fitted with 300 first class and 244 tourist class berths, as well as six holds for cargo, which included 700 tons of refrigerated space. Her first year was marked by two events of note. In March 1939, while outbound from Hong Kong, she collided with the French *Marechal Joffre* of Messageries Maritimes. The P&O liner had to spend three weeks in the local Taikoo Dockyard undergoing repairs. Two months later, in May, she rescued the passengers and some crew from the burning Danish ship *Alsia* off Ceylon.

Called to military duty almost immediately after hostilities began in September 1939, the *Canton* was totally rebuilt at her builder's yard as the HMS *Canton*, an armed merchant cruiser, complete with guns, aircraft and a catapult. Until 1944, she did patrol work from end to end of the Atlantic and in the Indian Ocean, but afterwards was converted, at Capetown, to a troop transport. She was returned to P&O with a valiant record in September 1947. Thirteen months later, following a thorough refit, she reopened P&O's Far Eastern commercial service as far as Hong Kong. Soon after, she would be joined by the prewar sisters *Corfu* and *Carthage*, and later the brand-new *Chusan*,

Richard K Morse Collection

*The* Canton *(left) and the* Strathnaver *are shown at anchor in Hong Kong, in the spring of 1962, awaiting available berths at the breaker's yard. Most of the lifeboats, some rigging and many of the internal fittings have already been removed from these ships, both veterans of the 1930s.*

the last and largest of the Far Eastern liners.

In her final years, her routing was from London and then Southampton to Port Said, Aden, Bombay, Colombo, Penang, Singapore, Hong Kong, Kobe and Yokohama. Captain Philip Jackson served in the ship at the time. 'On board the *Canton* in those years [the late fifties], I recall lots of Government and service people in first class and artisans in tourist class. We also had a very substantial inter-port business in the East, especially with Chinese and Malay passengers.' The *Canton* was among those prewar ships selected for disposal after the P&O and Orient Line merger. Sold to the Leung Yau Shipbreaking Company in the summer of 1962, she left London on 31 August under the care of a small crew on a final, empty sailing out to Hong Kong.

The ORCADES

Soon after the armistice in 1945, both the management of P&O and the Orient Line set out to create replacement tonnage for their passenger routes. P&O were slightly more cautious in their approach, a sensible path considering that India was soon to become independent and the once important and very lucrative passenger and mail trades to Bombay would decline considerably. Furthermore, apart from the Australian and Far Eastern routes, cruising could not be resumed for some time, especially in view of the hard-pressed state of postwar Britain. In fact, P&O still had a rather impressive fleet: the four surviving 'Straths', the sisters *Mooltan* and *Maloja* and several other passenger ships refitted for the migrant trade. The Orient Line had only two luxury ships, the *Orontes* of 1929 and the *Orion* from 1935, along with two low-fare, austerity ships, the *Otranto* and *Ormonde*. Consequently, their plans called for no less than three successively larger and more luxurious ships, the *Orcades* of 1948, the *Oronsay* of 1951 and finally the *Orsova* of 1954.

Costing an impressive £9 million, the *Orcades* came from a good friend to the Orient Line, the Vickers-Armstrongs yard at Barrow. Launched on 14 October 1947, she was delivered in the following December, just in time for a maiden voyage over Christmas to Fremantle, Melbourne and Sydney. Propelled by steam turbines that could produce a service speed of 22 knots, she cut the passage time between London and Sydney from thirty-six to twenty-six days. A new, faster era had begun.

The design for the *Orcades* was clearly based upon the favourable experience her owners had with the *Orion* and previous *Orcades* of 1935–37. She was the first major liner to group her single mast and single funnel in a compact space just abaft the bridge. C M Squarey, the noted British connoisseur, wrote of the new *Orcades* soon after her maiden sailing. 'In her sense of spaciousness, this corn-coloured ship maintains splendidly the excellent tradition of the Orient Line ships for featuring wide open spaces. One feels that tremendous thoroughness has gone into every detail of this ship; there is no playing up to popular appeal for the mere sake of being popular, but rather does one sense the whole object had been to produce the right answer to the question. Convention had been given the respect it deserves in this ship, but modern conceptions also have decided advantages over old conventions. One sees this in a striking degree in the location of the bridge, constructed as near amidships as possible. It is a striking innovation that gives this ship a distinct personality, just as the tilt of some men's hats often gives them an independent air.'

The passenger accommodation aboard the *Orcades* was balanced between 773 berths in first class and 772 in tourist class. Along with substantial open-air deck spaces and separate swimming pools, each class had its own public rooms, dining saloons and such amenities as children's playrooms, hairdressers and a gift shop. Cabin space ranged from a special suite on B Deck that consisted of a bedroom, sitting room, verandah, pantry, bathroom and trunk room to inside six-berth 'family' cabins in tourist class.

In 1955, a year after the three new Orient liners were in service, the *Orcades* was selected for an experimental voyage: to Australia via the Panama Canal. It quickly proved a popular alternate to the Suez Canal route and was planned so as to provide a routing from London to Bermuda, Port Everglades, Nassau, Kingston, the Panama Canal, Los Angeles, San Francisco, Vancouver, Honolulu, Fiji, Auckland or Wellington and finally across to Sydney and Melbourne. Otherwise, the *Orcades* used the traditional routing: through the Mediterranean and Red Sea, Aden and Colombo, and then onwards to Australia and New Zealand. Like all of the major postwar liners, she was also used for periodic cruising, to the Medietrranean, West Africa, the Atlantic Isles and even across the Atlantic to the Caribbean on three- and four-week sailings.

By the late fifties, the postwar liners of both the P&O and Orient lines were taken in hand for

*A trend-setter in the later forties, the* Orcades *was the first of the Orient liners to have her funnel and shortish mast grouped just abaft the bridge. Seen sailing from Sydney, she cut the passage time from London from five to four weeks.*

P&O Group

modernization and improvement. The *Orcades* was sent to the Harland & Wolff yards at Belfast and, among other alterations, was fitted with a complete air-conditioning system and revised berthing for 631 first class and 734 tourist class passengers. Four years later, however, she was given a slight demotion upon the retirement of the last of the 'Straths'. She was made into an all-tourist class ship, with 1635 berths, that would be useful for outbound migrant sailings. As all of the prewar liners had now been retired, the *Orcades* – at sixteen – was the eldest in the P&O-Orient passenger fleet. Bob Cummins served aboard the *Orcades* as a steward in the late sixties. 'I spent two years in her and did six trips around the world. We were carrying diverse passengers, from the titled rich in first class to immigrants in tourist class who were going out to Australia on a £10 fare assistance scheme. Outbound, we were always "chock-a-block". I was aboard the *Orcades* in 1967 when the Suez Canal was

suddenly and dramatically closed. We were outward bound in the Mediterranean, sailing from London to Port Said. The captain was ordered to return to Gibraltar and await further instructions. We were then ordered to Dakar, then Capetown and Durban, and then onward to Bombay, Colombo, Singapore, Fremantle, Adelaide, Melbourne and Sydney. Our regular four-week sailing became a seven-week voyage.'

The final years of the *Orcades* were marked by disappointment and problems. In 1968, soon after

*A very rare photograph of the Kaohsiung scrapyards, taken on 6 February 1973. Mr P T Chang of Nan Feng Steel casts a backwards glance at his latest acquisition, Orcades, which has just arrived for breaking. Signal flags still fly and the ship's Red Duster hangs limply over the stern railings. The Orcades has but four more months left before her last bottom plates will be cut up for scrap on a nearby mudbank.*

James L Shaw

26

new, very stringent safety regulations were enacted in the United States, she could no longer carry passengers to or from American ports. In fact, she virtually disappeared from P&O advertising in North America. In 1970, on 23 June, she was damaged in a violent storm off Fremantle. Two years later, on 17 April, she had a boiler fire at Hong Kong. Her advancing years combined with some deferred maintenance were becoming problems, but above all, the P&O passenger division had just been hard-hit by jet competition and ships such as the *Orcades* had fallen on very hard times. Captain Philip Jackson recalled this tense period. 'In the early seventies, we were faced with some major decisions. Ships such as the big *Orcades* and *Canberra* of 1960–61 had been built primarily for our fast UK–Australia migrant and tourist services. Then, quite suddenly and most dramatically, Mr Boeing's jumbo jet appeared in regions east of the Suez. We abruptly lost the bulk of our trade. Our passenger ships were sent roving around the world (including more and more to North American shores) looking for business. In fact, the older liners – such as the *Orcades* [1948], *Himalaya* [1949] and *Chusan* [1950] – were soon all to be sent to the junk-yards of Taiwan. Their good life's work, their economic well-being, had ended.'

The *Orcades* was only temporarily repaired following her fire at Hong Kong. In fact, spare parts had been brought over from P&O's *Iberia*, which was actually the first of the postwar liners to be retired and which was then just about to be delivered to the breakers at Kaohsiung. The *Orcades* lasted only a few months longer, being laid-up at Southampton on 13 October. With a dwindling worldwide passenger trade, coupled later with rising costs for fuel oil and staffing, she had little hope of finding a buyer. She was sold off to Taiwanese breakers and reached Kaohsiung on 6 February 1973.

## The HIMALAYA

P&O's first new postwar liner, also coming from the Vickers yard at Barrow, was commissioned as the *Himalaya* in October 1949. At nearly 28,000-tons, she was not only the company's largest ship as well as being flagship, but was also the fastest yet, reaching 23.13 knots during her trial runs. With her basic hull and superstructure following the design of the prewar 'Straths', she had a single, forward mast and therein copied the *Orion* of the Orient Line. Furthermore, she was given a quite unusual berthing arrangement: 758 in first class and a rather meagre 401 in tourist class. However, her cargo capacity, of nearly 450,000 cubic feet, was the biggest ever in the P&O liner fleet, a

distinction that she retained until the very end of her days.

Initially used on the prescribed P&O routing, from London to Gibraltar, Port Said, Aden, Bombay, Colombo, Fremantle, Melbourne and Sydney, and for periodic cruises, the *Himalaya*'s sailings were occasionally extended to include Penang, Singapore, Auckland or Wellington. In 1958, she was selected as the experimental ship to sail from Melbourne, Sydney and Auckland to Fiji, Honolulu, Vancouver, San Francisco and Los Angeles. A new South Pacific run to North America had opened for the P&O-Orient Lines. A year later, she pioneered a transpacific run for her owners, from Los Angeles, San Francisco and Vancouver to Honolulu, Yokohama, Kobe, Hong Kong and Singapore, and then sailed homeward to London via Colombo, Bombay, Aden, Port Said, Naples, Marseilles and Gibraltar.

Given full air-conditioning and other improvements during a major refit at Flushing, Holland, during the winter of 1959–60, the *Himalaya* was, along with the *Orcades*, selected to become an all-tourist class ship at the end of 1963. Thereafter, she would be used more often for low-fare migrant sailings. Her revised capacity was listed as 1416 berths. Her very final years, in the early seventies, were marked with something of a renewed popularity as she was used more and more frequently on cruises from Sydney. To the Australian cruising public, the warmth and friendliness of the *Himalaya* made her a beloved ship. However, sparked off partially by the extreme fuel oil price increase of 1973, when the cost per ton rocketed from $35 to $95, it was decided the *Himalaya* had outlived her economic profitability. She followed several of her original company's running-mates to the scrapyards on Taiwan. She reached Kaohsiung on 28 November 1974, just three weeks before demolition began on the *Orsova*, anchored at a nearby berth.

## The CHUSAN

P&O planned their second postwar replacement liner for the Far Eastern trade. She was in fact the largest and fastest liner ever designed for that trade for a British firm. Furthermore, as postwar economic conditions brightened, the company keenly anticipated the resumption of lucrative two-week cruise voyages. Consequently, this ship was kept at a slightly smaller size, at 24,200-tons, rather than the 28–29,000-tons of the other postwar liners. She would, in fact, become the last company ship purposely designed for the Far Eastern service.

Named *Chusan* during her launch ceremonies on 28 June 1949, she too came from the Vickers yard at

Barrow-in-Furness. She was delivered to P&O in June 1950, following a series of highly successful trials. Her commercial maiden voyage was, in fact, a cruise to the Atlantic Isles and Lisbon. Three Mediterranean cruises from Southampton followed. In September, she set off on her maiden long-distance sailing, from London to Gibraltar, Naples, Port Said, Aden and Bombay and then a return voyage to Britain. Two months later, in November, after a rather exceptionally long delay, she entered her intended service, from London to Gibraltar, Port Said, Aden, Bombay, Colombo, Penang, Singapore, Hong Kong, Kobe and Yokohama. She won high praise from the start and developed a rather special rapport with the sea-going public. The *Chusan* was always one of the best loved liners in the P&O fleet.

In 1952, similar to several other company ships, her appearance was changed slightly by the addition of a smoke-deflecting Thornycroft top to her single funnel. Fortunately, it was both an eye-pleasing as well as effective addition. In 1959, she was sent to the Harland & Wolff yards at Belfast for her most thorough refit, which included the installation of complete air-conditioning, additional private plumbing to her cabins and a reworked berthing pattern from 475 to 464 in first class and from 551 to 541 in tourist class. That same year, she undertook P&O's first full round-the-world sailing, calling at 24 ports in 92 days and covering nearly 32,000 miles. Her itinerary included such stop-overs as Bombay, Singapore, Manila, Hong Kong, Yokohama, Vancouver, San Francisco, Los Angeles, Acapulco, the Panama Canal, Trinidad and Las Palmas. Several years later, in July 1963, as the Far Eastern run began to diminish and as the company expanded its liner services into a full worldwide operation, the *Chusan* made her first visit to Melbourne and Sydney. Thereafter, she would make a number of visits to this continent already familiar to P&O-Orient schedules. Cruising also increasingly developed into a viable alternative operation, as suggested by this late summer listing from 1966:

*When completed in late 1949, the 27,900-ton* Himalaya *was the largest and fastest passenger liner in the extensive P&O fleet. To the very end of her days, in 1974, she was noted as having the biggest cargo capacity of any of the P&O-Orient passenger ships.*

After 1969, the *Chusan* was used almost exclusively for cruising. A year later, on 8 February, on one of her last 'line voyages', she made the final scheduled P&O call at Bombay. Well over a century's link with India was over. Shortly thereafter, the *Chusan* – seeking more profitable employment – was time-chartered to a South African tourist firm for cruising. Amongst short-distance runs to Durban and the Seychelles, one long-distance cruise brought the ship to New York in October 1971 – a most unexpected sight. America's largest port had seen very few P&O-Orient visitors since the Second World War. The *Stratheden* had called four times in the summer of 1950 while under a brief charter to Cunard for 'special demand' sailings from Southampton. Both the *Arcadia* and *Iberia* had called in 1959, during cruises, and the *Canberra* visited on several occasions between 1962–64, also as part of cruise sailings.

Junior officer David Carr was among the eighty crew members who took the twenty-three-year-old *Chusan* out to the ship-breakers at Kaohsiung, Taiwan, in the spring of 1973. 'We sailed from Southampton to Hong Kong via Dakar, Durban and Singapore. There was simply no space at the Kaohsiung scrapyards, so we were ordered to temporarily wait at Hong Kong, just off Green Island and next to the wrecked *Queen Elizabeth*, which had been ruinously destroyed by fire and then capsizing while being converted to the floating university-cruise ship *Seawise University* [on 8 January 1972]. We sat there for a week. It was a haunting wait – the fire-gutted, former *Elizabeth* and the empty, death-bound *Chusan*.

'The voyage out to the East in the *Chusan* was quite sad. She was like the other P&O liners on their way to the bone-yards: completely stripped. The officers sat at the two surviving tables in the corner of the first

| | | |
|---|---|---|
| *Orcades* (August 5) | 16 days Mediterranean, from £88 | |
| *Chusan* (August 7) | 12 days North Cape, from £76 | |
| *Canberra* (August 8) | 11 days Mediterranean, from £71 | |
| *Oronsay* (August 19) | 22 days Mediterranean, from £121 | |
| *Canberra* (August 20) | 10 days Mediterranean, from £64 | |
| *Chusan* (August 20) | 13 days Mediterranean, from £83 | |
| *Orcades* (August 22) | 12 days Atlantic Isles, from £66 | |
| *Chusan* (September 5) | 15 days Mediterranean, from £95 | |

*The burning* Oronsay *heels over dangerously against a quay. Fire broke out on the brand-new liner on 28 October 1950 as she lay in a fitting-out berth at Vickers-Armstrongs in Barrow.*

class restaurant. There was still white linen on the table, but otherwise the room was an empty steel barn. There was nothing else left.

'We were finally cleared to take the *Chusan* into Kaohsiung harbour, and I shall always remember the sight along the river banks. Ships lined both sides, all tightly squeezed together and all secured stern first. They were each waiting for the scrap crews that would finish them off. We berthed next to an American freighter, but were temporarily moored to buoys rather than being deliberately run aground, which was so often the case with the other liners.

'We then had to wait for several days aboard the *Chusan* until London signalled that the final payment for the ship had been made. I remember sailing back down the river to Kaohsiung in a launch and spotting an inbound tug towing a long, flat double-bottom and a protruding piece of bow. I noticed the name *Orcades*. It was the remains of yet another postwar P&O liner. Her last pieces were being towed up river to be blown-up.'

## The Oronsay

The *Oronsay* was the second of the Orient Line's three-ship postwar rebuilding programme. She was a slightly altered version of the *Orcades* although overall a very similar design: a single mast and funnel mounted amidships together with the wheelhouse and bridge, and exceptional open spaces below for the passengers. She was launched at the Vickers yard at Barrow, on 30 June 1950, and cost a total of $9.6 million. Several months later, on 28 October, while lying at her fitting-out berth, the *Oronsay* was damaged by a fire that began in her No 2 cargo hold. The blaze spread, smoke poured from the brand-new liner and fire-fighting continued well into the night and next day. When the outbreak was extinguished, the *Oronsay* – her stability upset by the quantities of water pumped into her during efforts to control the fire – canted over against the shipyard quay. There was, of course, the lingering threat of capsizing. Damage necessitated the replacement of numerous steel pieces in the decks, girders and beams.

Finally commissioned in May 1951, the *Oronsay* was employed on the traditional run from London to Australia via the Suez Canal and for occasional cruises. In January 1954, she was selected to undertake P&O-Orient's first major experimental sailing away from their customary routes, from Melbourne, Sydney and Auckland to Honolulu, Vancouver, San Francisco and Los Angeles. This was a huge success, and she promptly replaced the veteran Union liner *Aorangi* on the run, and soon more sailings were offered in P&O-Orient liners. By the late fifties, a regular run to North America had begun.

The accommodation aboard the *Oronsay* was listed as 612 berths in first class and 804 in tourist class. The arrangement of these was similar to almost all of the postwar liners for both firms. There were nine passenger decks: Sun, Stadium, Verandah, A, B, C, D, E and F. She was fully air-conditioned (installed during her major refit in 1959) and equipped with stabilizers. There was an outdoor pool for each class, a cinema, gift shop, beauty salon and barber shop. On B Deck there was a two-berth deluxe suite, fitted with a bedroom, sitting room, trunk room, pantry and full bathroom. The first class quarters included one-, two- and three-berth cabins, many of which had private facilities, located on A, B, C, and D Decks. Their public rooms consisted of a grill, library, main lounge, ballroom, verandah bar, two galleries, a second lounge, a tavern and the restaurant (with two adjoining private rooms with one being solely for children). The tourist class accommodation included two-, three- and four-berth staterooms, located on B, D, E and F Decks, few of which had private facilities. Public rooms consisted of a lounge, library and the restaurant.

*A stern view of the* Oronsay *on a very unusual occasion: she is in the Gladstone Dock at Liverpool, a port very rarely used by P&O-Orient liners.*

F Leonard Jackson

In 1964, the *Oronsay*, like all of the surviving former Orient Line ships, lost part of her distinctive identity: her corn-coloured hull. P&O had decided that all of the liners would be made to look similar and have all-white hulls. By the end of that year, the *Oronsay*, *Orcades*, *Orsova* and the new *Oriana* were 'white ships'.

The *Oronsay* became the subject of considerable attention from the press, after 14 January 1970. While visiting the North American West Coast, at Vancouver, an outbreak of typhoid was discovered. The ship was quarantined until 4 February, causing considerable discomfort to her passengers and crew as well as her intended sailing schedule. The entire affair cost P&O in excess of $1.3 million.

The *Oronsay* was among the last of the postwar liners to go to the breakers. She continued to sail until September 1975, and was withdrawn at Hong Kong rather than going through the customary procedure of being retired and partially stripped at Southampton. A month later, on 6 October, she departed on the overnight passage to Kaohsiung. Demolition began in earnest in the following April.

### The Arcadia and Iberia

The *Arcadia* was one of P&O's most popular and beloved liners. She and her near-sister, the *Iberia*, were ordered in 1953, the culmination of the company's postwar liner rebuilding prgramme. They were, however, ordered from different yards: the *Arcadia* from John Brown & Company at Clydebank (builders of the three big Cunard Queens among many others) and the *Iberia* from Harland & Wolff at Belfast (builders of the *Titanic* and later the equally large P&O flagship *Canberra*). The only other, and very apparent difference between the pair was that they were fitted with different stacks: the *Arcadia*'s was domed and had a black-painted top whereas the *Iberia*'s was curved and had some open grating.

The *Arcadia* and *Iberia* were the biggest liners yet seen on the Australian run. At 721 feet in length (the *Iberia* was for some reason two feet shorter) and with a capacity for some 1390 passengers (655 in first class and 735 tourist class), they were easily equivalent to many of the notable North Atlantic liners, such as the *America*, the *Andrea Doria* and the *Caronia*. The *Arcadia* was launched on 14 May 1953, the same day the Orient Line's flagship and largest ship, the *Orsova*, was launched at the Vickers yard at Barrow-in-Furness. Later, when the *Arcadia* was moved to a fitting-out berth, she lay alongside another incomplete ship: the royal yacht *Britannia*, which was to be presented to a young Queen Elizabeth II as a coronation present from the Royal Navy.

The *Arcadia* entered service in February 1954, sailing from London's Tilbury Docks to Gibraltar, Port Said, Aden, Colombo and then onwards to Melbourne and Sydney. Later, there followed extended voyages: to India, calls in South Africa, to the Caribbean and Panama Canal, along the North American West Coast, to the Orient and considerable cruising, including a special cruise to New York in 1959 and the first summertime P&O cruises to Alaska in 1969. With her polished veneers, brasswork, soft chairs and large open-air deck spaces, she established a special, long-lasting rapport with her passengers. Rather strangely, the *Iberia*, which entered service in September 1954, never quite had the same charmed relationship with the travelling public. One *Arcadia* loyalist later reported, 'She was a ship of tremendous charm and personality. Actually, this is a certain, undefinable something that pervades throughout just a handful of ships, very few of them in fact, and which lingers in the most beautiful, evocative memories. The *Arcadia* was always my absolute favourite.'

Travel writer C M Squarey wrote of the *Arcadia* soon after her delivery, 'As ships go, there is nothing notably sensational about the *Arcadia*. Her owners are too shrewd to dabble in sensationalism. She follows a postwar pattern of considerable experience. The P&O Company do not like their ships to be described as luxurious; the *Arcadia* is not luxurious, but I believe that she will leave a happy and most satisfied impression on all who voyage in her. And it is that that matters.'

David Carr gained his second mate's ticket in the early sixties as the P&O-Orient passenger division grew more diverse and far-flung. 'I joined the *Iberia* and made a special cruise in her from Los Angeles to Yokohama for the 1964 Olympic Games in Tokyo. There were all sorts of cruises to Japan that year, many of them in P&O liners. In those days, a P&O voyage might last as long as five months. We'd sail out to Australia (from Britain), then go to Hong Kong and Japan, then cross to North America, recross to Japan, then down to Australia again and then finally home to England by way of Ceylon, India, the Suez and the Med. Of course, there were many alternatives as well. After the Suez Canal closed in 1967, we were often routed via South Africa. Also, we almost always stopped at either Bombay or Colombo for Indian crew changes. I must have been King Neptune at least fourteen times.'

In the early seventies, the P&O liner fleet was greatly reduced – a result of competition from the jet, shifts in cargo transport, new Board of Trade regulations on ocean liner stability and general difficulties

*A day of excitement and pride, 14 May 1953, the* Arcadia *is launched at the John Brown yards at Clydebank.*

with the older ships themselves. The *Iberia*, bothered by stability problems for most of her sea-going career, seemed to have no end of misfortune towards the end. She endured a rather exceptional voyage in October 1969. Homeward bound from Australia to England via Panama, her funnel caught fire at Pago Pago. There was an electrical failure at Honolulu and then engine problems at Acapulco. Finally, there was a fuel leak at Curaçao. David Carr recalled the end of the *Iberia*. 'Although only eighteen years old at the time, she was the first to go. I made her last voyage in the

spring of 1972 and then looked after her at the Southampton Docks as the Japanese scrap merchants came aboard for inspection. Once the final deal was completed, the *Iberia* was stripped of all fittings, even down to the linen. This was put in storage at Southampton and later sold to collectors.'

The *Iberia* was routed via South Africa for her final, empty sailing, and reached Kaohsiung on 5 September. The scrappers were soon aboard. One by one, all of the other postwar liners went to the scrapyards. After 1976, the sole survivor of these earlier ships was the much loved *Arcadia*. She had something of a reprieve and was used for South Pacific cruising from Sydney until early 1979. Then, she too made her final run up to Taiwan to meet the inevitable ship-breakers. However, unlike most other company liners, the *Arcadia* was not completely stripped for her last run.

James Shaw, a noted American shipping journalist, went aboard the ship at Kaohsiung in March 1979. He later wrote, 'At the time of my visit, the 29,700-ton *Arcadia* was positioned alongside the 99,400-ton Greek tanker *Andros Apollon*, as the P&O ship's final berth was not yet available. At that time, stripping operations were in progress. Furniture and bedding were being lowered over the side and being taken ashore in two lifeboats. Two other lifeboats were being used as "tankers" to take off excess fuel oil. The same fuel oil would be used to heat the ship's plate in furnaces ashore so that it could be formed into steel re-enforcement bars.

'Onboard the liner, Taiwanese work crews were already engaged in taking-up the hardwood desks aft. Carpeting in most public rooms had been cut and rolled up. The officers' cabins on the bridge and the chartroom had already been stripped of most equipment. The radio room and all radio instruments had been sealed by local government inspectors.

'Most "nautical antiques" – such as the large P&O world route-map from the aft bar and the B Deck wood-engraving of the *Arcadia* – had been removed by the Rainbow Enterprise Company. This firm, based at Kaohsiung, buys the interior decorations of most liners that come to Taiwan for breaking. These items are then exported to nautical shops around the world. As for the ship itself, I was told that she was purchased at the market rate of $100 per light displacement ton (she was 23,060 light displacement tons) and that it would take approximately eight to ten weeks for complete dismantling.'

## The Orsova

The last of the postwar Orient Line trio was a unique ship, especially created by her owners and the designers at Vickers-Armstrongs. She was the world's first 'mastless' liner. All of her necessary rigging was attached from the forward kingpost to the large single funnel. Otherwise, her design was once again similar, being closely copied from both the *Orcades* of 1948 and then the *Oronsay* of 1951. She was slightly larger, being 28,700 tons compared to the 28,300 of the *Orcades* and 27,600 of the *Oronsay*. Both of the earlier ships measured 709 feet in length while the new company flagship, named *Orsova* during the launch ceremonies on 14 May 1953, was 723 feet. Her accommodation consisted of 694 berths in first class and 809 in tourist class.

*The* Arcadia *at Pago Pago on American Samoa. She was an exceptionally handsome liner.*

Delivered to the Orient Line in the spring of 1954, her maiden voyage included a most interesting rendez-vous. Charles F Morris in his book *Origins, Orient and Oriana* recorded the occasion. 'I was aboard the *Orsova* on her maiden voyage when, on the evening of April 5th, we were about to pass the *Gothic* [chartered from Shaw Savill Line to act as temporary royal yacht] which was homeward bound from Australia [and the around-the-world coronation tour] with Her Majesty Queen Elizabeth and HRH Prince Philip onboard. Captain Whinfield, aware of this, sensed an occasion, and ordered the plumber to make some rocket directors out of pieces of plumber's pipe. These were to be mounted on the guard rails at the starboard side of the navigating bridge.

'The night was dark, and there was some movement of the ship caused by wind and sea while hundreds of passengers and, I think, of the crew remained on deck to enjoy the occasion. The Captain then sent a cable to the *Gothic*: "We send warm and loyal greetings to your Majesty and Prince Philip from 1011 passengers en route to Australia and New Zealand. We also wish you both a happy reunion with your children [Prince Charles and Princess Anne] at Tobruk and a quiet leave when you reach home."

'Then – up went the fireworks! It was certainly effective as it was equally unconventional. Certainly, there was no element of distress – it was just Captain Whinfield! It had been interesting to observe what was going on, and I believe that every light was burning in our ship, while we could see those of the *Gothic* and her escorting cruiser quite clearly. Then, to the delight of the passengers and surprise – if not consternation – of those accustomed to the ways of the sea, the *Orsova* was swung towards the *Gothic*, when the ships were still a mile or two apart, though I found it difficult to judge with the naked eye, but readers will be aware of the implications of this manoeuvre but then, as I have said earlier, Captain Whinfield was a man to make the most of such occasions! Almost simultaneously, the cabled reply came from the *Gothic*: "Please thank your officers, passengers and crew for your kind and loyal message which I have received with great pleasure. Elizabeth R."

'At the same time, the cruiser quickly took action: increased speed and moved between the two liners, while the *Orsova* resumed her former course and ended a thrilling experience for all on board. It must be left to the imagination what message the captain of

P&O Group

*The Orsova of 1954 was the first major liner to dispense entirely with the conventional mast, and instead to have her rigging and necessary wireless lines attached between her forward kingpost and her single stack.*

the cruiser may have had in his mind!'

A year later, in July 1955, the *Orsova* completed the longest P&O-Orient passenger sailing to date, a trip round the world of some 46,000 miles. It, too, was an experimental journey, part of the combined company efforts to expand their liner operations and reach especially into the Pacific, and by the late fifties, several circumnavigations were offered annually in the P&O-Orient schedules.

In 1973, after nearly twenty years of regular liner and cruise service, the *Orsova* was up for retirement. Although she had just been given a £225,000 refit at Southampton, there was considerable uncertainty about her future. In London, P&O Cruises Limited had just been created to replace what remained of the P&O Lines, of the former P&O-Orient combination. Single-class holiday cruising was the primary thrust of the future and would be the only way of survival for firms such as P&O. While almost all of the postwar group that included the *Orsova* were relegated to the ship-breakers, there was even some thought given to scrapping the relatively new 45,700-ton *Canberra*, dating from 1961. The plan being considered was to retire the *Canberra*, which had just had a most

*A busy day, typical of Southampton until the early 1970s, showing (from left to right) the Canberra, Oriana, Himalaya and Union-Castle/Safmarine's S.A. Vaal.*

unsuccessful trial season of short cruising from New York, and rebuild the *Orsova* as a more contemporary cruise ship. She would be paired, so it was thought, alongside her Orient Line successor, the 41,900-ton *Oriana* of 1960. However, in rethinking this scheme, it was decided to retain the *Canberra*. The *Orsova* was retired in November 1973, and briefly laid-up along the Southampton Docks. Soon afterwards, she too was sold to the Taiwanese breakers, arriving at Kaohsiung on 7 February 1974. Owing to a huge backlog of unwanted freighters, tankers and other liners, scrapping did not begin for ten months, until 17 December. In the space of three years, beginning in September 1972, Kaohsiung harbour had witnesed the arrival of five P&O liners: the *Iberia*, *Orcades*, *Chusan*, *Orsova* and *Himalaya*.

### The ORIANA

In the fifties, decisions came from the London boardrooms of both the P&O and Orient Lines to develop the biggest and fastest liners ever to sail the Australian route. In fact, the large size, great capacity and especially the high speeds that would characterise these new liners (the first to be designed and built in Britain which could actually understudy for the giant Cunard 'Queens' of the late thirties), were determined by P&O-Orient's interest in new frontiers of ocean travel, namely the Pacific and North America. There was, of course, another important aspect: the forecast for the continued demand for space in tourist class used by outbound migrants, return travellers from Australia and an ever-rising number of pleasure-seeking tourists. Two large liners would, according to

H J Wood

the best company calulations, be nothing less than highly profitable.

The Orient liner would come first, being ordered from Vickers-Armstrongs at Barrow-in-Furness, a company with whom they had a long-standing association. Delivery was set for the end of 1960. Although the designers would opt for something rather radical in overall design, they carefully reviewed the plans for the *Orsova*, that first 'mastless' liner introduced in 1954. In fact, initial drawings for the new flagship showed a modified and larger *Orsova*, with one funnel as well. This was later altered to include a second funnel-device, actually a ventilator, which was located aft and on a lower deck. The new *Oriana* thus appeared to have two stacks. However, much like the *Orsova*, she did not have a dominant mast, but instead had her rigging attached between a short radar mast and the highly-placed 'working' funnel.

At 41,900 tons and 804 feet in overall length, she was a most impressive liner. When launched, on 3 November 1959, by Princess Alexandra of Kent, she was dubiously noted as being the largest liner yet built in England. All earlier and larger British liners were constructed in either Northern Ireland or in Scotland. During the trials, held a year later, in November 1960, everyone felt nothing short of pride and delight. On her trial runs, speeds as high as 30.64 knots were recorded, another extreme novelty for a passenger liner not intended for transatlantic sailings. Her owners had asked for a 27.5 knot service speed, a mere single knot less than the operating speeds of Cunard's mighty *Queen Mary* and *Queen Elizabeth*. More specifically, the new *Oriana* would cut the passage time between Southampton and Sydney by seven days, from four to three weeks. This would be the supreme competitive edge and together with P&O's projected *Canberra*, they would become the most popular and successful of the final liners on the Australian route. However, soon after the *Oriana*'s maiden run to Fremantle, Melbourne and Sydney, in which she gained the 'Golden Cockerel' award for the fastest passage (a record which, in fact, she still holds), she was sent, as part of the expanded P&O-Orient programme, to such ports as Hong Kong, Yokohama and Kobe, and then across to Honolulu, Vancouver, San Francisco and Los Angeles. Sailing outward from the UK via Suez, she would return either through the Panama Canal and the Caribbean or, in later years, via South Africa. In addition to her 'line voyages' she would also cruise, initially as a two-class ship and then as an all-first class liner, for two weeks in the Mediterranean or Atlantic Isles, three weeks to the West Indies or on short runs from Sydney to nearby Pacific islands.

The Orient Line house flag was lowered for the last time, in 1966, on board the *Oriana*. Thereafter, the P&O-Orient name would be dropped and all of the remaining 'O Boats', *Orcades*, *Oronsay*, *Orsova* and the *Oriana* herself, would be officially tranferred to the P&O Company. With a berthing capacity listed as 638 in first class and 1496 in tourist class, the *Oriana* might have enjoyed a decade of high profit in 'liner service' before being hard-hit, similar to so many other two-class passenger ships, by aircraft competition. She was, in fact, struggling to find passengers by the early seventies. However, to avoid the possibilities of selling her or, far worse, giving her to the scrappers, the P&O Group created P&O Cruises and, with very little alteration, converted the liner to a 1700-capacity cruise ship. Thereafter, she would sail almost exclusively on two- and three-week holiday cruises, first from Southampton and later, after 1981, only from Sydney. She remains in this service to date, is still popular and has several years of life ahead of her. According to Captain Philip Jackson, master of the *Oriana* in 1984–85, 'At the age of twenty-four [July 1984], I believe that *Oriana* can look forward to several further years on the Australian cruise run. [The rumour was that she will last until late 1987.] Recently, we've made some alterations on board – such as reducing the cruise capacity from 1750 to 1550, and the total staff from 790 to 690. In 1985, she will have been given a $12 million, two-week refit at Singapore. We have a thirty per cent repeat passenger factor here in Australia, but we feel that there is a huge untapped market. Ideally, we need to go to different Pacific ports, but then with such a big liner, which is also essential, we are obviously quite limited when considering anchorages, depths and wharf conditions. Recently, we have strengthened our on board entertainment programme, added special theme cruises (such as the Variety Club and Melbourne Cup cruises) and hope to tap into the opening of the big Australian convention trade.' In the summer of 1984, the P&O managers evidently rethought their earlier plans and announced that the *Oriana* would be withdrawn and sold off in March 1986. This will be the end not only of a well-known liner but the last of the Orient liners.

The CANBERRA

If the Orient Line's new flagship (and last liner) was to be the fastest ever to sail on the Australian run, P&O's intended flagship – scheduled for delivery six months later, in the late spring of 1961 – would rank as the

*An exciting day for Cornerbrook, Newfoundland: the maiden visit, during a transatlantic cruise from Southampton to Boston and New York, of the* Oriana. *Even at 41,900 tons and 804 feet, the liner seems dwarfed by the impressive landscape in the background. The date is August 1979.*

largest liner ever built for a service other than the North Atlantic. Harland & Wolff at Belfast were contracted for this huge project, the creation of the biggest British liner since the 83,600-ton *Queen Elizabeth* of 1940. She was to be named *Canberra*, in honour of the Australian capital, and would represent the high-point of a final 'golden age' in British passenger shipping, being constructed just as new

Photo by Jim Fost

flagships were coming off the ways for Union-Castle, Shaw Savill and Canadian Pacific.

At her launch on 16 March 1960, some initial and most embarassing difficulties were discovered. According to David Carr, 'The 818-foot long liner was found, soon after she first hit the waters, to be as much as 18 inches lower in the stern than intended. P&O was less than satisfied, especially since the ship now required a counter-balance, which meant tons of cement in the bow. Consequently, her depth would be, instead of the projected 32 feet, as much as 35 feet, a dilemma that would later be a problem in mooring in smaller harbours. It also led to some stability problems. Ironically, the *Iberia*, also Belfast built, had stability problems as well whereas her Clydebank-built sister *Arcadia* had none.'

Driven by steam turbo-electric engines, linked to a twin-screw design, the *Canberra* joined the *Oriana* and other P&O-Orient liners when she departed from Southampton on a capacity-filled maiden voyage, on 2 June 1961. The number of berths was adjustable to suit demand, increasing from 556 to 596 in first class and from 1616 to 1716 in tourist class. Her passenger accommodation was spread over ten decks and she was fully air-conditioned, stabilized and fitted with three outdoor pools and a fourth just for children. There was also a theatre, teenage and children's facilities, several gift shops, a barber and a beauty salon. The deluxe accommodation included four verandah suites, all of them doubles, located on C Deck, which consisted of a bedroom, verandah and bathroom. Also on C Deck, were eight deluxe cabins, each of which had a sitting room, bedroom and bathroom. All of the other first class staterooms, with one to four berths, had private bathrooms. First class public rooms included the Crow's Nest Bar-Lounge, the Stadium, Bonito Club, Verandah Promenade, Century Bar, Meridian Room, Writing Room, Menzies Room, Crystal Room, Ladies Salon and the restaurant. Tourist class, with cabins for either two or four, included the Playground, Island Room, Alice Springs Lounge, Peacock Room, Cricketer's Tavern, two writing rooms, a library and reading room, the William Fawcett Room and the restaurant with a seating capacity of 704.

Once in service, the *Canberra* followed a sailing pattern very similar to her running-mate, the *Oriana*, and her schedules might include sailing to as many as a hundred ports on five continents. While her official

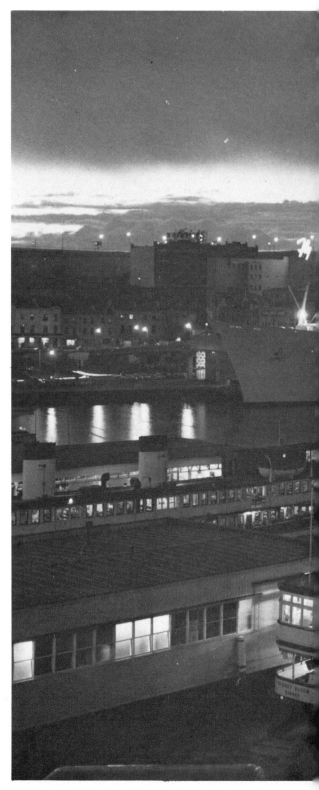

*The largest P&O-Orient liner of all, the* Canberra, *berthed at Circular Quay in Sydney. The ferry* Sydney Queen *is in the foreground.*

40

Luis Miguel Correia

operation was listed as the Australian service, she also sailed to the Caribbean, North America, the Far East, Middle East, South Africa and the Pacific Islands. Some of her earliest cruises included round-trip transatlantic sailings to New York spending as much as seventy-two hours in port. These well-patronized trips were run between 1962–64. During her early years, the *Canberra* also suffered from another embarrassment: a sizeable mechanical failure occurred on 5 January 1963 off Malta, while outbound for the Suez. David Carr was then serving aboard one of the oldest P&O liners. 'On board the *Strathmore*, we offered to tow the *Canberra* home to Britain. The offer was refused, but we stood by and sent food across to the stricken new flagship in our lifeboats. Ironically, the aged *Strathmore* was then on her final homeward sailing.'

The *Canberra* was left, like almost the entire P&O passenger fleet, without passengers by 1972, as the jets made serious inroads into areas east of the Suez. In a snap but misplaced decision, she was sent to New York, in early 1973, for a ten-month series of Caribbean cruises. The entire affair was a dismal failure, so much so that the liner spent some weeks in

*Assuredly one of the most beautiful of modern liners, the* Canberra *shown outbound at Lisbon.*

*Traditionally, a musical farewell has been given to every P&O liner departing from Southampton. In this view, the Royal Marines are 'sending off' the* Canberra, *bound for a ten-week voyage to Australia and the Pacific.*

*Prepared for the first sitting of the evening meal, the* Canberra's *first class restaurant was decorated in a very contemporary style, with a Pacific theme.*

P&O Group

P&O Group

lay-up at Wilmington, North Carolina. Among other marketing problems, neither P&O or the *Canberra* were well known names in the American north-east. Quickly sent back to Southampton, there was considerable rumour that she might go to the breakers after only twelve years of service. Fortunately, there was a last minute redecision; the plan to convert the smaller *Orsova* into a cruise ship was abandoned and the *Canberra* kept in her place. She has been cruising full time from Southampton ever since, except for her service in the Falklands War.

Each winter, as the P&O flagship shifted to several months' cruising from Sydney, she would run something like the earlier 'line voyages', sailing either via Suez or Panama. Ironically, it sometimes proved difficult to fully book these runs. More recently, as the *Canberra* approaches her twenty-fifth year, she has begun to suffer from mechanical problems and, possibly worse still, from declining cost efficiency. A new generation of managers at P&O headquarters in London are studying plans for her replacement. Once she is retired, it will be the end of the traditional P&O 'line voyage' fleet. Thereafter, the company's passenger interests will be solely in cruising.

## The CHITRAL and the CATHAY

Soon after the P&O and Orient lines merged in 1960, there were numerous decisions to be made. One was to retire the veteran prewar liners *Corfu*, *Carthage* and *Canton* from the Far Eastern trade. While the 24,200-ton *Chusan* of 1950 was also used on that service, she was often detoured for cruising and subsequently the demands on that service no longer required so large a passenger liner. The practical approach would be toward more moderate tonnage with less capacity. P&O-Orient were not, however, wanting to build new ships. Consequently, they were extremely fortunate when, at the end of 1960, in the face of a new, independent Belgian Congo and therefore a abruptly dwindling trade, the Compagnie Maritime Belge of Antwerp placed their two newest and largest passenger-cargo ships on the sales lists. The *Jadotville* (built in 1956, at Chantiers et Ateliers de St Nazaire in France) and the *Baudouinville* (finished a year later at the Cockerill-Ougree shipyards at Hoboken in Belgium) were quickly bought for a mere £3 million. In fact, very little alteration was needed for either ship with the exception of a fresh coat of paint and new names: the *Jadotville* became the *Chitral* and the *Baudouinville* changed to *Cathay*. The former left London on her first Far Eastern sailing on 2 March 1961 and the latter followed a month later, on 12 April.

David Carr, then a junior officer with P&O, joined the *Cathay* in her first season. 'I was very lucky to have as one of my first assingments a combination liner such as this. She was like a private yacht, carrying 240 first class passengers only. She was also a very fine sea boat. We had a ten-week round-trip: London, Rotterdam and Southampton (which was occasionally extended to other ports for cargo) to Port Said, Aden, Colombo, Penang, Port Swettenham, Singapore, Hong Kong, Yokohama, Kobe and then reverse. Homebound, there might be a call at Naples. We would carry lots of service people – the Hong Kong police and civil servants, for example. We used the King George V Docks, the "KGV" docks as they were called, at London and had a two-week turnaround. This seems so improbable by today's rapid, overnight container ship standards. After London, we stopped briefly at Southampton. It was mostly for the passengers. They would have had an easier train ride down from London.

'Of course, cargo was very important to ships such as the *Cathay*. Outwards, we carried lots of general freight, which often included many crated cars. Homebound, there was more general cargo, but most of it was for Woolworths in Britain. This included

umbrellas, toys – mostly inexpensive plastic items. On every homeward voyage, Woolworths reserved at least one full hatch.'

Captain Philip Jackson served as chief officer in the *Chitral*. 'I looked after 240 or so passengers. Eight out of my ten-hour days were spent in planning and organizing passenger entertainment. The quartermaster served as my assistant, the daytime children's attendant alternated as a night-time hostess and there was a three-piece band. We'd have deck games and sports, late afternoon bingo, concerts and the occasional film presentation. Because of the rather small numbers, the entire ship had something of a club-like atmosphere. Older, well-heeled passengers loved a ship like the *Chitral* and her sister, the *Cathay*. The

*Together at the Yokohama Ocean Terminal in Japan, P&O's combination liner* Cathay *is berthed just ahead of the* Arcadia. *The* Cathay *was on a 'line voyage' from London whereas the* Arcadia *had just crossed from the American West Coast.*

Yokkaichi, Nagoya, Kobe, Yokohama and then homeward via Guam. At the same time, it was first rumoured that the *Chitral* would be converted to a permanently moored hotel ship and then to a twelve passenger freighter. In 1970, in a miscalculated decision, she was withdrawn from the Far Eastern run, the last P&O passenger ship on that trade, and sent to Genoa for a series of April–October cruises in the Mediterranean. She could not have been less suitable: a mere 240 passengers at maximum against six empty cargo holds. At the end of the year, twelve months after her sister, she too was handed over to Eastern & Australian for further service in the Pacific. Both ships replaced the earlier *Aramac*, the former Cunarder *Parthia* of 1948, which then went to the breakers.

By 1975, however, both the *Chitral* and *Cathay* were again out-of-step, traditional passenger-cargo ships in the jet and container era. They were unprofitable, and were retired by December of that year. The *Chitral* was unable to find a buyer and subsequently went to the scrappers at Kaohsiung, Taiwan. The *Cathay* was more fortunate and was sold to Nan Yang Shipping Company of Macao for use as an officers' training ship. However, she was soon passed to the China Ocean Shipping Company of the People's Republic of China and was renamed *Kengshin*, which was changed to *Shanghai* shortly thereafter. She remains in service at the time of writing.

P&O Group

Sultan of Selangor often travelled with us, taking ten to fifteen berths for his entourage, for shopping trips from Singapore to Hong Kong and return.'

While these sisters were quite popular with passengers, they began to lose their cargo trade and therefore much of their profit by the late 1960s. Most freight was being lured into new, very large and very fast container ships. P&O briefly considered converting them with larger passenger capacities, but the idea never left the boardroom. The *Cathay* was sold off in November 1969, to a member of the P&O Group, the Eastern & Australian Steamship Company. Staffed by Australian officers and Chinese crew, she now sailed on something of a triangular routing: from Melbourne, Sydney and Brisbane to Manila, Hong Kong,

# CHAPTER TWO

# UNION-CASTLE TO AFRICA

John Havers had been a passionate ocean liner enthusiast since his youth, watching ships in the 1920s and 1930s at the bustling port of Southampton. In the years after the Second World War, just as the devastation and destruction began to fade, Mr Havers began fourteen years with the illustrious Union-Castle Mail Steamship Company Limited, the foremost passenger firm to Africa.

Britain's giant passenger ship network began gradually to re-emerge (and rebuild) soon after the end of the war. Simultaneously, many people left the armed forces and the nation slipped into a bleak era of gloom, continued rationing, lingering bomb and fire damage, and considerable unemployment. Many sought work with 'career firms', those noted prewar companies that offered a bright, productive future. In 1947, John Havers was very fortunate to join Union-Castle. It was also a rather convenient decision as many of the big Castle liners were based at Southampton, which remained his home.

The ARUNDEL CASTLE, CARNARVON CASTLE, WINCHESTER CASTLE, ATHLONE CASTLE, STIRLING CASTLE, CAPETOWN CASTLE, PRETORIA CASTLE and EDINBURGH CASTLE

John Havers began as an assistant purser, a prime assignment in those hectic years, and was posted to the 20,063-ton *Carnarvon Castle*, a well known prewar liner dating from 1926. 'I joined her in drydock, where she was undergoing postwar repairs, but not yet her full refit and conversion for luxury service. She had served during the war as an armed merchant cruiser, an AMC, and had been engaged in action off Uruguay, in December 1940, with the Nazi raider *Thor*. The *Carnarvon Castle* was hit by thirty-eight shells and temporary repairs were made at Montevideo, ironically using some plates salvaged from the

*Originally built with four funnels, the* Arundel Castle *was rebuilt with twin stacks in 1937. Her twin masts were said to be the tallest in the Union-Castle fleet.*

Vincent Messina Collection

German pocket battleship *Graf Spee*, which had been sunk in the area. Later, in 1944, she was more thoroughly repaired and converted to a troop ship at New York.

'When I joined the *Carnarvon Castle*, although she had been repainted in company colours, she was still in her wartime guise with a large, ungainly tripod mast stepped forward of the funnel. Her original twin masts had been cut down in size during the war and, at least temporarily, she had lost her handsome good looks that so well matched the other Castle liners of the period. Actually, I had first visited the *Carnarvon Castle* in the early 1930s, as a young boy who spent hours and hours along the Southampton Docks. Then, she had her original twin squat stacks, placed aboard from her completion, but which were replaced during a major rebuilding and re-engining in 1936. To increase her speed and to bring her into conformity with the newer Castle liners, namely the *Athlone Castle* and *Stirling Castle* of 1935–36, she was given more powerful Burmeister & Wain diesels, lengthened [by 30 feet, from 656 to 686 feet] and given a single, wide, rather flat funnel.'

Although designed for and used on the famed Cape Mail Express, between Southampton, Capetown, Port Elizabeth, East London and Durban, the *Carnarvon Castle* – like so many other British liners – was not immediately restored for commercial, luxury service. She had more pressing postwar duties. John

*The* Carnarvon Castle *in the late forties, with her masts stumped and her wartime tripod mast still in place.*

Havers recalled, 'She was urgently needed to handle the flood of British migrants bound for South and East Africa. There had been considerable economic development in South Africa during the war and this was coupled with a huge gold discovery in the Orange Free State in 1946. There was also a ground-nut project in Tanganyika as well as prosperous expansion in both Northern and Southern Rhodesia. Consequently, the *Carnarvon Castle* was used for low-fare resettlement voyages. Her wartime troop accommodation was only slightly upgraded, for 607 passengers in cabins and 671 in dormitories. I did eleven voyages in the *Carnarvon Castle*, carrying full loads of these fare-assisted passengers outbound and then coming homewards practically empty. The only northbound passengers we might have were political and social undesirables, distressed British seamen and the occasional refugee former Nazi.'

The *Carnarvon Castle* was one of the three oldest mail ships to survive the war. The oldest of all was the *Arundel Castle*, which dated from 1921. Actually, she had been laid down in 1915, her intended name *Amroth Castel*, but she was delayed owing to the First World War. She and her twin sistership, the *Windsor Castle* (sunk in March 1943), were noteworthy in being the only 'four stackers' built for a service away from

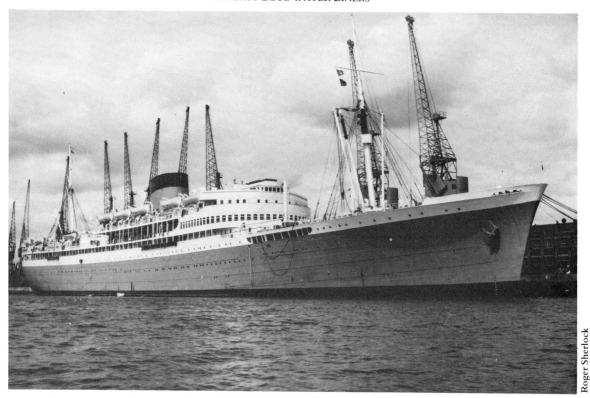

Roger Sherlock

the North Atlantic. In fact, they were the last to have as many stacks. Both were the first-rate ships on the Cape Mail Express until the advent in the later twenties of a new generation of motor liners, a group that included the *Carnarvon Castle*. In the company's large modernization and fleet acceleration programme of 1936–37, both the *Arundel Castle* and *Windsor Castle* were taken in hand by Harland & Wolff at Belfast for improvements. The original four funnels were replaced in a streamlining effort that gave each ship two wider, more contemporary and more attractive stacks. New turbines were fitted that increased their service speeds from 17 to 20 knots. They were also lengthened, from 661 to 686 feet by being given a new bow. The accommodation on the *Arundel Castle* was arranged as 219 berths in first class, 167 in second class and 194 in tourist class. The three-class quarters would disappear from postwar Castle liners and the *Arundel Castle* would become the firm's last twin-stacker. She came through the war unscathed and was restored by her builders at Belfast in 1949–50. She resumed sailings to the Cape in September 1950.

The *Carnarvon Castle*, after war duties as an armed merchant cruiser, then a troop transport, and finally as a postwar austerity migrant ship, was reconditioned at the Harland & Wolff yards at Belfast in 1949–50.

*In the classically handsome Union-Castle style, the* Stirling Castle – *shown at the Southampton Docks – had twin masts, a wide flattish funnel and a long, low superstructure.*

With revised berthing for 216 in first class and 401 in tourist (a reduction from her original total of 853), she resumed luxury sailings just three months prior to the return of the *Arundel Castle*, in June 1950.

The *Winchester Castle* was the third oldest of the prewar mail ships. Completed by Harland & Wolff in October 1930, she too was built, as a successor to the *Carnarvon Castle* generation of motor liners, with two squat stacks. Eight years later, she went back to her builders yard for modernization. A new wide single stack went aboard, new diesels were fitted (increasing her service speed from 16 to 20 knots) and passenger accommodation improved. She was, however, not fitted with a new raked bow. She retained her straight stem to the very end of her days.

John Havers was next assigned, in 1949, to the sisterships *Athlone Castle* and *Stirling Castle*, 25,500-tonners dating from 1935–36. He rose to the rank of senior assistant purser in charge of the tourist class (these ships carried approximately 250 in first class and 540 in tourist). 'These fine identical sisters first introduced what became Union-Castle's standard

Luis Miguel Correia

passenger liner look: a long, low superstructure and flat funnel, and a very long look on the waterline. They were practically the same length as Canadian Pacific's famed *Empress of Britain* of 1931 (742 feet compared to the Castle's 725 feet), but our ships had far less tonnage. They had powerful Danish-built Burmeister & Wain diesels to give their 20-knot service speeds and were, of course, a clever blend of pure economics: 790 or so passengers and about 8400 tons of freight. The company's naval architects were so delighted both with their good looks and high performance that consequently all of our liners followed their design style. The 27,000-ton *Capetown Castle* appeared next, in April 1938, and ranked for all of her years as the longest motor liner afloat'.

All of the big Castle mail ships gave yeoman service during the Second World War. The more recent liners, the *Athlone Castle*, *Stirling Castle* and *Capetown Castle*, were especially distinguished in their service as fast troop transports. Mr E Drummond of Leeds recalled meeting the *Athlone Castle* in the final months of the war. 'In January 1945, at Liverpool, I boarded one of the "Queens of the Pacific", the *Reina Del Pacifico*, along with many other RN, RAF and Army personnel for destination unknown. As we sailed out of the Mersey into the Atlantic to rendezvous with the

*At the time of completion, in 1937, the* Capetown Castle *became the longest motor liner in the world. She survived until 1967.*

convoy and escorts with a zig-zag course, we knew only too well what to except. On station on the starboard side was the *Athlone Castle*, a grey, darkened hulk gliding through the waves of a force 10 – or so it seemed, but in naval terms "a real drop of rough sea". We parted company at Gibraltar.

'On 30 August 1946, returning from the Far East on board HMS *Serene*, a fleet minesweeper, we were steaming at a steady 12 knots through the Suez Straits enjoying an off-watch period after the scorching heat of the Red Sea. Directly astern, in the distance, a ship's masthead light appeared, followed by port and starboard lights. The distance quickly closed in and at 1945 hrs the *Athlone Castle* passed down the port side – a breathtaking sight, with all porthole lights and deck lights blazing. As "ships that pass in the night", it made a fine sight; a marked contrast to her convoy duty days.

'We reached Suez the next morning at 0800. Once again, the *Athlone Castle* lay at anchor awaiting entry to the Suez Canal. The small minesweeper HMS *Serene*, with a certain amount of arrogance by comparison, steamed past the *Athlone Castle* as she weighed anchor, as if making the gesture: "Catch us if you can!" and entered the Suez Canal to sail its length, with *Athlone Castle* proceeding astern. We arrived at Port Said at 2230, where *Serene* was destined to spend two days.

'The *Athlone Castle* slipped quietly out of the breakwater into the Mediterranean, disappearing into the night as quickly as she had arrived astern of *Serene* and with an indignant blast of her siren as if to say: "Catch *us* if you can!"'

The three newest Castle mail ships were reconditioned in 1946 and resumed commercial service a year later, the same time that John Havers joined the Union-Castle Company. 'The Cape Mail Express run was then being sailed by a mixture of prewar liners, some of which were specially allocated from our alternate, but slower and smaller round Africa service. The company had lost eight passenger ships during

the war and so considerable rebuilding was the order of the day. Eight liners, carrying upwards of 700 passengers each and from 6000 tons of freight, were needed to make weekly mail deliveries inside a fortnight. The ships sailed from Southampton every Thursday afternoon at 4 o'clock with absolute clockwork precision. [It was often said, especially in later years, that you could set your watch by a Thursday afternoon Union-Castle sailing.] It was quite an extraordinary service. With printed schedules of perhaps a year or more in advance, and with the priority of a guaranteed berth in South African ports, however great the shipping congestion, all passengers and freight shippers knew to the day when they or

*The postwar Union-Castle 'sensations', the* Edinburgh Castle *(shown here) and her twin sister, the* Pretoria Castle, *were, in the late forties the largest liners yet built for the extensive Cape route.*

Roger Sherlock

Roger Sherlock

*With the forward mast stumped, aft mast removed and a new mast placed just abaft the bridge, both the* Edinburgh Castle *and* Pretoria Castle *lost their very handsome appearance. The latter is shown, after 1966, in her Safmarine colours as the* S. A. Oranje.

their goods would be delivered to any of the Cape ports. I doubt if this service with its exact regularity and superb record had an equal anywhere in the annals of long-haul passenger-cargo runs.'

In the early fifties, with all of the prewar mail liners restored, the Cape Mail run included the 28,705-ton sisterships *Edinburgh Castle* and *Pretoria Castle*, both completed in 1948 and the largest Castle liners yet; the 27,000-ton *Capetown Castle* completed in 1938; another set of sisters, the 25,500-ton *Stirling Castle* and *Athlone Castle*, completed in 1936; the 20,000-ton *Winchester Castle*, finished in 1930; another 20,000-tonner, the *Carnarvon Castle*, delivered in 1926; and finally, the eldest, the 19,200-ton *Arundel Castle*, which first went to sea in 1921. These totalled some 195,000-tons of passenger shipping. John Havers has varied recollections of this enormous collection of liners, all of them painted in the distinctive livery of red-and-black funnels, white superstructure and lavender hulls. Ships' names were spelled out in gold lettering.

'The *Edinburgh Castle* and *Pretoria Castle* [both delivered by Harland & Wolff in 1948] were the postwar sensations. The best people travelled in them, served by the company's hand-picked staff. Princess Margaret had named the *Edinburgh Castle* while Mrs Smuts did the honours for the *Pretoria*

*Castle*, but by radio telephone from South Africa. These ships were, of course, larger versions, repeats in fact, of the *Capetown Castle* from a decade before. However, one major difference was that these new ships were given steam turbines rather than the customary prewar diesels. This actually represented considerable foresight as the company envisaged an even faster future mail service, being reduced from 13½ to 11½ days in each direction [this finally came about some fifteen years later, in 1965, when five liners and two high-speed freighters replaced the traditional eight passenger ships.]

'The *Capetown Castle* was the biggest of the prewar group and was, in fact, the first Castle liner not to be named after a place in the British Isles. The *Athlone Castle* and *Stirling Castle*, being only smaller versions of the *Capetown Castle*, were especially popular ships. The eldest group, the *Winchester Castle*, *Carnarvon Castle* and *Arundel Castle*, retained much of their prewar décor, a style favoured by many of our passengers who had sailed with Union-Castle in the 1920s and 1930s. As the years passed, these ships became "period pieces" of ocean liner decoration. Also I remember especially the *Arundel Castle*, our only two-stacker, for her two towering masts.'

John Havers also recalled the established routing of the Cape Mail Express run. 'After leaving Southampton on Thursday afternoons, we proceeded to Madeira and/or Las Palmas [the latter being mostly for refuelling] and then sailed directly for Capetown, arriving there on Thursday of the second week, some fourteen days later. On Friday, we would sail again, bound for Port Elizabeth on Sunday, East London on

Monday and then a turnaround at Durban from Tuesday to Thursday. We revisited East London on Friday, Port Elizabeth on Saturday and then often made a special call at Mossel Bay. This last-named port was added strictly according to inducement, of either sufficient passengers or cargo. The passengers used tenders and then were lifted on board in a large wicker basket that had a little door. We returned to Capetown on Monday and remained there until Thursday. We arrived at Southampton fourteen days later, early on a Friday morning. The ships remained alongside the Southampton Docks for thirteen days, until their next scheduled Thursday afternoon departure. The mail ships crossed one another near the Equator and generally passed quite close, at an equivalent of a combined 40 mph. It gave the passengers aboard both ships a thirty second thrill! As a purser, who worked sixteen to eighteen hours each day, it would take it least four days of rest to recover from one of these six-week roundtrip Cape Mail Express voyages.'

During the fifties, all of the Union-Castle mail liners were divided between rather deluxe first class quarters and comfortable if less expensive accommodation in tourist class. John Havers recounted, 'In first class, we had the equivalent of first and club classes on today's jet aircraft: the high professionals, bankers, industrialists, corporate chairmen, aristocracy and the older, well-heeled "winter dodgers", who made an early January sailing, stayed a fortnight or so in South Africa, returned in early March and thereby missed the very worst of the English winter. Frequently, we had Princess Alice, the Countess of Athlone, who was the last of Queen Victoria's grandchildren and the great aunt to our present Queen. She had, of course, named the *Athlone Castle* [in November 1935]. Often, the Princess preferred to sail on the *Athlone Castle*, but when impractical, she readily accepted the scheduled mail ship. We also took Harold Macmillan from Capetown to Las Palmas and later had the President of South Africa as well. Very often, we carried various South African Government ministers on the Cape inter-coastal voyages.

'Outbound, in tourist class, we had the settlers, the tourists who couldn't – or wouldn't – afford first class (often going on South African bus tours or to see friends) and British businessmen and their families. It was the equivalent of airline coach class travellers of today. Once, we even had the Soviet Ambassador travelling in tourist class. It was during Stalin's regime and evidently first class was considered too expensive, too capitalistic. It was all rather ironic, however, that on the South African passenger run, the 107-passenger combination liners of the Ellerman Lines tended to be the first choice for many travellers. They were superbly-run ships, much like cosy, private yachts. The Holland–Africa liners were usually second choice. Union-Castle liners, despite their size, speed and fame, were often in third place!'

'Life on board was very different than on today's cruise ships. There was very little, if any air-conditioning, possibly only in the restaurants on the newer ships. Consequently, on board many of the older, prewar liners, many of the public rooms were two decks high to counter the lack of air. Also on the elder ships, the uncooled dining rooms were especially awful. As purser, I can readily recall sitting in a hard-boiled shirt, drinking hot soup and all the while I was expected to look totally composed and at ease. The portholes tended to be always opened. Wind-scoops were essential and either you were lucky to obtain one or made some alternative, artificial version. However, many captains hated these improvised scoops and complained that they made the ships look dreadful.'

Cargo played a very important economic and profit-making role in the operations of these Castle mail liners, which were, in fact, very large passenger-cargo liners. John Havers remembered this aspect of the Cape Mail run as well. 'Outbound, we usually took general cargo: machinery, automobiles, spare parts for the General Motors plant at Port Elizabeth, Scotch whisky, agricultural goods, passenger crates and motor cars, and – most importantly – the mail, which gave us a priority everywhere. Homewards, gold bullion was very important – several hundred, very heavy ingots per trip and all of them bound for the Bank of England in London. There were three keys for three separate locks to the specie room, one key each being held by the captain, the chief officer and the purser. Each day, whether in port or at sea, together we inspected this cargo – counting each ingot and then checking each coded number against a corresponding manifest. We also carried a considerable quantity of fruit, namely apples and oranges. Our heavy-duty cargo was copper, which always went to the bottom of the holds. It was usually loaded at Durban, after having been brought by rail or aboard a small coastal freighter from Beira.'

The Union-Castle Line underwent considerable change after 1955, which was three years after its centenary. After many previously unsuccessful attempts, the company was finally taken over, by Cayzer, Irvine & Company, owners of the big Clan Line of freighters. They merged their interests with

*The traditional Crossing the Line ceremony on board a Union-Castle liner, with purser John Havers on the left, dressed as King Neptune.*

John Havers Collection

yet other British shipping firms, the Houston Line, Scottish Shire Line, King Line and Bullard King Line. Together, these formed the British & Commonwealth Shipping Group. While Union-Castle retained its separate identity, the overall union created one of the largest merchant ship fleets under the British flag. At the end of 1955, the Group controlled ninety-nine deep-sea ships. (A decade later, this had slipped to seventy-one ships, and by 1985 to a mere six freighters, all of which were used for charter services.)

This merger prompted the modernization and acceleration of the Cape Mail run. The older liners were scheduled for retirement, to be replaced by three brand-new passenger ships, the largest yet in the fleet. The first of the mail ships to go was appropriately the oldest of all, the thirty-seven-year-old *Arundel Castle* at the end of 1958. Authors W H Mitchell and L A Sawyer of *The Cape Run*, the history of Union-Castle and its ships published in 1984, wrote: 'On Friday, 5th

December 1958, the *Arundel Castle* left Cape Town on her 211th and final voyage and some 10,000 people gathered at the docks to see her go. Ships in port sounded their customary farewells and dipped ensigns, tugs formed an accompanying flotilla and aircraft dipped in salute. It has been a long, long tradition with the people of South Africa that liners sailed festooned with streamers – but this was something different. She arrived at Southampton on 19th December and left again on the 30th for Kowloon to be broken up after a distinguished career during which she had steamed 2,850,000 miles in peace and 625,565 as a troop ship.'

The *Winchester Castle* was next to be retired; in November 1960 she arrived at Mihara in Japan, to be

taken in hand by ship-breakers from the Nichimen Company. The *Carnarvon Castle* followed in September 1962, when she went to Japanese breakers at Mihara. In 1965 when the fast mail service finally came into effect, the last three prewar liners were scheduled for disposal. The *Athlone Castle* reached Southampton for the last time on 6 August 1965, concluding her 141st round voyage to South Africa. She then went to breakers at Kaohsiung, Taiwan. The *Stirling Castle* was decommissioned three months later, on 30 November. She was sold to Japanese breakers, leaving Southampton on 1 February 1966 and reaching Mihara on 3 March.

The *Capetown Castle* became the last existing member of the prewar fleet and was reduced to a 'relief ship' on the Cape run for two years (1965–67) and also used for periodic cruises. Earlier, on 17 October 1960, she made headline news when she was

*The* Pendennis Castle, *the first of three brand-new liners for Union-Castle, which were destined to be the last built for their South African trade.*

seriously damaged by an engine room explosion off Las Palmas – an unfortunate incident which claimed the lives of seven crew. The *Capetown Castle* underwent repairs and was replaced for one round-trip by the 17,000-ton *Braemer Castle*, temporarily withdrawn from the Round Africa service. In 1965, she was again in the news when £100,000 worth of gold was stolen from her strong-room. Detectives later discovered the ingots, which had been cemented into the bottoms of her sand lockers and in a space between her two cargo holds. When finally retired in the late summer of 1967, the *Capetown Castle* had a far shorter distance to travel than many of her contemporaries for her demise. Instead of going out to the Far East, she was bought by Italian breakers and broken-up in the harbour of La Spezia, a port just south of Genoa.

With all of the prewar liners now gone, the *Edinburgh Castle* and *Pretoria Castle* became the oldest mail ships in the fleet. Used in the new faster schedules, they would survive for another decade, until 1975–76, when they too would sail out to the East for breaking-up.

### The PENDENNIS CASTLE, the WINDSOR CASTLE and the TRANSVAAL CASTLE/S. A. VAAL

Replacing the three oldest prewar liners, the *Arundel Castle, Carnarvon Castle* and *Winchester Castle*, were three large ships, the biggest and fastest yet built for the company. It was planned they should enter service at about two-yearly intervals, in 1958, 1960 and 1962. According to John Havers, 'The first of these, the 28,582-ton *Pendennis Castle* of 1958, was an improved version of the earlier *Edinburgh Castle* and *Pretoria Castle* of 1948. All of them came from the same builder, Harland & Wolff at Belfast. There were, of course, alterations and improvements in the new vessel's décor and she was in fact lengthened while still on the slipways, being increased from 748 to 763 feet, especially for stabilizers [the first set ever incorporated in a Castle liner] and for speed. The increased length was to accelerate the 'Cape Mail' run from 13½ to 11½ days. The *Pendennis Castle* was, in fact, the last liner to be ordered directly by Union-Castle, coming just prior to its integration into the British & Commonwealth Group.'

The 36,123-ton *Windsor Castle*, the largest Union-Castle liner of all, followed – but came from the Cammell Laird shipyard at Birkenhead, just across the River Mersey from Liverpool. She was named by Her Majesty Queen Elizabeth the Queen Mother, who used a special bottle of South African wine for the ceremony held on 23 June 1959. She left Southampton on her maiden voyage to the Cape a year later, on 18 August. She ranked briefly as the largest liner to be built in Britain since the mighty 83,600-ton *Queen Elizabeth* of 1940. This record passed to the P&O-Orient Lines' 41,900-ton *Oriana* that December and then to their 45,770-ton *Canberra* in the following June.

Costing over £10 million, the *Windsor Castle* became

*The* Windsor Castle, *preparing for her maiden voyage in August 1960, is shown alongside at Southampton Docks; behind her, the* Winchester Castle, *the* Pretoria Castle *and farther back still, the troop ship* Nevasa.

Roger Sherlock

55

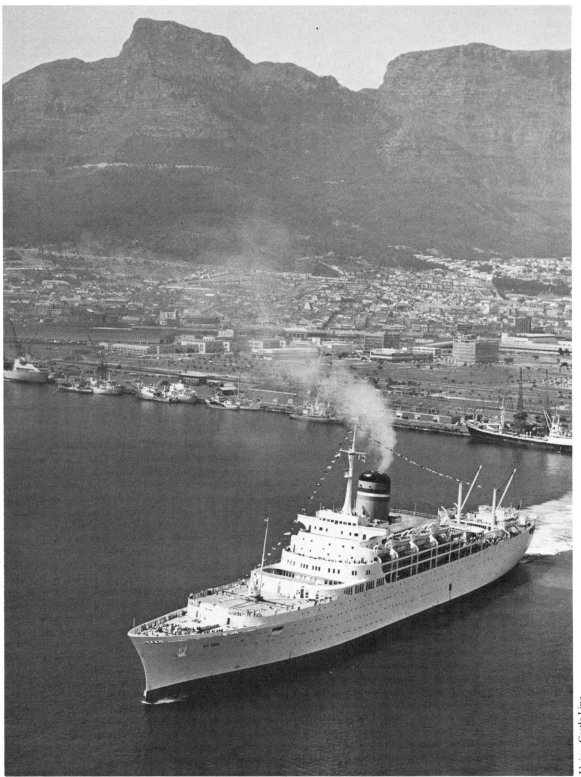

*The last of the Union-Castle liners, the* Transvaal Castle, *later became the* S. A. Vaal *for the Safmarine Lines. She is seen departing from Capetown.*

the company flagship and fastest liner ever to sail on the South African run. Her passengers were divided between 237 in first class and 585 in tourist class but these figures could be adjusted to suit demand. She had a large cargo capacity of some 623,000 cubic feet, of which 352,000 were in refrigerated compartments. Her accommodation was considered the most luxuriously modern on the Cape Mail run. Bob Cummins, who served aboard the *Windsor Castle* in her early years, recalled, 'She was a very fine liner, some years ahead in design and decoration. She was incredibly spacious [most liners of equal size carried well over 1200 passengers whereas the *Windsor Castle*'s total capacity was 822], which so suited her routing and the nearly two weeks at sea. I especially recall the top suites, which were so lavish and well-fitted that the occupants never had to leave them. Even their meals could be served in luxurious privacy.' Each class had separate public rooms but shared a large cinema. Each also had their own open-air swimming pool, verandah lido and deck spaces. All of the first class staterooms had private bathroom facilities. Sample fares for the *Windsor Castle*'s thirty-eight day round-trip to the Cape, over the Christmas-New Year holidays in 1965, were listed as £508 for first class and £231 for tourist class.

The 32,697-ton *Transvaal Castle* completed this new and final Union-Castle trio when she entered service in January 1962. She had come from the John Brown yards on the Clyde. According to John Havers, 'She was specially planned as a follow-up to our all-one-class *Braemar Castle* threesome of 1951-52. The company felt they would like to try a one-class ship, with a range of accommodation from deluxe suites to inexpensive three- and four-berth rooms, on the mail service. In more contemporary fashion, they called it "hotel class" and it was, in actuality, somewhere between normal first class and tourist class. Another innovation aboard this liner was the introduction of waitresses, the first ever on a Union-Castle liner. Unfortunately, however, she proved to be our final new liner.'

To complement the faster mail service, the company added two 13,100-ton cargo liners, which ranked as the fastest diesel-driven freighters afloat at the time. Named *Southampton Castle* and *Good Hope Castle*, and commissioned in 1965, they were put on the Mail run, but without any passenger accommodation. Cargo was to be their sole income – a hint of the future. Built

to make 22½ knots in service and 25 knots at top speed, John Havers reported, 'They did 28 knots on their speed trials, which made them quite incredible ships. Twenty-eight knots was the service speed of the record-breaking *Queen Mary*!'

The new, faster Cape Mail run was introduced in July 1965, using five liners and the two new freighters. To meet the new standards, the *Edinburgh Castle* and *Pretoria Castle* were refitted extensively and improved. According to John Havers, 'When pushed at even higher speeds [over 20 knots], they tended to snake-about and wobble far too much. Consequently, their foremasts were halved because of violent shaking and the aft masts removed completely. Altogether, this destroyed their postwar generation good looks. It marked the end of that traditional Union-Castle appearance of a wide flat funnel offset by twin masts. Hereafter, it was single masts perched above the bridge and mostly domed stacks.'

The regular Thursday afternoon sailings at four were now changed to Fridays at one o'clock. It was to be the final chapter in Union-Castle's passenger history. Another change, also in 1965, was the transfer of the *Transvaal Castle* and *Pretoria Castle* to the South African Marine Corporation (Safmarine). The ships were renamed *S. A. Vaal* and *S. A. Oranje* respectively, repainted in Safmarine colours, but were actually retained by a London-based holding company until 1969. In that year they were transferred formally to the South African flag and registered at Capetown, which replaced London as the home port. John Havers remembered this transfer. 'It was something of an internal trade. South Africa had become more economically independent and increasingly nationalistic. Since we were carrying more and more South African passengers, the Government wanted a national crew that spoke Afrikaans. The two liners were consequently transferred, with the intention that Safmarine Lines would build the next mail liner (which in fact, never came about as a passenger ship, but as a huge container carrier). Although these two ships had a South African flag and registry at Capetown, they were, in fact, always managed by our London office.'

The demise of the famed Cape Mail passenger service was quite evident by the mid-seventies. The *Edinburgh Castle* and *S. A. Oranje* (ex-*Pretoria Castle*) were sold to Taiwanese scrappers in 1975-76. The *Pendennis Castle* was sold as well, in 1976, but to Hong Kong buyers for further trading. However, soon after reaching her Far Eastern home port, she rarely left her moorings. Renamed *Ocean Queen* for the Ocean Queen Navigation Corporation, flying Panamanian colours, she seems to have changed hands a year later (in 1977), joining the Kinvara Bay Shipping company Limited and being renamed *Sindbad I*. Neglected and with few future prospects, she sailed across to Kaohsiung on Taiwan in April 1980 and was promptly broken-up.

For the final year or so (1976–77), the *Windsor Castle* and the *S. A. Vaal* (ex-*Transvaal Castle*) sailed alone as the passenger-carrying mail ships. Weekly liner service to South Africa, once the company's prized tradition, was gone forever. Large and powerful container ships filled out the other weekly sailings. Passenger service ended completely in October 1977. The *Windsor Castle* was sold to the Greek-owned, Panama-flag Latsis Line and was renamed *Margarita L.* Refitted in Greece, she was sent off, in January 1979, to Jeddah, Saudi Arabia for service as a permanently-moored oil workers' hotel and recreation ship. The *S. A. Vaal*, which made the final arrival at Southampton on 10 October, went to the Carnival Cruise Lines of Miami, which also used Panamanian registry. Sent out to the Kawasaki shipyards at Kobe, Japan, she spent nearly eleven months being rebuilt as an all-first class, tropical cruise ship with 1432 berths, which was double her original Union-Castle capacity of 728 berths. The author recalls seeing her at Kobe in the summer of 1978 and a diary entry read, 'The former *S. A. Vaal* seemed out of place in such distant waters, so far from the Atlantic run to South Africa that she steadily plied. Her large funnel was painted over in blue while the under decks and hull were masses of scaffolding and large pieces of vinyl covering. Workmen crawled about her like ants. She was assuredly a ship undergoing an extensive transformation.' Renamed *Festivale*, she entered weekly cruise service from Miami, in October of that same year. Reportedly, she has been such a success for her owners, sailing in seven days to San Juan, St Thomas and Nassau, that they approached the Latsis Line in an effort to buy the former *Windsor Castle* as the ideal companion ship after a similar conversion. The sale never materialized and instead the Carnival Cruise Lines ordered the first of four new liners in 1980.

John Havers feels that there were many factors which contributed to the demise of the Union-Castle passenger service. 'The jet is, of course, the most obvious – a strong, ferocious competitor. This was accompanied by a dwindling number of sea passengers. Then, container ships took the cargo, which eliminated that source of revenue. Of course, there were ever-increasing labour costs, the fuel oil crisis of the early seventies [the ships were doing 22 knots under steam and were incredibly expensive] and even the isolation of South Africa itself contributed. The Union-Castle "Cape Mail" was the last big, long-haul ocean liner run in the world. It was very sad to see it go.'

*The unsuccessful* Bloemfontein Castle *of 1950, shown in her later years as the Greek-owned Adriatic ferry* Mediterranean Star.

Antonio Scrimali

## The BLOEMFONTEIN CASTLE

One of John Havers' other assignments was to sail in a rather odd passenger ship in the Union-Castle fleet, the 18,400-ton *Bloemfontein Castle*, completed in 1950 and which, quite uniquely, had space for 739 passengers in all-tourist class quarters. Previously, all Castle liners had at least two classes, including luxurious, upper-deck first class accommodation. However, this new ship was created especially for the low-fare migrant trade, to follow-up on the postwar austerity services of ships such as the *Carnarvon Castle* and *Winchester Castle*. John Havers remembers 'The Belfast-built *Bloemfontein Castle* – "Bloemph" as we called her – arrived just too late for the continuation of a booming migrant trade. As Britain reached full postwar employment, the flow of South and East Africa-bound settlers declined substantially. Consequently, we put this ship, an "odd duckling" at best, on an alternate to the Cape Mail Express and Round Africa runs that was known as our Intermediate Service. She sailed from London, called at Rotterdam and then went southward to Las Palmas, Lobito, Walvis Bay, Capetown, Port Elizabeth, East London, Durban and then finally to Lourenço Marques and Beira. We ran something of a special mini-cruise service as well, between Durban and Beira. The Lourenço Marques Radio Station always came aboard at Durban, held a broadcast quiz in the lounge and this gave the passengers the chance to participate and be heard throughout South Africa.'

The *Bloemfontein Castle* was not without some historic moments, however. 'She heroically rescued all hands, 234 in all, from the wrecked Holland-Africa liner *Klipfontein*, which broke in half off the Mozambique coast in January 1953. Later, we had a much pursued London diamond thief aboard, who had actually signed aboard as part of our deck department. Our high seas capture and arrest caught the full attention of the press. However, the police did not want his identity uncovered and so we had to smuggle him ashore at Capetown. He was taken off the ship on the "off quay" side of the ship by a large tug and then delivered to the far reaches of the Duncan Dock, all while hordes of reporters and photographers were left howling along the ordinary quayside.

'The *Bloemfontein Castle* also took part in a fruitless search for a downed American troop transport plane in the mid-Atlantic, which was on a flight from a European base to the Azores. The search took place at night and there were dozens of flares, aeroplanes and countless sightings of whales and unconnected debris, but no luck with our laborious "square" search.'

Unfortunately, the 18-knot, 595-foot long *Bloemfontein Castle* was never a successful ship and was the first of the postwar-built Union-Castle liners to be withdrawn. In fact, it was the beginning of the slow decline and demise of this mighty passenger fleet. John Havers recounted her end, 'There was nothing very startling about her. She had very basic accommodation that was aimed at the lower end of the tourist class market from the start. She never seemed to fit in and was finally sold off in 1959, after only nine years of service, to the Chandris Group of Companies. Renamed *Patris* for their new Europe-Australia Line migrant service, she was a huge success in this trade and was the first of many second-hand liners to join that firm.'

## The RHODESIA CASTLE, the KENYA CASTLE and the BRAEMAR CASTLE

Union-Castle's Round Africa passenger service was unique to ocean liner shipping. It completely circumnavigated Africa. John Havers spent a decade on this trade, serving as purser aboard the prewar *Llandovery Castle*, *Dunnottar Castle*, *Durban Castle* and *Warwick Castle*, and the last to be purposely designed for this trade, a postwar trio named *Rhodesia Castle*, *Kenya Castle* and *Braemar Castle*. 'The Round Africa voyage – "the RA run" as we called it – encircled Africa, either by going out via the west coast or out by the way of the east coast. From the purser's point of view, it was easier to go out on the eastern side as you then had the long Atlantic voyage home to get things, namely the paperwork, sorted out. Ports of call "out west" began with London, then Rotterdam and onwards to Las Palmas, Ascension, St Helena, Capetown, Port Elizabeth, East London, Durban, Lourenço Marques, Beira, Dar-es-Salaam, Zanzibar, Tanga, Mombasa, Aden, Port Sudan, Suez, Port Said, Genoa, Marseilles, Gibraltar and then homeward to London. Occasional variations for cargo or military reasons included calls at Naples, Djibouti and ports in Portuguese East Africa such as Nacala. The entire round-trip took about eight weeks, which necessitated a full week's rest and recovery after returning to England.'

Shipboard operations seem to have been far more complicated then, especially from this distance in time, and compared to contemporary cruise ship services. According to John Havers, 'During the Suez Canal transits in the 1950s, in the regime of Colonel Nasser, it was necessary to have an armoured car or light tank positioned on the foredeck as protection for the ship. Of course, this ceased when the British Army left the Suez zone. My responsibilities on a large passenger-cargo liner like the 17,041-ton *Rhodesia Castle* were quite different from a purser's role on a present day ship. It was commercial in every sense and one was running a sort of bus between ports. We did, however, have passengers – including American tourists – who made the whole round trip. As pursers, we had to take it as it came: lost baggage, heavy baggage, endless cleaning and re-cleaning of cabins for new occupants, strange meal times adjusted to varying ever-changing schedules, lots of changes in currencies and postage, enormous quantities of mail on and off, masses of letters from the head office [in

*Shown during her trials off Scotland, in November 1952, the* Braemar Castle *was the last of three specially-designed Round Africa liners for Union-Castle.*

London], flowers and fruit baskets for newcomers which had to be delivered to their cabins, loads of visitors seeing people off and often packing the ship solid, crew pay and other matters, defaulters, tours to places of interest that needed special arrangements, ship's business in general, port forms, crew lists, entertaining shore officials, entertaining the passengers and then those 1001 different problems with the inevitably unexpected – breaks of journey, overbooking, drunkeness, births and deaths. It was all go!'

The ports themselves were often a problem. 'On the East African coast, the noise of cargo loading and off-loading was awful. At Beira, for example, the port itself was built around a swamp that often reached 110–120°F and with the deepest, thickest humidity. It was also full of insects and cockroaches that were half

*Coronation Day on* Rhodesia Castle

| | |
|---|---|
| 9.30–10.00am | Church service in the lounge |
| 11.00–11.45am | Crossing the Line ceremony |
| 12 noon–1.00pm | Luncheon in two sittings |
| 1.15–3.45pm | Westminster Abbey Service Broadcast |
| 4.30pm | Film Show for Children in the Smoke Room |
| 5.30pm | Children's Tea Party in the Saloon |
| 7.30pm | Dinner |
| 7.40pm | Toast: "THE QUEEN" Proposed by The Commander, followed by the National Anthem |
| 8.45pm | Gala Dance |
| 10.30pm | Buffet in the Smoke Room |
| 10.50pm | Prime Minister's Speech Broadcast |
| 11.00pm | The Queen's Speech Broadcast |

Richard K Morse Collection

the size of a man's foot and known as "tiger tanks". We often tried to shoot them by using large rubber bands.

'While the cargo was being worked, the passengers often went to the beach, to escape both the noise and the heat. We might have as many as three days in some ports or even five days at Beira. Then, we organized special overland excursions to the Tsavo Game Reserve or into Nairobi. However, these were very long, very hot, very adventurous drives. It was long before the era of air-conditioned coaches.'

The passengers tended to be a mixed lot during the 1950s when fares for a full round-trip began at £50. John Havers recalled, 'We carried the civil servants, the tea and coffee planters, copper workers, mine managers, civilian troops, the missionaries and priests, local inter-port passengers and the occasional special passenger such as His Excellency the Governor of the Sudan. Of course, the purser arranged all of the onboard entertainment in those days: cricket matches and games on deck, horse-racing, the Crossing of the Line ceremony, dancing (to a live band on some ships, to records on others), indoor games, cards, fancy dress (held separately for both adults and children), films, the ship's concert (in fact, a passenger talent show) and then prize night. On Voyage 7 for the *Rhodesia Castle*, the programme for Tuesday, 2 June 1953 was entitled "Coronation Day" [see above].

'As pursers, we did a sixteen to eighteen hour day yet the salaries seem incredible – £30 a month for an assistant purser in 1947 to £300 a month for a full purser by 1961.

'On the East African service, we tended to cater for the middle-grade civil servants. Lloyd Triestino's *Africa* and *Europa* – with their thorough air-conditioning, superb first class and light, comfortable décor – were the superior ships. The upper-grade civil servants tended to go in British India's *Kenya* and *Uganda*. Union-Castle liners were actually behind the times when it came to the comforts of air-conditioning. Some of our ships simply didn't have so important an amenity, yet the P&O "Strath" liners had air-conditioned restaurants in the 1930s!'

Long before the intrusion of the jet, container cargo shipping and sky-rocketing fuel oil and labour costs, areas like the South and East African coasts employed dozens of passenger ships. 'There were plenty of chances to see a wide range of commercial liners when on the Round Africa route. There were the Anchor liners, bound to and from India – a race with their *Cilicia* for the last berth at Port Sudan comes readily to mind – we just won. There were the Italian beauties at Genoa, with my favourites being the *Conte Biancamano*, *Conte Grande*, *Saturnia*, *Vulcania*, *Federico C*, *Venezuela* (ex-*De Grasse*), the graceful four-masters of the East Asiatic Company and even P&O's old *Mongolia* then sailing as the *Nassau*. We also came across Cunard-White Star's *Georgic* on the migrant run to Australia, various P&O passenger ships like the *Himalaya* at Aden and *Maloja* at Port Said, the Dutch *Volendam* as a trooper going out to troubled Indonesia, the luxurious *Andrea Doria* at Gibraltar, the French *Pasteur* and *Champollion* at Marseilles, and Muslim pilgrim ships at Suez such as Blue Funnel's *Talthybius* and the Japanese Railways' twin-stacker *Koan Maru*, which somehow escaped the US Navy's wartime torpedoes. Other ships seen included the Indian *State of Madras* at Mombasa and such British India liners as the three-funnel *Tairea* and little *Amra*. On all of the Union-Castle services, we would come across the Portuguese colonial liners *Imperio*, *Patria*, *Mocambique*, *Angola* and the old *Nyassa*. Farrell Lines' *African Enterprise* and *African Endeavor*, British India's *Karanja* and *Kampala* and Bank Line's *Isipingo* were also familiar sights. There was also Ellerman's *City of Exeter*, *City of York*, *City of Durban*, *City of Port Elizabeth* and the veteran *City of Paris*, which dated from 1921, Shaw Savill's *Dominion Monarch*, and the aforementioned *Kenya*, *Uganda*, *Africa* and *Europa*. Union-Castle's Round Africa liners usually met at one of the East African ports, one going eastabout and the other westabout.

'All of the above-named passenger liners should not obscure the fact that hundreds and hundreds of interesting cargo ships in their well known colour schemes could be seen almost everywhere. There were the Farrell and Robin lines from the United States, Ellerman and Harrison ships, tankers, whalers and so on.'

There were, of course, those special, quite notable incidents that remain vivid in John Havers' memory. 'I recall a blizzard in the Straits of Dover when the *Kenya Castle* drifted rather than sailed. In April 1954, we met the *Gothic*, chartered from Shaw Savill and acting as a royal yacht, carrying Her Majesty the Queen and her coronation tour party. At Aden, it was 100°F at three in the afternoon and we asked if we might salute by siren. The response was that the ship's commander preferred not. It seemed that the Queen was napping. Consequently, we simply dipped our flags and slipped past quietly. On another occasion, during a docker's strike in London, I took 250 crewmembers by ferry and then train to Hamburg to staff the *Warwick Castle*, which had been detoured. We then went to Plymouth Roads and loaded our British passengers by tender.'

The Round Africa passenger service began its gradual decline by the late 1950s. The *Dunnottar Castle* (from 1936) was withdrawn at the end of 1958, and then sold off to the Liberian-flag Incres Line, who had her totally rebuilt as the luxury cruise ship *Victoria*. She still sails, now nearing her fiftieth year, but for the Chandris Lines. The *Warwick Castle*, which had been rebuilt as a small aircraft carried during the war and subsequently rebuilt as a passenger ship, and her sistership, the *Durban Castle*, both dating from the late 1930s, were next to go. They were sold for scrap in 1962; the *Warwick Castle* being broken-up at Barcelona and the *Durban Castle* at Hamburg.

The final Round Africa ships were the Harland & Wolff-built trio, the *Rhodesia Castle*, *Kenya Castle* and *Braemar Castle*. John Havers fondly remembered this threesome. 'They were built [1951–52] to replace three elderly prewar Round Africa liners, the *Llandovery Castle* [1925], *Llanstephen Castle* [1914] and *Llangibby Castle* [1929]. The new ships represented contemporary ideas, each having accommodation for about 550 passengers in one class which, in standard, was between first and tourist class. It was often referred to as cabin class. It was, of course, much easier for the passengers, especially on such long voyages, to have full run of the ship. In the two-class combination liners, the tourist class passengers alway seemed to suffer somewhat.

'Powered by steam turbines, giving them a 17½ knot service speed, I recall that the *Rhodesia Castle* also had a special third, auxiliary boiler, to be used only for emergency speed, but for which we always needed special permission from London. Once, when we pushed her to absolute maximum, the *Rhodesia Castle* registered 22 knots!'

The Round Africa service was terminated in 1962. Thereafter, the three surviving ships went outwards

only by way of the east coast and then turned around at Durban, where there were scheduled connections on the same day with one of the big Cape Mail Express liners, which sailed homeward via the Atlantic. Of the surviving ships, the *Braemar Castle* – which it was briefly through might become a cruise ship – was withdrawn in the face of a dwindling trade and then sold to scrappers at Faslane in Scotland at the end of 1965. She had reached the very slight age of fourteen. The *Rhodesia Castle* and *Kenya Castle* thereafter had their sailings timed with British India's *Kenya* and *Uganda*. However, it was all to be quite short-lived. Primarily as a result of the decline of Britain's East African colonies, the surge of nationalization in Africa and then a general shift to air travel, the previous passenger requirements – particularly among those earlier civil servants, traders and their families – all but vanished completely. In 1967, the two lone survivors were withdrawn, finishing-off what remained of the old Round Africa service. The

*The* Rhodesia Castle *and her two sisterships were given extended refits during 1960–61, which included the addition of domes to their single funnels.*

*Rhodesia Castle*, unable to find a foreign buyer for further trading, went to Taiwanese scrappers while the *Kenya Castle* found new life with the Chandris Lines, under the Greek flag, vastly rebuilt as the cruise ship *Amerikanis*, which translates to 'American Lady'. She remains in North American cruise service to date.

# CHAPTER THREE

# THE AFRICAN ROUTES

## ELLERMAN LINES

The CITY OF PORT ELIZABETH, CITY OF EXETER, CITY OF YORK and CITY OF DURBAN

Britain's Ellerman Lines once maintained one of the largest merchant fleets on earth. Their 'City' ships were known almost everywhere, from Southampton to Sydney, from Philadelphia to Port Elizabeth. Most of their freighters carried the customary dozen or so passengers, often in very fine quarters. However, there were four, quite distinct combination liners built in the early 1950s for the run to South and East Africa. They were the *City of Port Elizabeth*, *City of Exeter*, *City of York* and *City of Durban*.

These four 'City' liners were built at the Vickers-Armstrongs yard at Newcastle-upon-Tyne between 1952 and 1954. At 13,300 tons and 541 feet in length, they were driven by Doxford diesels that rendered service speeds of up to 16½ knots. By comparison, present-day 55,000-ton container ships plying the

same African routes make up to 25 knots. In the older quartet, there were five holds for cargo – for items such as South African gold, fruit and timber. They carried their cargo (and passengers) out of London (and occasionally from Middlesbrough, Hamburg, Rotterdam and Antwerp as well) via Las Palmas to Capetown, Port Elizabeth, East London, Durban, Lourenço Marques and then turnaround at Beira.

The four sisters could carry 107 passengers each, all in first class. They were considered leisurely and yacht-like, especially when compared to big, speedy ships like the Union-Castle liners, which plied very similar routes. The Ellerman liners' accommodation

*The* City of Port Elizabeth *departing from Hull, a cargo call between her arrival and then final departure from London. The passenger accommodation has been 'curtained off' by canvas coverings until the ship returns to London.*

J K Byass

was of quite a high standard. C M Squarey described two of the public rooms aboard the *City of Port Elizabeth*: 'The drawing room is delightfully proportioned and carries all of the charm of the Queen Anne period in its scheme of decoration. A fine portrait of Queen Anne hangs over the mantlepiece. The Smoke Room is amidships and access to it can be gained either internally or externally through double doors each side, which opens up on to the Promenade Deck. Pleasant panelling prevails all round this room, the Jacobean period influencing its decoration and successfully producing a congenial atmosphere. The curtains, made of dark velvet, are a rather unusual selection, however, for a ship spending the greater part of its time in tropical climates. This ship is not air-conditioned; there is, however, abundant ventilation in the form of punkah louvres, and variations of that even down to the old three-bladed fans.'

Mr Leslie Shaw of Rainham in Kent, who began travelling by ship in 1932, made voyages in at least three dozen or so passenger liners, including the *City of Exeter* and *City of Durban*. 'They had the best service ever. Morning tea requested at 7.30am was punctually delivered each day by the steward or stewardess. Both ships offered the finest menus for dinner I've ever experienced and the *City of Durban* had the most magnificent sweet trolley.'

*The former* City of York, *fully rebuilt as the Mediterranean ferry-cruise ship* Mediterranean Sky. *Her passenger capacity was increased from 107 to 850 berths.*

The four 'City' liners had profitable, popular lives on the African run for over fifteen years, a rather good investment by contemporary shipping standards. However, by the early 1970s, such ships were quite out-of-step with the times. The advent of ever-growing, ever-faster container ships brought a revolution of sorts to runs like South and East Africa. Furthermore, the passenger trade had withered in the face of competitive jet-plane travel. The *City of York* made the last voyage of the Ellerman passenger service when she sailed from Capetown on 4 June 1971 – an historic link, first made in 1892, was ending.

The four ships were soon laid-up and offered for sale. They attracted Greek buyers, commanding approximately $700,000 each. They joined the Karageorgis Group through a series of holding companies. All were then brought to Greek ports for intended conversion to Aegean ferries and cruise ships. However, only two were transformed and have survived.

The *City of Exeter* and *City of York* were fully rebuilt, at a cost of over $12 million each. They became the futuristic-looking *Mediterranean Sea* and *Mediterranean*

*Sky.* The original accommodation and cargo spaces were gutted to make way for some 350 cars and 850 passengers. Both now ply the eastern Mediterranean and once, during the late seventies, the *Mediterranean Sea* even served as a venue for a floating trade fair in the Middle East.

The *City of Durban*, renamed *Mediterranean Dolphin*, and the *City of Port Elizabeth* renamed the *Mediterranean Island* and later *Mediterranean Sun*, were kept initially in reserve, awaiting conversion, but this never came to pass. The former *City of Durban* was sold to Taiwanese scrappers in the spring of 1974; the ex-*City of Port Elizabeth* met the same fate in 1980.

The Karageorgis ferries still sail at present, the last survivors of the Ellerman 'City' liners.

## ELDER DEMPSTER LINES

### The ACCRA and APAPA

The Elder Dempster Lines was the foremost British shipping firm on the West African route, one which was a stronghold of colonial possessions until the 1960s. Following war losses in its passenger fleet, the company contracted for three new passenger-cargo ships, two being sisterships and the third, the firm's largest liner and flagship.

The smaller pair, named the *Accra* and *Apapa*, were built by Vickers-Armstrongs at Barrow and commissioned in September 1947 and March 1948 respectively. At 11,600 tons each, they had accommodation for 259 passengers in first class and a small third class

section with 24 berths. Housed on five decks, the first class public rooms and facilities included an outdoor pool and games area on the Sports Deck; the Forward Lounge, library, card room, gift shop, beauty salon, barber shop, bar and the Smoke Room on the Promenade Deck; cabins on C and D decks; and the dining saloon forward on E Deck, the lowest passenger deck. The cabin accommodation included a suite, comprising a sitting room, bedroom and full bathroom, and a series of single- and double-berth rooms, some of which had extra Pullman berths and all but one of them fitted with private shower and toilet. Third class consisted of six four-berth rooms located aft on E Deck and a small covered promenade area and saloon just above on D Deck.

Later joined by the larger *Aureol* of 1951, the *Accra* and *Apapa* worked on a monthly timetable, sailing from Liverpool with the passage taking five days to Las Palmas in the Canaries, seven days to Bathurst in The Gambia, nine days to Freetown in Sierra Leone, twelve days to Tema and Takoradi in Ghana, and thirteen days to Lagos, Nigeria. The round-trip fare, with seven nights ashore in Accra or five nights in Lagos, was £245 in January 1966. While round-trip holiday passengers were important clientele, especially by the mid- and late sixties, the company relied heavily on one-way traffic: civil servants, businessmen and their families, traders, scientists and engineers, and West Africans travelling to and from Britain for their education.

Cargo was also an important aspect of this trade, even for the passenger ships. Roland Hasell, who later became chief officer on *Queen Elizabeth 2*, sailed with Elder Dempster in the 1960s. 'While the passenger ships sailed according to a prescribed schedule, the twelve-passenger freighters out of London ran three- and four-month round-trips to many backwater ports in West Africa. I especially recall at one of them that the local pilot was lifted out of the water in his canoe by the ship's crane. A pilot, who was a father, often directed his children to steer the ship. Our outbound cargos tended to be general goods – second-hand lorries and lots of junk machinery. Homeward, we had the important revenue items: logs, palm kernel nuts, nut oil and palm oil [kept in deep tanks on board], bales of rubber and liquid latex.'

The *Accra* and *Apapa*, like so many British-flag passenger-cargo ships, were adversely affected by the abrupt decline of Britain's political and economic status in former colonial outposts by the 1960s. The passenger trade dwindled considerably, not only due to the loss of a near-constant flow of civil servants and other Government personnel, but also because of the appearance of airline competition. The West African student trade, for example, made the transition to air travel.

The *Accra* was withdrawn first and, unable to find any appropriate buyers despite her being only twenty years of age, went to Spanish ship-breakers. She arrived at Cartagena on 13 November 1967. Just under a year later, on 20 September 1968, the *Apapa* left Liverpool on her final sailing. In her two decades, she had carried 100,000 passengers, 750,000 tons of cargo and made 177 round voyages to West Africa. She was

*Flagship of the Elder Dempster Lines, the* Aureol, *on the Mersey, outbound for a month-long round voyage to West Africa.*

Elder Dempster Lines

more fortunate than *Accra*, however, and found a new career with the Shun Cheong Steam Navigation Company of Hong Kong. Renamed *Taiphooshan*, she was sent out to the Far East for further trading, mostly in local waters and to Singapore and Penang. She was broken-up in the winter of 1975 at Kaoshiung by the Fu Chiang Steel & Iron Company.

## The Aureol

Delivered in the autumn of 1951, from Alexander Stephen & Sons at Glasgow, the appearance of the *Aureol* enabled Elder Dempster Lines to have a schedule of fortnightly sailings from Liverpool. She was paired with the *Accra* and *Apapa*. The *Aureol*, at 14,083 tons, had larger, more spacious accommodation than the two earlier ships – 253 in first class, 76 in cabin class and 24 in third class. She too was driven by Doxford-type diesels, which provided an adequate service speed of 16 knots. Her round voyages also took 30 days but her routing was slightly different, however, from the two earlier ships, as she called at Monrovia instead of Bathurst.

C M Squarey was quite pleased with the design of this new ship, which was in fact the last passenger liner to be built for Elder Dempster. 'The Elder Dempster fleet is well known and held in high regard by those who occupy their business in the West African waters as well as by quite a few others; from years of experience they know what the trade wants and their target has always been to please the passenger in a non-sensational way. There is nothing sensational about this latest addition to their fleet except, perhaps, her external appearance. Her white hull with the gold band around it, her almost clipper bow, her nicely rounded bridge, abaft of which is her single mast, and her stocky yellow funnel all unite to give her a most pleasing profile. My forecast is that many people will reckon that she is the prettiest ship based on the Mersey.'

The *Aureol* made the first cruise in Elder Dempster history, over the New Year's holiday in 1967, from Lagos. Her passenger loads on the West African trade began to drop, even after the withdrawal of the *Accra* and *Apapa* left her as the sole remaining Elder Dempster liner, so in April 1972 she was transferred to Southampton, in an effort to recruit more passengers. It was a short-lived reprieve. Just over two years later, in October 1974, she was withdrawn completely and thus ended her owner's passenger trade. She was decommissioned at Southampton on 18 October.

Initial rumours were that the *Aureol* was to be sold to Pakistani buyers, to become an Indian Ocean pilgrim ship, but this never materialized. Instead she went to the Marianna Shipping & Trading Company of Panama, a division of the John S Latsis Line of Greece, who had earlier bought the P&O liners *Strathmore* and *Stratheden* and who would later buy Union-Castle's *Windsor Castle* (in 1977). The *Aureol* was renamed *Marianna VI*, sent to Piraeus for some refitting and alterations, and then dispatched to Jeddah in Saudi Arabia for use as a workers' accommodation centre. She was permanently moored there until February 1979, when she was brought back to Piraeus and then laid-up in Perama Bay with a large assortment of either out-of-work or retired passenger ships, freighters, tankers and coasters. A year later, however, another Arabian lease was arranged and she was taken to Rabegh, where she remains to date.

# BRITISH INDIA LINE

## The Kenya and Uganda

In January 1983, just after finishing emergency duty in the Falklands as a hospital ship, the thirty-year-old educational cruise ship *Uganda* was rechartered by the British Government for two years of further duty as a relay ship between Ascension Island and the Falklands. It was a charter worth over $85 million. P&O Cruises, as parent of *Uganda*, the last British India (BI) liner, could hardly refuse. However, it spelled the commercial end for a most beloved ship.

The 16,000-ton *Uganda* was Britain's last old colonial liner. At least one preservationist group was formed to help save her in April 1985 when the charter ended. She was built at the Barclay Curle yards at Glasgow in 1952, for the British India Steam Navigation Company Limited. Alone that corporate title conjures up images of the Imperial Raj. However, the *Uganda* and her sistership, the *Kenya* of 1951, initially worked the company's alternate passenger service: to East Africa via the Suez. Sailing out of London, the two ships plied an exotic route: Gibraltar, Port Said, the Suez Canal, Aden, Mombasa, Tanga, Zanzibar, Dar-es-Salaam, Beira and then a turnaround at southern Durban. Britain's dominant political links in that area at the time made such a passenger and freight service quite prosperous. The *Uganda*, for example, carried 299 passengers, 190 in first class and 109 in tourist class, and nearly 400,000 cubic feet of cargo.

However, by the mid-sixties, with the political character of the area greatly changed, the trade began to wane. The *Uganda* was converted to a schools' cruise ship, a concept pioneered by some earlier and otherwise out-of-work British India liner/troop ships of the 1930s. Extraordinarily popular for many years, she terminated this service in January 1983 and, after some extended charter service for the British Government between Ascension and the Falklands, was laid-up pending disposal in April 1985. The *Kenya* was not as fortunate, however. While brief thought was given to converting her into a globe-trotting display ship for British industrial products, she terminated BI's East Africa service at London, on 9 June 1969. Shortly thereafter, she was scrapped at La Spezia in Italy.

*A stern view of British India's* Kenya, *loading cargo at London. She terminated her owner's East African passenger run in the summer of 1969.*

British India Line

Luis Miguel Correia

## ——— HOLLAND-AFRICA LINE ———

### The JAGERSFONTEIN and ORANJEFONTEIN

The Holland-Africa Line was once famous for its sizeable fleet of freighters with names ending in 'fontein' and 'kerk'. Today, at a time of dramatic change in the shipping industry – from containerization to corporate reorganization to a worldwide slump in trading conditions in the early 1980s – the history of the company and its ships are largely forgotten. Holland-Africa, part of the United Netherlands Steamship Company, was eventually merged into the giant Nedlloyd Group and subsequently lost its identity. The company also once maintained a passenger service to South and East Africa – one with an extremely high reputation.

To supplement its existing prewar tonnage, two combination passenger-cargo liners were ordered in that fateful year of 1939. The first of these, the *Rietfontein*, was laid down at the Schichau shipyards at Danzig in 1939. Just prior to launching on 30 March the following spring, her name was changed to *Elandsfontein*. Soon thereafter, the incomplete ship was seized by the German Navy, but strangely she was never completed. She sat out most of the war untouched. On 14 March 1945, having been moved to

*The* Uganda *was extensively rebuilt from a passenger-cargo liner as an educational cruise ship, at a major refit at Hamburg in 1967–68. She remained in schools' cruising until early 1983.*

Gdynia, she was seriously damaged by artillery fire and then left to sink at the mouth of the Vistula. She might have been left as an abandoned wreck, but the shortages of adequate shipping after the war, particularly for the battered Dutch, were such that her owners sent an examination team to Gdynia. Two years after the sinking, on 20 March 1947, she was raised and towed to a nearby berth for temporary patching. Five months later, on 9 August, under the care of a sturdy ocean-going tug, the remains of the *Elandsfontein* underwent a sensitive and cautious tow to Holland, to the De Schelde shipyard at Vlissingen. To reduce the memories of wartime and her capture, she was given a new name, *Jagersfontein*. However, because of shortages of materials and even a reduction in the number of available skilled personnel, the reconstruction of the ship was a long, sluggish affair. It took well over two years before she was actually commissioned, in March 1950, for her planned service to African ports.

The intended sistership, named *Oranjefontein* from

her conception, was ordered from a Dutch yard, P Smit Jr at Rotterdam. She too was launched in the spring of 1940, but then also fell into German hands. Completed that December, she was transferred to the German navy, only to be damaged by the Allied bombing of Rotterdam, on 28 August 1941. Her captors had the ship repaired and then transferred her operations and management to the German-Africa Line, which had run combination passenger-cargo liners on the same South and East African run before the war. She seems to have done little actual sailing, but was instead used for target practice by U-boats and the *Luftwaffe*. In the winter and spring of 1945, she is supposed to have participated in the evacuation of refugees from the German Eastern territories. Arnold Kludas, in his superb series *Great Passenger Ships of the World*, reported that she had been renamed *Pioneer* during this period, but that there was never any official confirmation of this change. However, soon after the Allied invasion of Germany, the *Oranjefontein* was returned to her intended owners, obviously with very little damage. By September, she had been sent off on a series of postwar repatriation sailings. She

brought Dutch nationals home from the Caribbean and made at least one sailing to the North American West Coast. In 1946, fully restored and reconditioned, she entered the African passenger trade for which she had been intended.

The *Jagersfontein* and *Oranjefontein* sailed as a team and were joined by the larger *Randfontein* in 1958. C M Squarey visited the *Jagersfontein* soon after her commissioning, in the spring of 1950. 'I liked particularly the panelled ceiling, the parchment walls and the distinctive high-backed chairs in the Smoke Room; the Cocktail Lounge is certainly a room with "barsonality", whilst the Main Lounge has a gentle, captivating charm of its own. The Forward Verandah is likely to be a favourite place of passengers. The Dining Saloon may be considered by some to be a little over-mirrored, and not all will dote on its "symphony in red" decorative scheme. Practically every cabin [in first class] has a shower or bath, which is a good and

*Designed and ordered in the late thirties, the* Jagersfontein *was not commissioned for the Holland-Africa Line's passenger-cargo services until as late as March 1950.*

Holland-Africa Line

distinctive feature of design.

'The tourist class accommodation [with 60 berths compared to the 100 beds in first class], which is right aft, is described by her owners as comparable to third class in large passenger liners; if it's a slight overstatement to call it tourist class, then perhaps it's as much an understatement to rank it third class. The Holland-Africa Line had long enjoyed an enviable reputation for running its ships really well; it is certain that this ship will not merely uphold, but enhance that reputation.'

The *Jagersfontein* and *Oranjefontein* were retired in 1967, prompted by a declining passenger trade and the gradual transition to the transportation of freight in faster cargo liners and then container ships. The former went to Greek buyers, the Embajada Compania Naviera SA, who renamed her *Devon*, but then promptly resold her to Taiwanese breakers. She arrived at Kaohsiung on 23 December. The *Oranjefontein* was sold to Spanish scrappers, who, for the delivery voyage from Amsterdam to Bilbao that August, renamed her *Fontein*.

## The RANDFONTEIN

The last of the Holland-Africa liners, the *Randfontein* of 1958, was also their largest pessenger ship. Delivered in January 1959, by the Wilton-Fijenoord shipyards at Schiedam, this 13,700-ton ship was fitted with six cargo holds, which included special tanks for

*The* Randfontein *of 1958 was the final passenger ship in the Holland-Africa fleet. Withdrawn in 1971, she was sold to the Royal Interocean Lines and later to the Chinese Government, for whom she still sails.*

Roger Sherlock

Richard K Morse Collection

*The Belgian* Albertville *and her four sisters were practical ships for the colonial run to the Congo. Her revenue was made from a combination of five cargo holds and accommodation for 207 one-class passengers.*

the transport of vegetable oils and refrigerated spaces for northbound South African fruits. Her passenger quarters were arranged for 123 in first class and 166 in tourist. Each class had its own public rooms, restaurant, open-air deck spaces and individual tiled swimming pools. All of the first class staterooms had a private bath or shower, and toilet. The air-conditioning system extended to all the cabins in both classes as well as the restaurants.

The *Randfontein* worked a sixty-five day schedule, with round-trip voyages that took her from Hamburg, Amsterdam, Antwerp and Southampton to Tenerife, Capetown, Port Elizabeth, East London, Durban, Lourenço Marques and then the same ports in reverse order. Round voyage fares in 1966 began at £408 for first class and £252 for tourist class.

After the earlier pair of ships, *Jagersfontein* and *Oranjefontein*, were withdrawn and scrapped in 1967, the *Randfontein* was teamed with several twelve-passenger freighters for another four years. Then, she too was withdrawn in the face of a greatly decreased passenger trade. She arrived at Amsterdam at the end of her final voyage to South Africa in April 1971. Three months later, she was transferred to another well known Dutch passenger shipper, the Royal Interocean Lines, who wanted her for their triangular Pacific Ocean service from Sydney and Melbourne to Yokkaichi, Kobe and Yokohama in Japan and then homeward via the Pacific islands. Renamed *Nieuw Holland*, she continued in Dutch-flag service for three

years, until 1974, when she was withdrawn, again a victim of a declining passenger operation and the transition from conventional freight to modern container ships. Placed on the sales lists, she soon joined the growing fleet belonging to the People's Republic of China. With Canton replacing Amsterdam as her home port, and being renamed *Yu Hua*, she was placed on the China–East Africa run, carrying materials, technicians and workers for the construction of a new East African railway system. Once this project was completed, she was placed on a far shorter run across to Hong Kong. Little is known of her actual overseas movements except that she was renamed in 1981 as the *Hai Xing*. She remains in service at the time of writing.

## COMPAGNIE MARITIME BELGE

The ALBERTVILLE, LEOPOLDVILLE, ELISABETHVILLE, THYSVILLE and CHARLESVILLE
Similar to Britain and to a lesser extent Portugal, France and Spain, the Belgians had a strong passenger-cargo ship link in the African trades – with a colonial outpost. The Congo route, from Antwerp to the ports of Matadi and Lobito, supported several generations of passenger liners. All of them were moderate in size, however, and did not exceed 15,000 tons. At the time, there was little need for larger ships.

Following substantial wartime losses, the Compagnie Maritime Belge, also well known as the Belgian Line, ordered no less than five identical 10,900-ton sisterships from the national shipbuilders, the Cockerill yards at Hoboken. Driven by Danish-built Burmeister & Wain diesels that rendered 15½ knots service speeds, they had six holds for cargo (including twin refrigerated compartments) and space for 207 one-class passengers (the *Thysville* and *Charlesville*, the last to be completed, were in fact given 248 berths).

The *Albertville* was the first of the five sisters, being launched on 1 July 1947 and completed in the following May. The *Leopoldville* was delivered in September 1948, the *Elisabethville* in January 1949, the *Baudouinville* (renamed *Thysville* in June 1957, in preparation for a brand-new, larger ship of that earlier name) in September 1950 and finally, the *Charlesville* in February 1951. Each ship was fitted with a set of public rooms, a restaurant, a children's nursery and play deck, a hairdresser, barber, gift shop and outdoor swimming pool. Some of the cabins had private shower or bath, and toilet.

In 1957, following the advent of the new *Baudouin-ville* and her sistership *Jadotville*, the service was accelerated slightly by giving engine refits to the five earlier vessels. After turbo-charging, their service speeds were increased by a full knot, to 16½ knots. The seven passenger ships offered a weekly service from Antwerp for at least a few more years. However, in the summer of 1960, as the Congo was granted

Compagnie Maritime Belge

Compagnie Maritime Belge

*Bound for Matadi and Lobito, after-dinner games in the Main Lounge aboard the* Charlesville.

political independence, trade demands changed suddenly. Three of the ships were immediately cleared for sale, with the three-year-old *Baudouinville* and *Jadotville* being sold to the P&O-Orient Lines, becoming their *Cathay* and *Chitral*, and the *Thysville*, the original *Baudouinville*, going to another British shipping company, the Booth Line, for their Liverpool–Amazon River service as the *Anselm*. This latter ship soon changed hands again, to another member of Britain's Vestey Group, the Blue Star Line. After rebuilding, she became the *Iberia Star* for the long-haul South American trade, from London to Rio de Janeiro, Santos, Montevideo and Buenos Aires. She lasted but a year before being transferred to a Blue Star affiliate, the Austasia Line, and became the *Australasia* for the Singapore–Australian service. She was finally broken-up in the summer of 1973, at Hualien on Taiwan.

The *Albertville, Leopoldville, Elisabethville* and *Charlesville* continued for some years thereafter, running a fortnightly instead of a weekly service, which included calls at Las Palmas and Tenerife. However, there was further change and disintegration by the late sixties; in 1967 the *Leopoldville* was transferred, to the 'sister' company on the same trade, the Compag-

nie Maritime Congolaise. She now flew the colours of Zaire and was renamed more nationalistically as the *P E Lumumba*. At about the same time, the *Charlesville* was withdrawn completely and sold to East Germany, to the VEB Deutsche Seereederei of Rostock. Renamed *Georg Buchner*, her former passenger accommodation was put to good use in her new capacity as a merchant training ship. She was laid-up in 1977.

Had the Belgians been able to foresee the future, they might have kept the *Charlesville*. Early in the following year, on 20 March 1968, the *Elisabethville* was badly damaged by fire at her Antwerp berth. The blaze raged throughout her midships accommodation and she was, in the final appraisal, not worthy of economic repairs. While already partially dismantled at Antwerp, the wreck was delivered to breakers at Ghent that December and finished-off.

The last two ships, the *Albertville* and *P E Lumumba* (ex-*Leopoldville*), continued in passenger service until 1972, when they too were withdrawn and were replaced by two brand-new 71-passenger ships, *Fabiolaville* and *Kananga*. The *Albertville* was sold to Taiwanese breakers and delivered at Kaohsiung on 19 April 1973. The *P E Lumumba* was sold to local Belgian scrappers at Tamise, but then was resold to another ship-breaker at Ghent. Partially dismantled, she was then sold for a third time, in the summer of 1974, to a Brazilian scrap firm and towed across the Atlantic to be broken-up at Rio Grande.

## The JADOTVILLE and BAUDOUINVILLE

This strikingly handsome pair of combination liners, which each had capacity for 300 one-class passengers, had rather a short-lived life in the Belgian Line fleet. Ordered from the Chantiers et Ateliers de St Nazaire in France for 1956 and from the Cockerill-Ougree yard at Hoboken for 1957 respectively, they saw less than four years of service on their Antwerp–Congo trade. Soon after independence was granted to the Congo in the summer of 1960, they became superfluous to the company's vastly changed trading requirements. They were swiftly sold to the P&O-Orient Lines who renamed the *Jadotville* as the *Chitral* and the *Baudouinville* as *Cathay* for their extensive London–Far East service. Continuing for nearly a decade, they later entered the Australian–Far East trade before their final dispositions: the former *Jadotville* was broken-up on Taiwan in 1975 and the ex-*Baudouinville* is now in Chinese hands as the *Shanghai*.

*A view of the open promenade aboard the* Leopoldville.

## MESSAGERIES MARITIMES

The FERDINAND DE LESSEPS, JEAN LABORDE, LA BOURDONNAIS and PIERRE LOTI

The Compagnie des Messageries Maritimes had the largest and most diverse passenger fleet under the French flag in the years following the Second World War. To replace such prewar liners as the *Felix Roussel*, *Athos II*, *Champollion* and *La Marseillaise*, the company built nine combination passenger-cargo liners in the early fifties. Deliveries began in 1952, with the final ship appearing two years later. An all-white trio, *Cambodge*, *Laos* and *Viet-Nam*, were built for the remains of the old colonial Indo-Chinese service which was extended to include the Far East. These ships used the Suez route. Two other ships, the *Caledonien* and *Tahitien*, were created for the Pacific, sailing to French Polynesia, the New Hebrides and New Caledonia via the Panama route. These ships had a turnaround at Sydney and also had colonial stop-overs in the Caribbean, at Guadeloupe and Martinique. Finally, a quartet of 10,900-tonners, the smallest liners of all, were designed especially for the African trade to Mauritius. These ships were named *Ferdinand de Lesseps*, *Jean Laborde*, *La Boudonnais* and *Pierre Loti*.

*La Bourdonnais* was the first of this class to be

*Built purposely for the Madagascar and East African trades, the* Pierre Loti *and her three sisters had some fifteen years of profitable service before being sold off in the overall dissolution of the Messageries Maritimes passenger division.*

Alex Duncan

Michael D J Lennon

*The former* Ferdinand de Lesseps*, greatly altered as the Mediterranean cruise ship* Delphi. *She now trades under the name* La Palma.

launched, on 5 July 1951, at the naval dockyard at Lorient. The *Ferdinand de Lesseps* followed, coming from the Forges et Chantiers de la Gironde yard at Bordeaux, then the *Pierre Loti* from the naval dock-yard at Bordeaux and finally, the *Jean Laborde*, also from Chantiers de la Gironde in Bordeaux. The ships were commissioned in March 1953, October 1952 and the last pair in July 1953. Propelled by Burmeister & Wain diesels which provided maximum speeds of 18½ knots, the quartet had five cargo holds, a third of which was for refrigerated items, and three-class accommodation for 88 first class passengers, 112 tourist class and 299 in third class, which was later reduced to 40 berths. First class consisted of several suites, large staterooms with private bathroom facilities, several attractive public rooms, a small restaurant and an outdoor pool. Tourist class was slightly less spacious and comfortable, and had more three- and four-berth cabins, while third class, being primarily for troops, police and workers, had only four-berth rooms and small dormitories.

The ships were routed from Marseilles to Port Said, Djibouti, Mombasa, Dar-es-Salaam, Majunga, Nossi-Be, Diego Suarez, Tamatave, Reunion and Mauritius. They sailed for some fifteen years. Inevitably, condi-tions had changed by the late 1960s, when aircraft had

secured more and more of the passenger trade, and fast freighters and then container ships lured the cargo trade. *La Bourdonnais* and the *Ferdinand de Lesseps* were retired in 1968, and, with the boom in Mediterranean tourist and cruise services, were sold off almost immediately to Greek buyers, the Efthy-miadis Lines. *La Bourdonnais*, with only slight mod-ifications, was placed on the Piraeus–Greek island trade and then often onwards to Cyprus and Israel. Renamed *Knossos*, her new career was comparatively brief, however. On 3 May 1973, during a passage from Piraeus to Limassol, her 212 passengers and crew had to abandon her following a fierce engine room fire. Scorched and blistered, the hulk was later towed back to Piraeus for inspection, but found to be unworthy of further repairs, she was laid-up in Perama Bay. Three years later, in 1976, she was finally sold to the breakers and towed to Spain for her demolition.

The *Ferdinand de Lesseps* was also sold to the Efthymiadis Lines, but very soon rebuilt as the 600-passenger cruise ship *Delphi*. Her original cargo area was gutted and fitted with passenger decks, cabins, public rooms and a large stern lido area. She was used mostly in the Aegean. Reports were that she was withdrawn in 1974 and then sold off to Spanish breakers as well. However, by 1976, she was seen in lay-up at Perama along with a large assortment of other, mostly undistinguishable former passenger ships and ferries. A year later, following the collapse of the Efthymiadis Lines after one of their ferries, the

*Heleanna*, was found to be unsafely loaded and sank in the Adriatic, the *Delphi* was auctioned-off by the Greek Government to Perla Cruises of Cyprus. She was renamed *La Perla* and her accommodation was refurbished and modernized. Three years later, she changed hands once again, to Intercruise Limited, another Cypriot-registered cruise company, and became the *La Palma*. She has been cruising ever since, often under charter and mostly in Mediterranean waters.

In January 1969, soon after *La Bourdonnais* and the *Ferdinand de Lesseps* were retired, Messageries Maritimes was given formal approval by the French Government to abandon all of its money-losing passenger ship services. Under a special timetable and reassignment plan, the Far East passenger run would be phased out by December 1969. The *Cambodge* and *Laos* would then be transferred to the Pacific–Australia run, replacing the *Caledonien* and *Tahitien*, which were to be retired and sold off. The *Jean Laborde* and *Pierre Loti*, still on the Mauritius trade, would be decommissioned during 1970. The *Pacifique*, the former *Viet-Nam* from the Far Eastern trade which was renamed in 1967, would terminate the Mauritius run in 1971. The *Cambodge* and *Laos* would end the

Australian service in 1972, and finally, the company's newest passenger ship, the *Pasteur* of 1966, would be retired in 1973 and end the South American service, which had been acquired from two other French passenger firms, Chargeurs Reunis and the Compagnie de Navigation Sud-Atlantique. This master plan would, of course, have nearly continuous changes before the final demise of the Messageries Maritimes passenger division. In fact, the passenger trade was declining so rapidly, the entire withdrawal schedule was accelerated by as much as a year. Following these radical changes, the company ran, at least for a few years, only one small passenger ship, the 3700-ton *Polynesie*, which sailed between Sydney, Noumea and the New Hebrides.

The *Pierre Loti* and *Jean Laborde*, after being laid-up at Marseilles in 1969, followed their earlier sisters and were sold to Efthymiadis Lines of Greece. Both ships were immediately assigned, with little alteration, to the very busy Greek inter-island trades. The *Pierre Loti*

*The former* Jean Laborde *served for a time, between 1974–76, as the* Eastern Princess, *sailing out of Singapore. She has since been extensively rebuilt as the Epirotiki Lines' cruise ship* Oceanos.

Roger Sherlock

became the *Olympia* and then two years later, in 1972, was renamed *Patra*. Shortly thereafter, she was rebuilt as a passenger-car ferry for the Adriatic service between Brindisi in Italy and Patras in Greece. She was assigned to an Efthymiadis subsidiary company, the Hellenic Italian Line. She changed hands in 1978, joined another Greek firm, Vanieros Ultramar Armadora SA and was rechristened *Chrysovalandou II*. A year later, she changed hands once again, to yet another Greek shipping concern known as the Amelia Martin Company, and became the *Eros*. She remains in Mediterranean service at the time of writing.

The *Jean Laborde* at first became the *Mykinai* for the Efthymiadis Company, being used in the local Aegean trades. A year later, she was renamed *Ancona* in preparation for her rebuilding and reassignment to the Adriatic ferry run between Italy and Greece. The renovations never quite took place, but in early 1974, in further preparation, she was renamed *Brindisi Express*. Soon afterwards, she was chartered to Far Eastern interests for use on the Singapore–Australia route. Renamed *Eastern Princess*, she first arrived at Singapore in September 1974. Then, following the collapse of the Efthymiadis Lines and the termination of her Eastern charter, she was sold off to the Epirotiki Lines, in fact to one of their subsidiary holding companies known as Pontos Navigation SA of Panama. She returned to Piraeus on 29 July 1976, and then was extensively rebuilt as the deluxe cruise ship *Oceanos*. Her greatly improved accommodation was extended to take as many as 800 passengers. On resuming service, she was chartered for cruising, including a phase for the Italian-flag Lauro Lines, within the Mediterranean, to West Africa, South America, the Caribbean and even to Scandinavia. She continues in service at present, although now sails for her owners, the Epirotiki Lines, on Aegean cruises out of Piraeus.

The other Messageries Maritimes passenger ships are listed under their appropriate geographic chapters.

## COMPANHIA COLONIAL

Portugal's African colonies, Angola and Mozambique, supported two large, very important passenger fleets, the Companhia Colonial and the Companhia Nacional, until independence was granted in 1975. By the early seventies Companhia Colonial had five passenger ships working on the African trades: their flagship and largest liner, the 23,300-ton *Infante Dom Henrique*, commissioned in 1961; the 13,200-ton twin sistership *Imperio* and *Patria* from the late forties; the 10,000-ton *Uige* of 1954, the smallest in the company's fleet and the 21,700-ton *Vera Cruz*, which was used for many years on the Lisbon-Bahia-Rio-Santos trade, but spending her final years as a troop transport to Angola. Companhia Nacional had four passenger ships in colonial African service: the 19,400-ton *Principe Perfeito*, dating from 1961; the 13,000-ton sisterships *Angola* and *Mocambique*, from 1948–49; and a modified version of that pair, the 10,700-ton *Niassa* of 1955. Companhia Colonial had one other large passenger ship, the 20,900-ton *Santa Maria* of 1953, but she was considered a transatlantic liner in view of her service between Lisbon, Caribbean ports and Port Everglades in Florida. Companhia Nacional ran two small combination ships, the 7600-ton sisters *India* and *Timor*, both completed in 1951, on a Far Eastern run from Lisbon via the Suez out to Hong Kong, Macao and Dili on Timor.

### The INFANTE DOM HENRIQUE

The *Infante Dom Henrique*, commissioned in September 1961, was the largest Portuguese liner ever to serve on the African colonial runs to Angola and Mozambique, sailing from Lisbon to Madeira, Luanda, Lobito, Capetown, Lourenço Marques and then home in reverse order. She carried 1010 passengers: 148 in first class and 862 in two grades of tourist class. To many, she was the best appointed and most comfortable of the Portuguese African liners. Each class had their separate open-air decks and swimming pool in addition to a series of public rooms, a chapel, three restaurants and hair salons. All of the first class staterooms had private bathroom facilities; very few in tourist class did.

In 1975, after the long-awaited independence of Portuguese Africa, ships like the *Infante* ( as she was more simply known) lost their work. While there had been some thought of converting her into a one-class cruise ship, the Portuguese Government had at the same time decided to develop the fishing village of Sines into a large industrial centre. Among other considerations, immediate accommodation for workers and their families would be needed. A rather large out-of-work passenger ship was perfect. Some $10 million was spent on refitting the *Infante*, bringing her into Sines, mooring her permanently and encasing

Luis Miguel Correia

*In a man-made basin, the rusting and neglected* Infante Dom Henrique, *once the pride of the Portuguese-African liner fleet, is now a sorry sight. She is located at Sines, along Portugal's Atlantic coast.*

her within a small man-made locked basin. Between her stern and the rolling waves of the eastern Atlantic, a small mountain of earth appeared. Only blasting could free her hereafter. Then, in 1977, shortly after the former flagship arrived, the overall project was suddenly abandoned. The role for which *Infante* was intended would go largely unfulfilled. In July 1983, I visited the idle former luxury liner.

The ship is now only partially used, providing basic accommodation ($6 a night for three, including breakfast, using a former first class triple-berth cabin) for anyone who just happens to drive along the ocean-side road. The surrounding landscape, greatly disturbed by heavy-duty machinery, resembles the surface of the moon. In unappealing greys, browns and blacks, the small mountains of soil created an even more solitary setting for this lonely liner. The ship itself had slipped into a very neglected state – great streaks of rust and peeling exterior paint, badly

faded funnel colours – an overall sense of lifelessness. Dozens of mooring lines seemed unnecessary in the tranquility and silence of her basin berth.

On board, the *Infante* was rather gloomy. A stale smell prevailed. Much of her furniture and artwork had been removed; the bronze of Prince Henry, for example, which once stood in the first class foyer, went to Companhia Colonial's home office in Lisbon, while chairs, some sofas and small tables met with less gentle endings – possibly even over the side. The remaining furniture was rather haphazardly scattered – several chairs here, a sofa and table there. The entire ship was swept, but not polished clean. There was no gleam and sparkle, just a lingering dullness.

Only the former first class cabins were in use for the occasional guests. The carpets were gone, leaving only bare steel floors. Again, it all just managed to seem presentable, hardly inviting or cheerful. The atmosphere was quite similar to a floating youth hostel. Also, only a portion of the former first class restaurant was in use: neatly set tables with white

*Furnished in a very modern style, the* Infante Dom Henrique *might have been converted for cruising had the industrialization scheme at Sines not been planned. The view above shows one of the ship's smaller public rooms, a bar-lounge.*

Companhia Portuguesa de Transportes Marítimas

linen were on the starboard side only while dozens of others, including what was evidently the captain's table, sat naked and barren. Once again, it was hardly a pleasant setting.

The bridge was another forgotten portion of the ship. Heaps of house and signal flags had been tossed in one corner, all of them weather-beaten and in tatters. The brass instruments had long since turned to a very dull silver-yellow. Odd pieces of litter were scattered about on the former chart tables, radio sets and bridge window ledges.

From shore, a swift Atlantic breeze rattled the remaining lines and blocks aboard the *Infante* – otherwise, there was a deep silence. One can only wonder what the future will hold for the *Infante Dom Henrique*.

### The IMPERIO and PATRIA

'Their plans were initially presented to the Anchor Line of Glasgow by the John Brown shipyards, as proposed new postwar liners for the Indian service', according to Luis Miguel Correia, the foremost authority on Portuguese merchant shipping and a native of Lisbon. Instead the ships were built at Clydebank in 1947–48, for the Portuguese, who wanted to reinforce their postwar African trades. Appropriately named as the *Imperio* and *Patria*, the 13,200-tonners were fitted with steam turbines that gave service speeds of 18 knots. Their passenger accommodation, ranging from a luxurious first class to very austere fourth class, was arranged as 114 in first class, 156 in tourist class, 120 in third class and finally 200 in fourth class, which was used mostly for either troops or Government work crews. Both ships were routed to West, South and then East Africa, sailing from Lisbon to Las Palmas, Sao Tome, Luanda, Lobito, Mossamedes, Capetown, Lourenço Marques, Beira, Nacala and Porto Amelia.

Similar to almost all of the Portuguese passenger ships used in the African trades, both aircraft competition and decolonization of Angola and Mozambique ended their profitability and usefulness. The *Patria* was delivered to Taiwanese breakers in August 1973; the *Imperio*, after a spell of idleness at Lisbon, ended her days at that same port in March 1974.

### The UIGE

This 10,000-ton ship was designed as an improvement of the earlier *Imperio* and *Patria*, and she followed the larger *Santa Maria* and *Vera Cruz* from the same Cockerill shipyards of Hoboken, Belgium. Named *Uige*, she was built alongside another Portuguese passenger-cargo liner, the *Niassa* for Companhia Nacional.

*A second class lounge aboard the* Imperio.

Companhia Portugesa de Transportes Marítimas

*Because of the exceptional similarity in the funnel colouring, ships like Companhia Colonial's* Imperio *were often thought to be part of the Holland-America Line. She and her sister, the* Patria, *were first designed for the Anchor Line's run to India.*

Built with a large capacity, having five holds, and space for 78 first class and 493 third class passengers, the *Uige* was commissioned in July 1954. John Havers remembered her from his sea-going days with Union Castle. 'I recall visiting the *Uige* in Lobito and found that she was streets ahead of her predecessors [the *Imperio* and *Patria*]. Fully air-conditioned and well-appointed, she was like the Union-Castle liners in being a big cargo carrier.'

The *Uige* was one of the last passenger ships to sail on the old colonial runs to East and West Africa before being retired and laid-up at Lisbon in January 1976, where she was broken-up four years later.

### THE VERA CRUZ

This ship and her sister, the *Santa Maria*, were the first large liners to be built for the Portuguese and both were designed for the Atlantic rather than African service. The *Vera Cruz*, built by the Cockerill yard at Hoboken, was delivered in February 1952, and was placed on the South American run, from Lisbon to

Luis Miguel Correia

Companhia Portugesa de Transportes Marítimas

*The library aboard the* Imperio.

Companhia Portugesa de Transportes Marítimas

*A corner of the first class saloon aboard the* **Patria.** *The paintings on the walls depicted the Portuguese settlement of Angola and Mozambique.*

Madeira, Recife, Salvador, Rio de Janeiro and Santos. The *Santa Maria*, having been built by the same Belgium shipbuilder, was introduced in September 1953, but was later employed on the run to the Caribbean and to Port Everglades, Florida.

The *Vera Cruz*, with accommodation for 150 in first class, 250 in second class, 232 in third class cabins and 664 in third class dormitories, was for a short time used on the Caribbean route, but after 1961 was re-routed almost permanently to the Angolan service. Used as a passenger ship, she often carried troops, especially when the political difficulties in that area erupted. She too was, of course, a victim of decolonization. She was laid-up at Lisbon in January 1972 and left that port on 4 March 1973 bound for the ship-breakers at Kaohsiung, arriving there on 19 April. Her sister, the *Santa Maria*, would finish her career that summer.

Luis Miguel Correia

The 10,000-ton Uige, completed in 1954, was an improved version of the earlier Imperio and Patria of the late forties. The newer ship was designed especially for the migrant and tourist trades to East and West Africa.

Companhia Portugesa de Transportes Marítimas

The first class main lounge aboard the Uige.

Luis Miguel Correia

Built for and used on the Brazilian trade from Lisbon, the Vera Cruz *sailed almost exclusively on the African colonial trades after 1961; mostly, she was used in 'Government service', especially for carrying troops and police.*

The last flagship for Companhia Nacional, the Principe Perfeito, *makes her final arrival at Lisbon, on 14 June 1975. She would rarely sail again, being used mostly as an accommodation ship in the Middle East.*

## COMPANHIA NACIONAL

### The PRINCIPE PERFEITO

Luis Miguel Correia recalled: 'In the early fifties, just as two brand-new large liners were being built for the rival Companhia Colonial [the sisterships *Vera Cruz* and *Santa Maria* of 1952–53], the Portuguese Government decided to establish a Lisbon–New York tourist service with two new 15–18,000 tonners. Delayed for some time, while ships such as Norwegian America Line's *Oslofjord* of 1949 and Holland-America Line's *Maasdam* of 1952 were studied, these two ships were intended to be a part of a large Government building programme to be enacted in the late fifties. It called for new flagships: the *Infante Dom Henrique* for Companhia Colonial, the *Principe Perfeito* for Companhia Nacional and the *Funchal* for Empresa Insulana, which traded to the Azores and Madeira only, as well as two Atlantic liners that would be operated by Companhia Nacional. However, the colonial struggle in Angola erupted in 1961, which created a serious new situation and necessitated a large sudden cash outlay from the Government in Lisbon, so the plan for the transatlantic ships was scrapped. Shortly thereafter, it was too late. The jet had taken over the Atlantic passenger trade. Companhia Nacional did receive, however, their new flagship and largest passenger liner, the *Principe Perfeito*, which was delivered in May 1961.'

The 19,400-ton *Principe Perfeito* was, like all Portuguese liners, built overseas. While the three largest Companhia Colonial liners came from the Cockerill shipyard in Belgium, the Nacional managers turned to one of the earlier masters of passenger ship construction, Swan, Hunter & Wigham Richardson Limited at Newcastle. Among many others, they had built the *Dominion Monarch* for the Shaw Savill Line, the *Bergensfjord* for the Norwegian-America Line, several passenger ships for the British India Line and an earlier Portuguese passenger ship, the *Mocambique* of 1949. Launched on 22 September 1961 and commissioned in the following spring, the new *Principe Perfeito* was given fully air-conditioned quarters for 200 first class and 800 tourist class passengers. In addition, there was auxiliary space for 200 troops if required. The first class section, dominated by twelve three-room suites, had upper deck spaces that included separate public rooms, a lido and outdoor pool, and cabins which all had private toilets (and mostly private showers as well). In tourist class, the

Luis Miguel Correia

cabins ranged in size from double to large eight-berth rooms. Cargo was carried in four holds and included a special refrigerated section.

Although the *Principe Perfeito* had been used for cruising, including two trips across the Atlantic to New York and other American East Coast ports in the summer of 1972 and a visit to New Orleans the following year, she was withdrawn from African service (between Lisbon, Madeira, Luanda, Lobito, Durban, Louranço Marques and Beira), and laid-up at Lisbon in January 1976. Since 1974 her owners had been merged with the once rival Companhia Colonial and together the companies were known as Compania Portugesa de Transportes Maritimas. Although there had been thought of refitting the *Principe Perfeito* for full-time cruise service, the idea never came to pass and, within three months, she was sold to the Global Transportation Company of Panama for use as a Middle Eastern accommodation ship. Sent to her builders for some modification and alteration, she was renamed *Al Hasa* and went out to Damman for her stationary duties. In 1980, she was sold to the Fairline Shipping Corporation, a subsidiary of Sitmar Cruises, also under the Panamanian flag, supposedly for lavish

*Built in 1948–49, the* Mocambique *and her twin sister, the* Angola, *were then the largest liners in the Companhia Nacional fleet. Both ships had large cargo capacities as well as three classes of passenger accommodation.*

Luis Miguel Correia

Roger Sherlock

*The very popular* Africa *and her sistership, the* Europa, *were among the finest liners on the East African trade. Both sailed for some twenty years until the dissolution of the once large Lloyd Triestino passenger fleet.*

rebuilding as the cruise ship *Fairsky*. She was to have been used in North American service, cruising to Alaska, Mexico and the Caribbean. However, plans changed soon and a brand-new *Fairsky*, at over 46,000 tons, was ordered from a French yard. The intended *Fairsky*, ex-*Principe Perfeito*, was kept in reserve as the *Vera*. In 1982, she was sold to Sappho Shipping & Trading Corporation, a part of the Latsis Group, renamed *Marianna IX* and then sent to Jeddah for further service as an accommodation ship. It seems rather unlikely that the former flagship of the Nacional fleet will ever sail again.

### The ANGOLA and MOCAMBIQUE

Both postwar creations, these twin sisters were designed and built by British yards, Hawthorn, Leslie & Company and Swan, Hunter & Wigham Richardson, both located in Newcastle. Large examples of the passenger-cargo design, at 13,000 tons each, they had a passenger capacity of 105 in first class, 141 in tourist class and 300 in third class. Fitted with Doxford diesels, they both had service speeds of 17 knots and were intended to offer an accelerated service schedule. The *Angola* left Lisbon on her maiden sailing, to Funchal, Sao Tome, Luanda, Lobito, Mossamedes, Capetown, Lourenço Marques, Beira and Nacala, in January 1949; the *Mocambique* followed in October. John Havers recalled visiting the *Mocambique* in the 1950s. 'As a purser with Union-Castle, I had the undoubted honour of being invited to lunch on this fine ship by the assistant port captain of Beira. A pleasant occasion, I was impressed by the comfort and service aboard, no less in one of the hottest and most humid ports in Africa. This ship and her sister had notable deluxe suites in first class.'

By the early 1970s, after uninterrupted careers in the African trades, the *Angola* and *Mocambique* were outmoded by both aircraft and larger cargo ships and then the decline of Portuguese Africa. The *Mocambique* was handed over to Taiwanese breakers in September 1972, the *Angola* in March 1974.

## The Niassa

Built alongside Colonial's *Uige* at the Cockerill yard at Hoboken, Belgium, the *Niassa* was added to the Nacional fleet, in August 1955, and first employed on the East African run. Years later, she was used solely on the West African route, sailing from Lisbon and Leixoes to Las Palmas, Sao Tome, Luanda, Lobito and Mossamedes. She was fitted with five cargo holds which included refrigerated space as well as tanks for palm oil. Her passenger quarters included a small, intimate first class, with only twenty-two berths, and a larger tourist section, with 284 berths, in four-, six- and eight-berth rooms. Both the *Niassa* and the *Uige* were designed to offer more comfortable emigrant travel to Africa as well as provide reasonable tourist class voyages.

Laid-up at Lisbon in March 1978, the *Niassa* was broken-up a year later at Bilbao in Spain.

# LLOYD TRIESTINO

## The Africa and Europa

One of Italy's largest passenger companies, the state-owned Lloyd Triestino, built seven fine motor liners in the early 1950s. Designed to replace their heavy war losses, the trio of *Australia*, *Neptunia* and *Oceania* was placed on the Australian run, the *Asia* and *Victoria* on the Middle and Far East run, and another pair of sisters, the *Africa* and *Europa*, on the East African trade. These latter ships, both commissioned in 1952, were built by Cantieri Riuniti dell'Adriatico at Monfalcone and the Ansaldo yards at Genoa respectively. These very handsome vessels had all-white hulls and raked bows, their upper-decks were crowned by a single domed funnel and a short radar mast placed above the bridge area. A pair of kingposts with booms and two electric cranes were positioned forward; another pair of kingposts and booms were aft. At 11,400 tons each, they were powered by Fiat diesels that gave a 19½ knot service speed. Accommodation, balanced with five holds for cargo, including some refrigerated spaces, was provided for 148 in first class and 298 in tourist class.

The *Africa* and *Europa* were routed on a monthly service, sailing from Trieste, Venice and Brindisi to Port Said, Aden, Mogadishu, Mombasa, Dar-es-Salaam, Beira, Durban, Capetown, Port Elizabeth, East London and then a return to Durban before reversing their course and returning to the Mediterranean. Beginning in 1967, after the temporary closing of the Suez Canal, both ships were routed via the Atlantic.

John Havers visited both ships during his service with the Union-Castle Line. 'Undoubedly, these were the top new buildings of the early 1950s on the East Africa route. They were superior to the new ships of British India, Messageries Maritimes and Union-Castle. They were fully air-conditioned and their cabins has private facilities – conditions considered essential today and as a much needed comfort in those times. For example, the three new one-class Union-Castle vessels [*Rhodesia Castle*, *Kenya Castle* and *Braemar Castle*] only had the dining saloon air-conditioned, a much appreciated improvement, but private bathrooms in cabins were rare. The purser berthed in the passenger areas, had no bath, shower or toilet and had to share and wait for these facilities with the passengers. This beautiful new Italian pair may have suited travellers fearing the heat experienced on the route from the Cape to Italy, but for British passengers it meant being landed in Venice. They may have been more expensive though I have no fair comparisons, but there was room for all four companies trading on this route in the pre-jumbo boom days of the Empire. The *Africa* and *Europa* were rather jealously called the "ice cream carts" by their crews.'

These ships continued in African service, well past their profitable days, until as late as 1976. The Italian Government had by then discontinued all subsidies to its deficit-ridden passenger fleet. The *Europa* was sold to Arabian interests, who renamed her the *Blue Sea* for Muslim pilgrim services. Most unfortunately, it proved to be a very short new career. On 12 November 1976, fire broke out while in Jeddah harbour. All passengers and crew were safely landed but the ship sank at her moorings within forty-eight hours. The *Africa* was kept by Lloyd Triestino, persumably for possible conversion to a cruise ship, but renamed *Protea*. However, no further plans developed and, in March 1980, she was sold to Taiwanese breakers at Kaohsiung.

# CHAPTER FOUR

# LATIN AMERICA

## ROYAL MAIL LINES

### The AMAZON, ARAGON and ARLANZA

The Latin American passenger trade was usually divided between a deluxe, demanding first-class market, who wanted nothing but the best in accommodation, if not for one-way travel then for round-trip cruise-like voyages, and a large, very lucrative, but undemanding market in tourist or third class travel. Mostly, these passengers travelled southbound, to new lives and employment on the South American continent. Aboard the passenger ships coming out of Northern waters, the greatest numbers of third class passengers would board at especially arranged calls in Spain and Portugal. Homebound, the lower deck quarters were often quite empty, filled possibly only with some students or budget tourists.

When Britain's Royal Mail Lines decided to retire the last of its prewar 'Highland class' of South American liners, the 14,200-ton *Highland Brigade*, *Highland Monarch* and *Highland Princess*, and then reassign their large flagship *Andes* to full-time cruising, the company's directors and designers agreed upon three rather modern and quite noteworthy passenger-cargo liners as replacements. The year was 1958. Firstly, the new trio would abandon the 'Highland' naming pattern (something acquired, in fact, in the earlier purchase of the old Nelson Line) and instead use three geographic selections: *Amazon*, *Aragon* and *Arlanza*. Secondly, in something of a throwback to earlier styles, the designers of the new trio 'broke' the superstructure with a cargo hold positioned between a deckhouse containing the bridge, wheelhouse and officers' quarters, and a separate, more extensive upper deck superstructure containing passenger accommodation. Overall, the new liners were very much of the combination passenger-cargo type – with five cargo holds and a capacity of 449 passengers. They were the last British-flag passenger ships to feature a third class section and, in fact, the final series of ships to carry three classes of passengers – first, cabin and third. Furthermore, they were the last group of British

passenger ships created as a group and the last to be built for the then 119-year-old Royal Mail Lines.

The trio was ordered from the famous Harland & Wolff yards at Belfast and represented a total investment of over $60 million. Their construction began in something of a final 'golden age' for Britain's liner industry. Just across the ways at Belfast, P&O's 44,000-ton *Canberra* was taking shape. She would be, when completed in the spring of 1961, Britain's largest liner since the 83,000-ton *Queen Elizabeth* of 1940. Further away, across the Irish Sea at Birkenhead, the Cammell Laird yards were hard at work on the 37,000-ton *Windsor Castle*, the largest liner ever built for the South African trade. At Barrow-in-Furness, the 41,000-ton *Oriana* was soon to be launched and establish herself as the fastest ever on the Australian run. Then, as if just for good measure, Union-Castle had contracted for the 32,000-ton *Transvaal Castle* from the John Brown yards at Clydebank, Shaw Savill had ordered the 24,000-ton *Northern Star*, Canadian Pacific was preparing for its new flagship *Empress of Canada* and last but by no means least Cunard was issuing reports about a possible 75,000-tonner dubbed Q3 that would replace the ageing *Queen Mary*. All seemed well and prosperous.

The *Amazon* was first of the three new Royal Mail ships to come off the ways, on 7 July 1959. The *Aragon* followed on 20 October, and the *Arlanza* on 13 April 1960. Their maiden voyages had a similar pattern: the *Amazon* made hers in January 1960, the *Aragon* in April and the *Arlanza* in October. Descriptive literature heralded the ships as the 'three graces'. John Draffin served in the purser's department aboard the *Amazon* and remembered her with particular fondness. 'The *Amazon* and her sisters were most distinctive and contemporary, in fact the first ships to have escalators. They were very much divided ships, however. The first class passenger quarters were very deluxe, even despite the extensive use of modern materials. Second class was less fancy. The third class section was very clean, but very simple. In the third class restaurants, the waiters would dish out food to twenty or thirty passengers at a table and then sit down and join them. Royal Mail employed Spanish and Portuguese staff in third class. Even the entertainment was arranged according to class. While the first class passengers might be having a film, second class would have bingo and third class would have a quiz. Other entertainments included fashion shows, horse-racing,

dances and concerts with records.'

These Royal Mail sisters used the port of London as their British terminus and sailed outwards via Cherbourg to Vigo, Lisbon, Las Palmas, Rio de Janeiro, Santos, Montevideo and Buenos Aires. The homeward voyage was identical except that Boulogne was substituted for Cherbourg. Passenger loads were derived from a variety of services including round-trip cruise-like voyages. In 1966 seven-week round-trip

sailings were offered at fares beginning at £391 in first class, £272 in cabin class and £182 in third class. Other traffic came from the particularly high loads of one-way traffic to and from South America. Of special importance was the southbound migrant trade from Vigo and Lisbon which used only the third class quarters. There was also a British tourist trade for the short-distance runs 'to the sun', to Spain, Portugal and the Canaries. The northbound, homeward

Furness Withy Group

voyages were less crowded, particularly in third class.

John Draffin, who worked aboard the *Amazon*, recalled the specialized sailing patterns of these ships and their revenue requirements: 'Being fast ships as well as good sea boats, but always tending to list somewhat, they were specialty designs with shallow draughts for the River Plate. After the ten-day turnaround at Buenos Aires, where they loaded the chilled beef for shipment to Britain, they had to make the return sailing within three weeks, which was the limit for the beef. We would repeat the same ports of call mostly, but returned often to Southampton to offload our passengers and then went to Rotterdam to discharge our European cargo before terminating the voyage at London, where the ships remained for ten days. The schedules were maintained like clockwork and each aspect of this extensive operation had a pattern. For example, always on the first day out of Rio, stowaways on the northbound ship were exchanged with her southbound sistership.'

Bob Cummins also served on the *Amazon*. 'Then a brand-new beauty [1961], she had the finest first class restaurant I've ever seen and which catered for all of the hundred or so first class passengers at a single sitting. We'd have older English diplomats, the Argentine land barons and aristocracy, wealthy Britons and some well-heeled round-trippers. There were 82 berths in the cabin class section and then 275 in third class. We took the outbound passengers by train down to Tilbury Landing Stage from London and then had a short tender call at Cherbourg. In South America, after landing the passengers at Buenos Aires and sending the round-trippers either to hotels or on extended excursions, the ship was moved to La Plata for five days to load the very important Argentine beef. We would then return to Buenos Aires, take on passengers and then reverse the same route. Unfortunately, British industrial problems killed these fine sisterships. Often, we would return to South America with half the cargo we brought up because of some dispute at the London Docks. As late examples of combination passenger-cargo ships, they never quite made it. Even later, when they were transferred within the Furness Group to Shaw Savill, they were equally as unsuccessful.'

The 'three graces' survived for close to a decade. After the great British Maritime Strike of 1966, when they were moored together in the London Docks, they began to suffer increasingly from those classic ills of so many passenger ships: declining passenger

*Aragon, on 21 April 1960 in London's King George V Dock, eight days before her maiden sailing on the 29th.*

loads, aircraft competition, increased operational costs and, in particular for these ships, new and improved methods of cargo shipping. Furthermore and quite importantly, the once lucrative Argentine beef trade had collapsed and this cast a substantial blow to Britain's shipping network to the east coast of South America.

The *Amazon*, the first of the class, was the first to go. She was transferred, in February 1968, to the Shaw Savill Line, quickly renamed *Akaroa* and despatched on their round-the-world and Australia/New Zealand services. The other sisters were soon to follow. The *Aragon* was laid-up for a time in Cornwall's River Fal, which was fast becoming something of a limbo for out-of-work British passenger ships. She was passed to Shaw Savill in February 1969 and hoisted their colours as the *Arawa*. The *Aragon*, the last to remain with Royal Mail, ended the firm's South American passenger service when she arrived at London on 21 February 1969. A long and distinguished era had closed. (In fact, the Royal Mail passenger service survived only for another two years, with the cruising schedule for the *Andes*.) The *Aragon* was sold to Shaw Savill soon afterward and became the *Aranda*. The second careers and ultimate demise of the 'three graces' is included in chapter 6.

*The first class writing-room aboard the* Amazon *was furnished in contemporary ship-board style, with vinyl-covered chairs, wood veneers and glass-encased lighting fixtures.*

Furness Withy Group

Alex Duncan

## BLUE STAR LINE

The ARGENTINA STAR, BRASIL STAR, URUGUAY STAR and PARAGUAY STAR

Another British shipping company deeply interested in the South American passenger trade was the Blue Star Line, a member of the large and diverse Vestey Group. Having lost all of their passenger ships during the Second World War, including the celebrated cruise ship *Arandora Star*, the company went to the Cammell Laird yards at Birkenhead for modified versions of their rather classic postwar refrigerated cargo ships. A quartet of ships was planned that would have extended superstructures and space for well beyond the customary dozen or so freighter passengers. The new ships, named appropriately the *Argentina Star*, *Brasil Star*, *Uruguay Star* and *Paraguay Star*, could each carry as many as 53 passengers, all in first class comfort. They were innovative for the late forties – almost all of the passenger cabins had private toilets and either a private bath or shower. The public space was distributed between a main lounge, smoking room and a restaurant as well as outdoor deck space and an open-air swimming pool. Completed at just under 10,800 tons and fitted with steam turbines that gave service speeds of 16 knots, the quartet was special in being among the first British merchant ships to have their machinery positioned farther aft than the usual midships position. Within a decade, the engines-aft design would become almost commonplace.

*Blue Star Line's passenger quartet, a group which included the* Paraguay Star, *carried some fifty first class passengers, outbound general freight and then large consignments of Argentine beef on the return sailings.*

The *Argentina Star* was the first of the four, being launched on 26 September 1946 and delivered in the following June. The *Brasil Star* followed in October, the *Uruguay Star* in May 1948 and finally, the *Paraguay Star* in October. Once in service, the quartet were familiar sights at the London Docks and appeared almost identical except that the latter two sisters had slightly taller funnels. While Blue Star continued to build a large fleet of twelve-passenger freighters, they were no longer concerned with either larger combination ships or luxury liners. These sisters were, in fact, the company's final passenger ships.

Their routing was quite similar to most liners on the South Atlantic run to the east coast of South America, sailing from London to Lisbon, Madeira, Las Palmas, Tenerife and then across to Recife, Salvador, Rio de Janeiro, Santos, Montevideo and Buenos Aires. Round-trip passengers were sent ashore at the Argentine capital as the ships spent as much as six days loading their most profitable cargo: northbound refrigerated beef. Often, the ships went to La Plata for their consignments. Sailings from London were offered at two to three week intervals and were scheduled as forty-seven day round-trips. In 1966 full fares began at £365.

Their lives changed little after the forties except that in 1959 their black hulls were repainted light grey. By the late sixties the ships seemed to begin losing their passengers and freight, and therefore their revenue. Almost simultaneous with the collapse of the Argentine meat trade, the *Paraguay Star* caught fire while lying in the London Docks, on 12 August 1969. She was badly damaged and would require costly repairs – with all this in addition to her twenty-one years, there was little hesitation in selling her to Hamburg scrappers. She was delivered on 19 September.

The *Argentina Star*, *Brasil Star* and *Uruguay Star* survived but another three years. I recall seeing two of them at anchor, both out of work and pending a final sale, off Gravesend in the late summer of 1972. The *Uruguay Star* was handed over to the Nan Fang Steel Enterprise Company at Kaohsiung on Taiwan, on 25 August 1972. The *Brasil Star* went to the Tung Seng Steel & Iron Works and was signed-over on 10 October and, nine days later, the last of the quartet, the *Argentina Star*, was delivered to the Hi Yo Steel & Iron Works. Soon afterward, Blue Star began a disposal programme of most of its twelve-passenger freighters as well. However, at the time of writing (spring 1985), the company is one of the very few surviving firms to still offer sailings in cargo ships. The 19,000-ton sisters *California Star* and *Columbia Star* each carried two passengers on a long-haul run between Britain and the North American West Coast. Also, from West Coast ports, the slightly smaller sisters *Southland Star* and *Wellington Star* (also with two berths each), sailed to the South Pacific and New Zealand.

## ——— ARGENTINE-ELMA LINES ———

### The ARGENTINA, URUGUAY and LIBERTAD

Argentina – despite its prominent position along the eastern coast of the South American continent – never actually expanded into the deep-sea passenger trades until after the Second World War. One of the first steps was to order a trio of very fine combination passenger-cargo ships from the famed Vickers-Armstrongs shipyards at Barrow-in-Furness. They emerged as three particularly handsome vessels.

Their original owners were the Compania Argentina de Navigacion Dodero, who were more simply known as the Dodero Line. As the company was state owned and controlled, the ships were given specific political names. The first came off the ways on 3 November 1948 as the *Presidente Peron*. She was followed in August 1949 by the *Eva Peron*. The third and last was launched in April 1950, as the *17 de Octubre*, the date of the Perons' rise to power in Argentina.

Each ship was approximately 12,500 tons with dimensions of 530 feet overall and 71 feet in width. They were driven by steam turbines geared to twin screws, which rendered service speeds of 18 knots. Their operations were coordinated on a three-ship schedule that had a sailing from either terminal port (London or Buenos Aires) every three weeks. The passage from London to Buenos Aires or vice versa took sixteen days. Intermediate ports of call included Le Havre, Lisbon, occasionally Madeira and then on to Rio de Janeiro, Santos and Montevideo.

The passenger accommodation was all first class. The *Presidente Peron* differed in that she carried a full capacity of 74; the other two could each carry 96 passengers. At the time of their completion, the standard of their accommodation was highly publicized. Mr C M Squarey referred to them as 'ships of quality and quantity – quantity in the generous space per passenger.' The accommodation was spread over five decks, all of which were positioned between four large cargo holds, two forward and two aft. He described the trio as follows: 'Everything about them is on a liberal scale. The public rooms are all air-conditioned. The dining room, in its shades of green, is a charming room while the main lounge, looking forward, is furnished in a delightful, essentially English style. The cocktail bar, running fore and aft, faces out onto the deck and is a distinct feature of the ships. There is a music room equipped with a dance floor, a well-appointed gymnasium, good deck space, a swimming pool of unusually large size and a deck area which forms a pleasant setting for an outdoor cinema.'

The passenger cabins were given particularly high praise in the ships' maiden seasons. 'The twin suites were each fitted with huge circular mirrors in their bedrooms, no doubt a strong consideration for the female occupants. Each of these rooms was further arranged with living areas that included soft chairs against windows overlooking the sea. All of the double-berth rooms were designed with rather extensive closet space and each had a special dressing table. Every double had a private shower and toilet while all of the singles had a full size bath and toilet. Furthermore, each ship was fitted with a complete laundry. It seems the only criticism, at least from the British travelling public in those years, was the ships' notices and signboards were posted only in Spanish and not bilingually.'

The trio settled down to successful and profitable lives – similar to the Argentine State Line threesome,

the *Rio de la Plata*, *Rio Jachal* and *Rio Tunuyan*, that were on the New York service. However, once the Peron regime toppled in 1955, little time was wasted in having the ships renamed. The *Presidente Peron* was rechristened *Argentina*, the *Eva Peron* was changed to *Uruguay* and the *17 de Octubre* to *Libertad*. At the same time, their owners were relisted as Flota Argentina de Navegacion de Ultramar, more simply known as the Ultramar Line. Sailings continued but were on occasions extended to include Hamburg, both for German passengers and additional cargo.

The lives of the three ships were marked particularly with considerable changes in funnel and hull colourings. The funnels were given a variety of different paint schemes over the years; at first the hulls were grey, then black and finally all-white. One last significant ownership change came in 1962 when the Ultramar Line and the Flota Mercante del Estado merged to form the Empresa Lineas Maritimas Argentinas, the ELMA Lines.

More changes were in the wind a year or so later. In 1962, the *Libertad* made several trips to New York as a substitute for the fire-gutted *Rio Jachal*. Then, with trade requirements changing, it was decided to convert both the *Libertad* and *Uruguay* to all-tourist class ships. The plan was to add to their accommodation and increase their capacities to 400 passengers each. The *Libertad* was taken in hand first and

*The* Eva Peron, *named in honour of the First Lady of Argentina, was renamed* Uruguay *in 1955, following the collapse of the Peron regime. She and her two sisters were very handsome examples of the combination passenger-cargo design. Here, the ship is in the colours of the Dodero Line, her original owners.*

converted at Buenos Aires in 1964. Then, the plans somehow altered. The projected refit for the *Uruguay* was cancelled and she reamained an all-first class vessel along with the third sister, the *Argentina*.

However, the Latin American run continued to show change. In 1966, both the *Argentina* and *Uruguay* were down-graded to pure cargo ships. The *Libertad* was left to operate alongside the enlarged *Rio Tunuyan*, which had been shifted to North European service from the passenger-declining New York trade. The *Argentina* and *Uruguay* later made some sailings southward, to the bottom of Argentina and to the Antarctic, both with supplies and research teams. They were finally laid-up for a time, being made redundant by more modern freighters in the ever-expanding Argentine fleet, until both were scrapped in Argentina in 1973. The *Libertad* ceased carrying European passengers by the early 1970s, and for a time made some Antarctic sailings as well. However, she too was laid-up, in 1974. A year later, she was broken-up at the Argentine port of Campana.

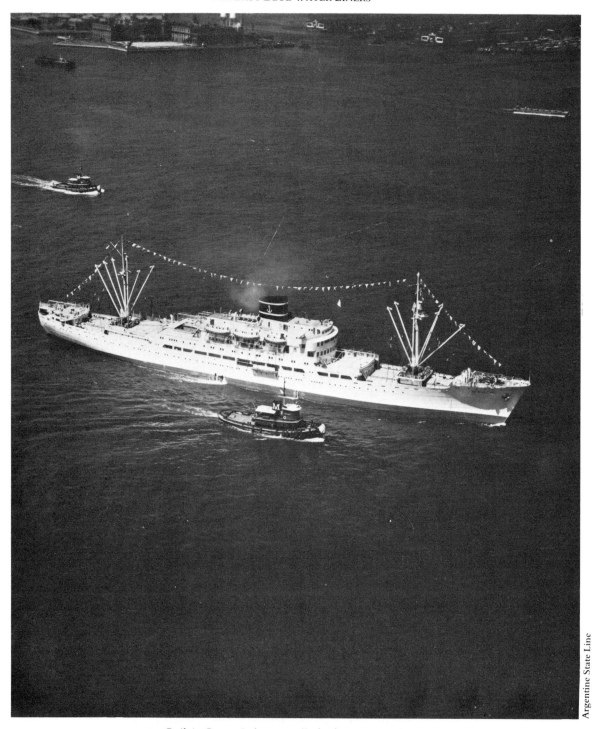

*Built in Genoa, Italy, especially for the east coast of South America–New York trade, the* Rio De La Plata *is shown arriving in New York harbour on her maiden voyage, in the spring of 1950.*

## The RIO DE LA PLATA, RIO JACHAL and RIO TUNUYAN

These three ships were designed especially for the North American service and to compete with the more established Moore McCormack Lines' trio of sistership, the *Argentina, Brasil* and *Uruguay*. The new trio were modified versions of the earlier Argentine threesome which had been built in England. Slightly larger, with 116 first class berths each, they came from Italian shipbuilders, the Ansaldo yards at Genoa. The *Rio de la Plata* was commissioned in April 1950, the *Rio Jachal* in the following September and the *Rio Tunuyan* in April 1951. A year later, following the death of Evita Peron, the *Rio Tunuyan* was renamed as *Evita*, a name she carried until the Peron regime was ousted in 1955. She then reverted to her original name.

Their routing was scheduled on a similar timetable to the earlier Argentine combination liners on the London service. There was a sailing from New York every third Friday, bound for Trinidad or La Guaira, Rio de Janeiro, Santos, Montevideo and Buenos Aires. At New York, the ships usually had a six-day stay in port, arriving on Saturday mornings and then sailing again on Friday afternoons. In 1960 the price of the forty-three day round-trip cruises began at $1080. Advertising campaigns were linked to 'the Route of the Rio liners'.

The accommodation was arranged on five decks: Sports, Promenade, Main, A and B. The public rooms included a forward lounge, a full cinema, a library and writing room, Smoking Room, restaurant and special children's dining room. On deck, there was a swimming pool and games area. The cabins, all of which were air-conditioned, had either private or semi-private bathroom facilities.

By the early sixties, the trade requirements for combination passenger-cargo ships on the South American trade from New York began to wane. Consquently, plans were made to rebuild both the *Rio de la Plata* and the *Rio Tunuyan* for an all-tourist class service to Hamburg. At the same time, in 1962, the ships's owners, the Argentine State Line (the Flota Mercante del Estado in Spanish) were merged with the Flota Argentina de Navegacion de Ultramar to form the ELMA Lines. Soon afterwards, on 28 September 1962, the *Rio Jachal* began the extended saga that ended her career. She was badly damaged by a night-time fire at her New York berth, at Pier 25, at the foot of Franklin Street in Lower Manhattan. With her upper-works scorched and badly damaged, she was taken to the Todd Shipyards in Brooklyn for examination and some very temporary repairs but was then laid-up, at an unused berth near 23rd Street in Brooklyn. Lifeless and neglected, she remained there for well over a year. In April 1964, under the care of a reduced crew, she was taken to Buenos Aires, presumably for full repairs, but then placed in further lay-up. Four years later, on 17 April 1968, she caught fire once more and this time was destroyed beyond economic repair. A year later, she was sold to local ship-breakers at Buenos Aires and demolition took place during 1970.

In 1963 the *Rio de la Plata* was refitted with 372 tourist class berths, but her new career on the North European run was quite brief. Late in the following year, on 19 November, while lying at a shipyard berth at Buenos Aires, she caught fire and burnt out completely. Her wreckage, although kept afloat for some time, was finally sold to local scrappers in 1968.

The *Rio Tunuyan* survived the longest and, following her 1963–64 refit with extended quarters for 372 tourist-class passengers, was assigned to the Hamburg run with the equally enlarged *Libertad*. Several years later, as the South American trade continued its decline, the *Rio Tunuyan* was teamed with the new French liner *Pasteur*. In the summer season, from May to November, the *Rio Tunuyan* sailed in the regular liner service; for the remainder of the year, she was used for cruising from Buenos Aires to the Straits of Magellan, the Antarctic and along the Brazilian coast. Following her last cruises, she was retired on 30 January 1972 and laid-up. She was broken-up five years later, in the spring of 1977, at San Pedro in Argentina.

## COSTA LINE

### The ANNA C.

At the end of the Second World War there was an extreme and pressing demand for low-fare passenger and migrant space to South America. The Costa Line of Genoa, which had previously limited its operations to coastal ships and freighters, recognized this situation and decided to enter the liner trade. It was the beginning of what would eventually become (by the mid-seventies) the largest passenger-cruise fleet in the western world. Their first ship was the idle British transport *Southern Prince*, built originally by Lithgows of Glasgow in 1929, for the Furness-Prince Line service between New York, Rio de Janeiro, Santos, Montevideo and Buenos Aires. With the Costa Line, she would be revisiting many of the same ports, although sailing out of the Mediterranean.

Transferred to her new Italian owners in 1947, the 10,900-ton ship, which had only 101 first class berths in her prewar service, was thoroughly rebuilt at

Roger Sherlock

Genoa as the *Anna C.* Her tonnage was increased to 11,736, the bow was extended by 8 feet to 524 feet overall and the accommodation space enlarged. Costa wanted to establish a strong reputation from the start and saw in this vessel the potential for taking advantage of the then pressing migrant/displaced persons trade to Latin America. She was rebuilt and refurbished not as a first class liner, but certainly in order to be more luxurious and comfortable than many of the austere migrant ships then sailing. With a high level of onboard ambiance and style, those cherished amenities such as good food and friendly service were recognized as important by Costa from the start. Furthermore, the *Anna C.* had a special distinction: she was Italy's first air-conditioned passenger ship.

Her maiden run from Italy, in March 1948, was booked to capacity – 850 passengers in all. Her success was immediate and led, within six months, to the acquisition and refit of the *Andrea C.* Although the ports of call were sometimes slightly varied, the routing for the *Anna C.* and most subsequent Costa liners on the South American route was from Naples, Genoa and Cannes to Lisbon, Madeira, Recife, Rio de Janeiro, Santos, Montevideo and Buenos Aires. In following years, she was consistently improved and upgraded. In 1952, she underwent a more extensive overhaul and had her original Burmeister & Wain diesels (16½ knots) replaced by new Fiat diesels (which would give as much as 20 knots). The accommodation was periodically extended as well and, during the winter of 1960–61, it was finally

*Costa Line's first passenger ship, the* Anna C., *which began her Italian-flag sailings to Latin America in the spring of 1948, was the former* Southern Prince *of the Furness-Prince Line, part of the Furness Withy Group.*

rearranged as 202 in first class and 864 in tourist class. She was then listed as 12,030 tons.

During the 1960s, the *Anna C.* was often re-routed to the West Indies, sailing from Naples, Genoa, Cannes and Barcelona to La Guaira and several Caribbean islands. She was also sent to the United States for winter cruising, being used on twice-weekly three- and four-day sailings from Port Everglades, Florida to Nassau in the Bahamas. Fares for the three-day voyages began at $69. Earlier, in the late 1950s, Costa had entered the American cruise trades with another of its greatly refitted second-hand passenger ships, the 6800-ton *Franca C.*, built originally in 1914. Being one of the first ships to offer Caribbean sailings from Florida and later as the first ship to offer air-sea cruises from San Juan, Puerto Rico, she is one of the pioneers of the $4 billion American cruise industry of the mid-eighties.

The *Anna C.* was, in her later years, kept in Mediterranean waters, sailing mostly on weekly summer season voyages from Genoa to Cannes, Barcelona, Palma de Majorca, Tripoli, Naples and Capri. After being laid-up for some time, she left Genoa under tow on 6 December 1971 for an overnight voyage to the scrappers at La Spezia. It was the end of the first of many Costa liners that followed.

## The ANDREA C.

In 1947, to replenish its depleted cargo fleet, the Costa Line added two 7100-ton American Liberty ships, which became the *Eugenio C.* and the *Enrico C.*, as well as the transport *Ocean Virtue*, which was one of 60 'Ocean class' freighters built in US yards for the British Government. All three ships were barely able to do more than 11 knots. Nevertheless, the blazing success of the *Anna C.* on the South American passenger run in 1948 led Costa immediately to consider acquiring a second passenger vessel. The former *Ocean Virtue*, renamed the *Andrea C.*, was selected and hurriedly rebuilt at Genoa with some 482 berths. By the fall of 1948, she too was sailing to Rio, Santos and Buenos Aires. The westbound migrant trade continued to boom to such an extent that the aged *Giovanna C.*, a 8300-tonner that was more of a tramp freighter, was given 1200 third class berths for temporary passenger service. Every outbound sailing from Naples and Genoa was booked to full capacity.

Like the *Anna C.*, the *Andrea C.* underwent periodic improvements and in 1959 was taken in hand at Genoa for a major refit. A new Fiat diesel was installed and raised her service speed to as much as 16 knots. The passenger quarters were altered as well, which included the addition of three outdoor pools, a cinema, strikingly modern public rooms, private bathroom facilities in all first class staterooms and a berthing plan that was arranged as either 122 or 234 in first class and 248 or 354 in tourist class. Like all Costa passenger ships by the early sixties, the *Andrea C.* was fully air-conditioned.

By the late sixties, as only larger ships were used on the run to Brazil and Argentina, the *Andrea C.* was periodically used on the Caribbean run, calling at several West Indian islands as well as La Guaira in Venezuela and Cartagena in Colombia. She also did considerable cruising, sailing not only from Genoa, Naples and Venice within the Mediterranean and to West Africa, but from Rio to the Brazilian coast and the Amazon region as well as from Buenos Aires to the Straits of Magellan. In her final years, during the mid-seventies, she cruised also from Cartagena to Caribbean ports and from Venice to the Dalmatian coast and Aegean isles. Kept in reserve for some time at Genoa, the forty-year-old *Andrea C.* was sold to breakers in La Spezia in late 1982.

## The FEDERICO C.

By the mid fifties, after refitting a string of second-hand passenger ships, the Costa family were enjoying substantial profits from their passenger division, one which had developed a very strong and sound reputation both in Europe and in South America. Thus, with sufficient cash reserves in hand, an agreement was reached with the Ansaldo Shipyards, a Genoa neighbour. The pact called for the company's first brand-new liner, which would become the 20,400-ton *Federico C.*, a top-flight luxury liner.

The South American trades were still very healthy at the time of the *Federico C.*'s maiden crossing, in March 1958. Ship appraisers gave the new Costa flagship high marks and easily spotted the high postwar Italian standard of passenger ship design and decoration. The Ansaldo yards had already built two superb liners for Italy's transatlantic service to New York, the 29,100-ton sisters *Andrea Doria* and *Cristoforo Colombo* of 1953–54, and were just starting work on the nation's largest and fastest postwar liner, the 33,300-ton *Leonardo da Vinci* of 1960. Laurence Dunn, in his well known first edition of *Passenger Liners*, published in 1961, wrote of the new Costa liner, 'Exceptional care was paid to the design and décor of accommodation and public rooms, which are in contemporary Italian style with rather restrained use of colours. Cabin class is but very little short of first class standards, and their several dining saloons are of identical décor and so partitioned that these can be divided to suit any variations in first and cabin class numbers. Each of the three classes [243 passengers in first class, 300 in cabin class and 736 in third class] has about five other public rooms, open and sheltered promenade deck space and also special decks for children. The three deck pools are particularly attractive, with novel irregular shape and surround. All of the first class cabins have their own bath or shower as do nearly all of those in cabin class.'

The *Federico C.*, with steam turbines that could produce a maximum speed of 23 knots, was designed to make the Genoa–Buenos Aires passage in fourteen days. The customary stopovers at Cannes, Barcelona, Lisbon, Rio de Janeiro, Santos and Montevideo were included en route. Assisted by several of the older and smaller liners, including the *Anna C.* and *Andrea C.*, the *Federico C.* proved a highly successful, very popular and most profitable liner and led, by the mid-sixties, to the creation of an even larger, new Costa flagship. In preparation for the commissioning of the 30,500-ton *Eugenio C.* in the summer of 1966, the *Federico C.* was reassigned. Several months earlier, in April, she began a new mid-Atlantic service from Naples, Genoa, Cannes, Barcelona, Lisbon and Madeira to Port Everglades, Florida. As transatlantic passenger shipping slumped deeper and deeper into decline, a temporary measure was taken in the attempt to recruit more passengers and the voyages

*Costa's first brand-new passenger liner was the superbly handsome Federico C., completed in 1958, especially for the three-class service to Brazil, Uruguay and Argentina. Notice the considerable open-air deck spaces as well as the three swimming pools, one for each class.*

were often extended to include La Guaira and some Caribbean ports. The accommodation was eventually re-organized for 186 passengers in first class and 1450 in tourist, and still later to carry approximately 800 all one-class 'cruise' passengers. By 1970, Costa had little alternative but to employ the *Federico C.* in continuous cruise service. As with most of the Costa liners, these voyages proved to be most diverse: ten- and eleven-day trips from Genoa to West Africa and the Atlantic Isles, longer Mediterranean and Black Sea cruises, several sailings to Northern Europe and Scandinavia, winter cruising from Port Everglades to the Caribbean and from Rio, Santos and Buenos Aires to South American coastal areas. The ship's overall amenities were listed as being completely air-conditioned, stabilized, with three outdoor swimming pools, closed circuit television system, children's facilities, a gift shop, beauty salon and barber shop. The staterooms were headed by four deluxe suites, each having five berths, that were located on the Promenade Deck. Each suite comprised of a bedroom, sitting room, dressing room, baggage area and twin bathrooms.

As Costa Cruises, the firm eventually became the largest cruise ship operator apart from the Soviets. The *Federico C.* was, for the most part, an important and useful ship. However, in 1983, the company decided to alter its fleet size and sell off some tonnage. The *Federico C.* was among the ships selected for disposal. After an extensive refit and modernization at Genoa, she was recommissioned for the Florida-based Premier Cruise Lines, a division of the well known Greyhound Bus & Tour Company. Based at Port Canaveral (which is quite near Walt Disney World and EPCOT Center), she sails as the *Royale*, wearing a bright-red hull and with multi-coloured lido decks, on three- and four-day cruises to Nassau and a Bahamian outer island port. Her sailings are linked specially to tours of the nearby tourist attractions which makes for popular seven- and ten-day combination travel. The *Royale* is now registered in Panama.

## THE MELANESIEN, BIANCA C. AND PROVENCE/ENRICO C.

When the *Federico C.* was introduced in 1958, the Costa Company was already looking into suitable

secondhand tonnage to supplement its Latin American services. In fact, most of these ships would be used in a variety of charter arrangements. First, they purchased the Dutch *Indrapoera*, a 9500-tonner left over from the colonial trade to Java. The capacity was increased from a scant 96 berths to 180, in two classes. However, instead of using the ship as the first *Bianca C.* as originally intended, she was time-chartered for six years to another Italian passenger firm, the Cogedar Line, who rechartered her to France's Messageries Maritimes. Captain Elvio Arimondo, who later became master of the Costa flagship *Eugenio C.*, served aboard this ship. 'She was aptly renamed as the *Melanesien* for the French charter. We had four-month round-trips that sailed from Marseilles, went across to Algeria, then on to Guadeloupe and Martinique in the Caribbean before passing through the Panama Canal and continuing to Tahiti, New Caledonia and finally a turnaround at Sydney. We carried mostly government passengers and lots of general cargo. The interiors were very old and very dark. We had two nationalities among the crew: French in the hotel department and Italians in the deck and engine areas.' When this charter ended in 1963, the thirty-eight-year-old *Melanesien* was sold to Italian breakers.

The name *Bianca C.* was quickly reused (the *Melanesien* was briefly renamed *Bianca C.*) for yet another Costa acquisition in late 1958. This 17,300-ton liner had been *Marechal Petain*, then *La Marseillaise*, also of Messageries Maritimes. She was the flagship of their colonial Indo-China run. Completed in 1949, she saw just seven years of service before passing on to the Swiss-owned, Panama-flag Arosa Line and becoming their *Arosa Sky* for North Atlantic tourist work. This phase of life was shortlived, however, as Arosa began to suffer from financial problems, caused mostly by rapid expansion. To survive and in an effort to gather some much-needed capital, they put their largest ship up for sale in little over a year. She quickly passed into Costa hands and was refitted.

Costa's interior décor was developing into some of the finest Mediterranean style afloat. This 'new' *Bianca C.* was superbly refitted, featuring rich velours, colourful works of art and particularly well-appointed cabins. Of course, as in all Italian passenger ships, lido decks and swimming pools (usually several of them, including one or two just for the children) were a highlight. Rich national cuisine, lively dance bands and a good number of well-stocked bars were also important elements to an Italian liner. Costa used all of these ingredients.

Although the *Bianca C.* was intended to be the

Alex Duncan

*Bought from Holland's Royal Rotterdam Lloyd, the former* Indrapoera *was owned by Costa, chartered to the Cogedar Line, and then to Messageries Maritimes who sailed her as the* Melanesien.

largest ship on Costa's Caribbean run, from Genoa and Naples to the West Indies and La Guaira, she was chartered to American interests soon after being commissioned. She spent the winter of 1959–60 cruising from New York to the Caribbean under the banner of a firm known as Wall Street Cruises. In the following winter, she sailed from Port Everglades, Florida, as part of a Costa subsidiary fleet then known as Atlantic Cruise Lines. While she periodically returned to regular liner service, carrying 202 in first class and 1030 in tourist, it was during one of these trips that she was to become a victim to an ill common to French and French-built ships – fire. While anchored off the Caribbean island of Grenada, on 22 October 1961, the *Bianca C.* caught fire following an explosion in the engine room. The flames soon spread to every deck and the ship had to be abandoned completely. All but one member of the crew survived the ordeal. Two days later, on the 24th, the empty, smoldering hulk was towed by the British frigate HMS *Londonderry* in an effort to run her

aground on a deserted beach. Unfortunately, the attempt failed when the 593-foot liner sprang a leak, flooded and then sank. The entire situation might have developed into a major tragedy, resulting in a large loss of life. In thanks to the citizens of Grenada, the Costa family erected a commemorative statue in the outer harbour at St George's. It remains in place to this day, although with a continuously eroding base.

Months after the *Bianca C.* tragedy, the Costa Line time-chartered the French-flag *Provence*, which had been sailing for Transports Maritimes of Marseilles since her completion in the spring of 1951. A 15,900-tonner, she was built as part of a set for the postwar Latin American trade. She came from the Swan, Hunter & Wigham Richardson yards at Newcastle while her sister, the *Bretagne* (which later became the Chandris *Brittany*), was built by Chantiers et Ateliers de St Nazaire in France. The *Provence*, designed with a wide range of accommodation, from deluxe suites in first class and large dormitories in third class, carried 157 first class passengers, 167 in tourist class, 508 in third class cabins and 470 in third class dormitories. Her routing was quite similar to the Costa passenger services, from Marseilles, Genoa, Naples and Barcelona to Dakar, Bahia, Rio de

Janeiro, Santos, Montevideo and Buenos Aires.

Several years later, on 18 February 1954, the *Provence* was involved in one of the most serious collisions involving a large passenger ship. While sailing in the River Plate, she collided with the Niarchos-owned, Liberian-flag tanker *Saxonsea*. Although both ships remained afloat, the 580ft long *Provence* was so badly damaged that she was not able to return to Marseilles for final repairs for nearly a year. She did not reappear at her French home-port until January 1955, and then did not resume her commercial sailings until 26 March.

After starting to sail under joint Costa/Transports Maritimes management in 1962, the *Provence* was gradually modernized and improved. Three years later, as the French company wished to close its passenger division, Costa bought the ship outright and renamed her *Enrico C.* Swiss-born Emile Girault, who later became the highest ranking *maître d'hotel* aboard the Costa cruise fleet, initially served in this French ship and recalled, 'I joined Transports Maritimes at Marseilles. I was assigned to the *Provence* and sent to New York for the ship's Caribbean cruise programme in the summer of 1963 [she was under charter to the shortlived Caribbean Cruise Lines]. Later, we sailed to South America, mostly with French and Italian passengers. However, the company did not readily accept my credentials [from the prestigious Ecole Hôtelière at Lausanne] or any of my other schooling, in fact. Instead, I became a busboy. The experience, however, was wonderful. It was the best, most diverse training that I could have received. I did cooking, waited on tables and even peeled potatoes in the kitchen. I did every part of the restaurant job.'

The *Enrico C.* underwent a very lengthy refit at Genoa, in 1965, and had most of her cargo spaces removed, a vast lido area built in the stern and a complete redecoration of her cabins and public rooms. Her berthing was rearranged in two-class fashion, with 218 first class and 980 in tourist class. She was then placed on the Genoa–Rio–Buenos Aires route as the consort to the brand-new *Eugenio C.*, which was commissioned in August 1966.

Like all of the Costa liners, she has since done

*Costa's* Enrico C., *the former French* Provence, *was refitted and modernized in the mid-sixties for continued service to the east coast of South America. Now refitted as a full-time cruise ship, she is shown outbound from Lisbon on a positioning voyage to Rio and Buenos Aires for their December–March cruise season.*

Luis Miguel Correia

considerable cruising, both from Genoa as well as Rio de Janeiro and Buenos Aires. She has even had a winter season working out of Capetown and Durban. Beginning in 1972, she was converted to an all-first class ship and used permanently in cruise service, thereby leaving the *Eugenio C.* on the traditional three-class liner run to South America. More recently, beginning in 1983, in a company reorganisation of what has become known as Costa Cruises, she has been advertised as the *Enrico Costa*, although seems not to have officially renamed. Other Costa cruise ships have undergone a similar 'renaming'. She now spends six months of the year, between spring and fall, on weekly cruises from Genoa to Barcelona, Palma de Majorca, Tunis, Palermo and Naples. Minimum fares began at $865 in 1985.

*Costa's largest liner and flagship, the* Eugenio C. *of 1966, copied the design of P&O's* Canberra *and had twin uptakes placed aft instead of the conventional funnel.*

The Eugenio C.

In the early sixties, the Costa liner fleet continued to grow, even as a third generation of the family took the helm. They worked in various capacities from offices on three continents, and made appearances on the ships themselves. More recently, in 1983, over one hundred Costa brothers, cousins and more distant family members were involved in the firm's operations.

The greatest success came in 1964 when they ordered their newest and largest passenger ship, the 30,500-ton *Eugenio C.*. Company designers examined closely the various elements of many ships: the then new *Leonardo da Vinci* (there was a striking resemblence in the interiors of the two ships), P&O's *Canberra* (certain external, upper-deck features are very similar), the sisters *Guglielmo Marconi* and *Galileo Galilei*, the even larger sisters *Michelangelo* and *Raffaello*, and finally the brilliant *Oceanic*, to which the end-result, the *Eugenio C.*, is certainly most closely related.

Although the new Costa flagship was called 'the ship of the future' (a rather over-used description in the 1960s) when she was commissioned in August 1966, she was most definitely startling, beautiful and quite advanced for the Europe-South America trade. In this service, she had no peers. She was the most modern, the fastest and certainly the best decorated. Like many other liners of the time, she was still primarily a port-to-port passenger ship carrying three classes of passengers on nine to ten monthly sailings between Naples, Genoa, Cannes and Barcelona and then across to Rio de Janeiro, Santos, Montevideo and Buenos Aires. In those early years, she was only used for occasional cruises, certainly the more deluxe voyages in the Costa schedules.

The passenger configuration on the *Eugenio C.* was balanced between 178 in first class, 356 in second class and 1102 in tourist class. There are nine passenger decks: Lido, Sun, Boat, Lounge, Restaurant, Foyer, A, B and C. Passenger cabins are on seven of these, with only the Lido and Lounge decks being reserved exclusively as public spaces. All in all, there are 579 cabins – 221 being outside and the remainder inside. Some 122 of these rooms are without private facilities (all of them in the original third class quarters); the others having either a full-size bath and/or shower and toilet. These rooms range from the eight deluxe apartments, which are forward on the Boat Deck and which consist of a bedroom, sitting area and full-size bath, to four-berth inside cabins on C Deck without private facilities.

The ship's most beautiful public room is the forward Ambra Lounge, decorated in silver-grey, rust and brown, all offset by curving windows with Viennese drapes. These windows look out onto the bow as well as the sea on both sides. Next, to this room is a foyer which extends into the Rubino Lounge, all made particularly attractive not only by the use of modern metallic pieces of art but by high-gloss black lino floors. In the Rubino Lounge, the flooring is rather handsomely accentuated by a large bone-white carpet. The ceilings are partially grated and give off attractive indirect lighting.

The décor – while always noticeably Italian-Mediterranean – grows simpler proceeding aft. The Opale Lounge follows, decorated in darker colours and with the continued use of marvellously comfortable velour chairs and sofas. There are very attractive Garden Verandahs on both sides of the ship, having substantial greenery and light wood furniture with bright yellow cushions. Rows of promenade windows face onto the sea.

Further aft on the Lounge Deck, there is a choice of bars, card rooms, quiet rooms and a library. The aft Turchese Lounge is used for the larger scale entertainments (such as International Night, the Talent Show, the Captain's Gala, etc), utilizing extra rows of folding chairs for the twin sittings. On other decks, four verandah lounges are placed adjacent to the three salt-water pools and lido areas. A disco and children's playroom are aft on the Boat Deck and there are two chapels, one forward and one aft, on the Restaurant Deck. There is also a beauty salon, barber shop and two boutiques. The restaurant is divided into three sections: the Magic Flute, the Etruscan and the Genova. The décor is similar throughout – more high-gloss floors, walls covered in metallic art, velour chairs and various sized tables (for seating two, four, eight and ten). The Magic Flute and Etruscan sections, used by the first and second class passengers respectively, feature 'grand carte' menus offering an extensive selection. The Genova Restaurant, used by the third class passengers, features a menu entitled 'un ala carte', a more limited selection.

Beginning in the mid-seventies, the *Eugenio C.* was used more often as a cruise ship. Her most extensive cruise voyage, a three-month trip around the world, was run in 1977. Emile Girault was *maître d'hotel* aboard the liner during her first circumnavigation: 'One outstanding memory for that trip was the supervision and preparation of the official banquet for the delegation from the People's Republic of China during the ship's call at Shanghai. Historically, it was quite interesting. Naturally, we served some macaroni and spaghetti dishes. Well, after all, the Chinese supposedly gave us [the Italians] the noodle-pasta concept to begin with, from the early travels of Marco Polo.'

Mr Girault continued to coordinate the food provision system as well for the *Eugenio C.*'s cruise voyages. 'Most of our supplies come from Italy. However, when the price is right, we buy elsewhere. This trip [a nine-day Mediterranean cruise, in July 1982], oranges were less expensive in Israel and so we made a sizeable purchase. Overall, our consumption is quite large, assuredly larger than any of the other Costa liners. For example, we have a daily use of at least 1200 bottles of mineral water, 600 bottles of wine and 300lbs of pasta.'

By the mid-eighties, the three-class South American sailings had all but disappeared completely. Motivated by the initial intrusion of airline competition, the Costa Line became Costa Cruises and began to concentrate solely on one-class pleasure voyages. During 1985, between May and September, the ship was used on ten-day Mediterranean cruises from

Genoa to Naples, Messina, Alexandria, Port Said, Ashdod, Limassol and Rhodes. Minimum fares began at $1075. For the remainder of the year, she cruises on more diverse voyages as well as on winter service from Buenos Aires and Rio de Janeiro. In more recent years, she has been advertised as the *Eugenio Costa*, in keeping with a newly developed Costa nomenclature, but without actually having been renamed. Costa Cruises remain one of the world's largest and most popular cruise firms. Captain Elvio Arimondo, who has been master of the *Eugenio C.*, added some insight into the success of the Costa passenger fleet. 'We have excellent administration within the Costa family. They are all very serious, work very hard and keep low profiles. Furthermore, we are a private company, which is very important in Italy. The government-owned firms, such as the Italian Line and Lloyd Triestino, did not have the same rate of success in passenger shipping for various reasons. Costa also keeps a good eye on the future of travel at sea. We are always willing to experiment. Of course, the Costa family has other vast interests: petro-chemicals, textiles, real estate (particularly in apartment housing in Italy) and even olive oil. Dante Olive Oil, which is now sold in North America, is a Costa product.

'These days [1982], we must be 90 per cent full or better. Operations, staffing and fuel have become very, very expensive. Actually, this has been a growing problem for some years. We looked at the *Michelangelo* and *Raffaello* [both 45,000 tons and built in 1965 for the Italian Line's transatlantic run to New York] when they were for sale [in 1975–76], but it was immediately apparent that they were too big, too expensive and especially hard on fuel. They were built to be run with the aid of an Italian Government subsidy at all times.

'We are much impressed with the *Oceanic* [39,000 tons, built 1965], which is, of course, a near-sister to the *Eugenio C.* They shared the same designer, a Mr Constanzo of Monfalcone, and were built at the same yard, just a year apart. We are intending that the *Eugenio C.* should get a major refit for full-time cruising and will be modelled after the *Oceanic*. We may put her in the short-distance trade in the Caribbean or even on the Miami-Nassau overnight run. We've even looked at Australian cruising, but it is simply too costly, necessitating crew changes by air.'

At the time of writing (1985), the *Eugenio C.*, or *Eugenio Costa* as she is advertised, remains the flagship of the Costa liner fleet. Other passenger ships include the aforementioned *Enrico C.*, the former *Provence*; the *Carla C.*, ex-*Flandre* of the French Line; the converted freighters *Daphne* and *Danae*, the former Port Line 'meat ships' *Port Sydney* and *Port Melbourne*; and, added in late 1985 after a lavish rebuilding, the former Lloyd Triestino *Guglielmo Marconi* as the *Costa Riviera*.

## ITALIAN LINE

### The CONTE BIANCAMANO and CONTE GRANDE

Built as near-sisters in the mid-twenties, the *Conte Biancamano*, which came from the William Beardmore yards at Glasgow in 1925, and the *Conte Grande*, delivered by Stabilimento Tecnico at Trieste in early 1928, were two of only four large Italian Line passenger ships to survive the Second World War. The other pair were the motor liner sisters *Saturnia* and *Vulcania*, also dating from the mid 1920s. The 'Two Counts', as the earlier ships were called, were fortunate to fall into American hands during the war and therefore received excellent care. The *Conte Biancamano* sailed for the US Navy as the troop transport USS *Hermitage*; the *Conte Grande* was re-named as well, becoming the USS *Monticello*. Both were returned to Italy in the summer of 1947 and, while extensively refitted and restored for peacetime service, many of their sumptuously grand prewar decorations and features were not revived. Instead,

*A glorious survivor of the Second World War, the Italian Line's* Conte Grande *was restored with wider funnels, a streamlined superstructure, a new bow and all-white livery. Although shown here at New York during some special North Atlantic sailings in 1956, she was used almost exclusively in the Latin American trade.*

while they retained their conventional appearances of twin funnels set between twin masts, their interiors were modernized almost completely. Frank Braynard, the noted American maritime historian, called the ships 'among the best conversions I have ever seen'. John Havers, who sailed in the Union-Castle liners, which frequently called at Genoa, remembered these large white-hulled Italian liners as well, 'I remember seeing the *Conte Grande* in Genoa berthed opposite to a Union-Castle liner at the Ponte de Mille. Undoubtedly, she was one of the finest looking ships ever, with her two large funnels, two masts and counter stern. She had perfection of line to a ship-lover. The *Conte Biancamano* just failed to come up to her sister's looks, having the original smaller funnels, but was a "looker" for all that. It was hard to visualize them in their original prewar Lloyd Sabaudo colours [they joined the Italian Line in a large national merger of passenger ships in 1932].'

While the express run to New York was considered the Italian Line's premier service, these ships were intended from the start of their postwar conversions to serve on the booming South American trade, from Naples, Genoa, Cannes, Barcelona, Lisbon and Dakar, and then across to Rio de Janeiro, Santos, Montevideo and Buenos Aires. The *Conte Grande* was completed first and resumed commercial sailings in July 1949; the *Conte Biancamano* followed in November. The latter ship soon divided her work, being used on the New York run in the peak summer months (from June through September) beginning in 1950. The *Conte Grande* had only one summer season on the North Atlantic, during 1956, when she served as a temporary replacement for the ill-fated *Andrea Doria*, the national flagship, which sank off the New England coast on 26 July 1956.

In addition to a difference in original builders and in their general exterior appearances, the *Conte Grande* at 667 feet was, in fact, 2 feet longer than her near-sister. The tonnage for the *Conte Biancamano* was placed at 23,842 whereas the *Conte Grande* was listed as being 23,562. Their passenger berthing arrangements also differed, being 215 in first class, 347 cabin class and 745 third class for the *Conte Biancamano* and 261 first class, 338 cabin class and 780 third class for the *Conte Grande*.

Although the 'Counts' were initially assisted by the 16,100-ton *Santa Cruz*, hurriedly acquired in 1947 and which had only 1200 third class berths for migrants, refugees, etc, in 1951–52 they were joined by the brand-new sisters *Augustus* and *Giulio Cesare*. They enjoyed great popularity and substantial profits in those early years. However, by the late fifties, as the

*Jeff Blinn, Moran Towing & Transportation Co*

first slight decline in the Latin American trade was noticed, the Italian Line opted not to replace the two older ships. They were retired in 1960, with the *Conte Biancamano* being laid-up at first and then going to the breakers at La Spezia. The *Conte Grande* was chartered to Lloyd Triestino for a single migrant sailing to Sydney before meeting her end at the same scrapyard in the autumn of 1961.

## The Augustus and Giulio Cesare

The Italians created some of the finest looking and best decorated passenger liners of the decade or so following the Second World War. Ahead of most others, the national shipyards, especially at Genoa and at Monfalcone, produced some exceptionally modern-looking ships. There was, in fact, a master plan created by Finmare, the Government-controlled consortium of shipping companies that included the Italian, Adriatica and Tirrenia Lines as well as Lloyd Triestino. The overall plan included building four large liners for the Italian Line services, two being destined for the South American trade and the next pair for the faster, more luxurious North Atlantic express route to New York. The Adriatica Line would be provided with no less than nine passenger-cargo ships ranging in size from the 4300-ton trio of the *Brennero* class (of 1958) to the 11,800-ton flagship *Ausonia* of 1957. The Tirrenia Line would receive a new series of ferries and short-sea passenger ships while Lloyd Triestino would be assigned seven combination liners: the *Australia*, *Neptunia* and *Oceania* for the Australian trade, the *Africa* and *Europa* for the East African run, and the *Asia* and *Victoria* for the Middle and Far Eastern routes. In a later, final review of deep-sea passenger shipping, the Italian Line would also build three exceptional ocean liners for the North Atlantic, the *Leonardo da Vinci* of 1960 and then the superliner twins *Michelangelo* and *Raffaello* of 1965, and Lloyd Triestino would add its largest and fastest ships of all, the *Galileo Galilei* and *Guglielmo Marconi*, in 1963.

Fitted with powerful Fiat diesels, which had actually been built some years before the ships themselves, the *Augustus* and *Giulio Cesare* ranked as two of the largest motor liners afloat at the time of their introduction. Being just over the 27,000-ton mark and at 680 feet in length, they were assuredly the largest,

*The* Augustus *was transferred to the New York run in February 1957, following the tragic loss of the* Andrea Doria *seven months before. She is shown being undocked by the tug* Carol Moran, *on 23 May 1957.*

fastest and most modern ships to sail out of the Mediterranean on the mid-Atlantic route to South America in the early fifties. Completely air-conditioned and fitted with such amenities as three outdoor pools and surrounding umbrella-filled lido decks, there were 180 berths in first class, 288 in cabin class and 714 in tourist class (634 of which had cabins while the remaining 80 slept in dormitories). Appropriately the term 'third class' disappeared with this new pair of Italian twins. Ship connoisseur C M Squarey visited the *Giulio Cesare* at Cannes in March 1952, soon after her maiden voyage, and was quite pleased with her accommodation. 'Perhaps the greatest progress of all in this ship has, in fact, been made in the tourist class quarters where the cabins and public rooms alike will seem like a dream to many a humble emigrant. The cabins are two-, four- and six-berth, all with hot and cold running water and even reading lamps over every berth. There is a splendid main lounge and smoke room and bar, whilst the dining room is of impressive proportions and nicely furnished; there are even some tables for two in it. Even this class has its own permanent mosaic swimming pool.'

Mr Squarey also noted the handsome exterior of the new ship. 'The hull (painted white) of this ship must be decidedly interesting to technicians, for the main frame is not up and down, and a little above the waterline she bulges out gracefully; she has also a bulbous bow; her funnel is high and she carries only one mast; she is, to look at, not unlike a larger edition of the prewar *Vulcania* and *Saturnia*. The Italians are masters at the art of ship-building, as well as masters at the art of hotel-keeping, and those two attributes when combined produce fine ships run in a manner that discerning public are not slow to appreciate.'

While both the *Augustus* and *Giulio Cesare* were intended for full-time services on the South American route, from Naples, Genoa, Cannes, Barcelona and Lisbon, and then across to Rio, Santos, Montevideo and Buenos Aires, they were re-routed to the North Atlantic for peak summer season service. The *Giulio Cesare* began periodic sailings to New York in June 1956, joining the *Andrea Doria*, *Cristoforo Colombo*, *Saturnia*, *Vulcania* and *Conte Biancamano*. Despite the more serious appearance of commercial aircraft, the Mediterranean tourist and westbound migrant trades were booming. A month later, on 25–26 July, the *Andrea Doria* sank after colliding with the Swedish liner *Stockholm*. It was not only a deep, most unfortunate blow to the Italian merchant marine, but created a considerable gap in scheduled services. While the *Conte Grande* was temporarily reassigned to the New

*Decorated in an exceptionally modern style for the early fifties, the first class Main Lounge aboard the* Augustus *was one of her finest public rooms.*

York run as a replacement, the *Augustus* was brought onto that service, in February 1957, as a more permanent substitute. For several years both the *Giulio Cesare* and *Augustus* would be familiar sights in New York harbour. However, once the new *Leonardo da Vinci* was delivered in the summer of 1960, both liners resumed South American service on a full-time basis. Four years later, during their annual refits, both ships were converted to two-class liners, retaining their original small first class sections, but with a combined cabin and tourist section that created 1000 berths in an enlarged tourist accommodation area.

By the late sixties, the Finmare Group of passenger companies began to show more obvious signs of decline in traffic. In April 1969, figures for 1966–68 were released which showed that the North Atlantic trade to New York had decreased by 15 per cent, the South American service dropped by 7.6 per cent for the same period and the South American Pacific service by 2.2 per cent. In addition, the Adriatica Line's Mediterranean passenger services had decreased substantially due to the Middle East crisis and the Lloyd Triestino liner runs dropped as well

Sal Scannella Collection

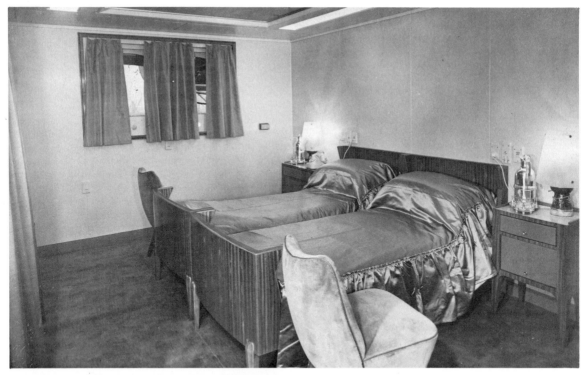

*Sal Scannella Collection*

The bedroom of a deluxe apartment aboard the **Augustus**.
Compared to the ornate style of the prewar Italian liners,
this décor might be considered to be exceptionally simple,
almost severe.

*Sal Scannella Collection*

*Sal Scannella Collection*

Also aboard the **Augustus**: an inside four-berth stateroom in
cabin class.

The first class Observation Lounge aboard the **Augustus**
and her sister, the **Giulio Cesare**, had windows that looked
out over the ship's forward section.

because of the closure of the Suez Canal. During 1967, the Finmare companies had carried 1.7 million passengers, which was a considerable decline from the 4.5 million passengers carried a decade earlier.

The first of several reorganization and reduction plans was announced by December 1969. This called for the immediate withdrawal of the *Augustus* and *Giulio Cesare* as well as the *Verdi* from the west coast of South America run. In addition, it was proposed that Lloyd Triestino's *Asia* and *Victoria* should be removed from the Far Eastern passenger trade and be converted to Mediterranean cruise ships. Soon afterwards the powerful and persistent Italian maritime unions bitterly protested to the government ministries in Rome. A string of timetable-disrupting schedules, work stoppages, slow-downs and other annoyances followed. The Italian Line ships, among others under the Finmare houseflag, were often as much as a week off schedule. As the situation became more confusing and difficult – the solution to it became more and more obvious.

Again under loud protests from the seamen's unions, Finmare announced a major 'reshuffling' scheme in February 1971. The *Raffaello* and *Leonardo da Vinci* were to be reassigned to the South American trade, replacing the *Giulio Cesare* and *Augustus*, which were to be retired and scrapped. Soon afterwards, the *Rossini*, *Verdi* and *Donizetti* were to be pulled off the South American Pacific link. The plan also called for the retirement of three Adriatica Line ships, the *Esperia*, *Messapia* and *Enotria*, which were to be replaced by four specially converted Mediterranean cruise ships, Lloyd Triestino's former *Asia*, *Victoria*, *Africa* and *Europa*. The Finmare directors' intended plan barely left the drawing board. There were more strikes, delays and some cancelled sailings. Embarrassing news stories began to report that the larger Finmare-controlled passenger ships were being subsidized by the Italian Government at a rate of $700 for every passenger carried. Especially in the case of the white-hulled Italian Line ships, these once glorious maritime queens had become a huge blemish. Their end and the termination of almost all overseas liner services were inevitable.

When the *Giulio Cesare* developed serious rudder problems during a South American voyage in December 1972, little effort was made to repair this twenty-year-old, uneconomic ship. Laid up for a time, she was scrapped at La Spezia in the following summer. In something of an emergency reassignment plan, the 29,191-ton *Cristoforo Colombo* was abruptly taken off the Trieste–Venice–New York run and sent southward to Rio, Santos, Montevideo and Buenos

Aires. At the best, it was a temporary reprieve for another ageing, fuel-hungry, half-filled liner.

The *Augustus* was finally retired in January 1976, and laid-up at Naples for a time. Months before, the giant *Michelangelo* and *Raffaello* had been withdrawn from the North Atlantic, and in the following June, the *Leonardo Da Vinci* would close out the New York service altogether. According to the best projections, the South American run would be terminated during 1977, and thereafter the Italian Line would concentrate on freight and container shipping. Some pessimists suggested that the busy scrappers at La Spezia would have even more work in the days ahead, breaking-up vessels such as the *Michelangelo*, *Raffaello*, *Augustus*, *Cristoforo Colombo*, *Leonardo da Vinci* and possibly even Lloyd Triestino's final pair of sisters, the *Guglielmo Marconi* and *Galileo Galilei*. The situation was that the world's passenger fleet had not yet recovered from the dramatic oil price increases of 1973–74, and there were further suggestions that even the lucrative North American cruise fleet had reached its peak. Among other bleak predictions, the Cunard Line felt they were accurate in reporting that their brand-new *Cunard Princess*, a 17,000-tonner delivered in the spring 1977, might well be the last deep-sea passenger liner. Certainly, the possibilities for the aged, operationally-expensive Italian liner fleet looked less than promising. The solution was, in fact, to sell them off – to rather unlikely buyers. The *Michelangelo* and *Raffaello* went to the Iranian Government to finish off their days as military accommodation ships in backwater ports, the *Cristoforo Colombo* was sold in the same year (1977) to Venezuelan interests for use as a floating workers' hostel along the Orinoco River, meanwhile the *Augustus* was sold to some unknown Hong Kong buyers with uncertain purposes. The *Leonardo da Vinci* was given a spark of fresh yet somewhat humiliating life. Passed over to Italian Line Cruises International, she was demoded to overnight passages between Miami and Nassau. Fuel-hungry and somewhat neglected, she was a great disappointment. She was sent to La Spezia within a year with the intention that she too be sold off to foreign buyers but she caught fire and then sank in local waters in July 1980. Once salvaged, she could only be cut-up for scrap – a sorrowful ending to the once magnificent postwar Italian passenger fleet.

Listed as under the ownership of Great Shipping Investment Limited, the former *Augustus*, renamed *Great Sea*, flew the flag of the remote Seychelles but rarely left her Hong Kong anchorage. For several years, apparently little happened except that she transferred to Panamanian registry and was later sold to the Ocean King Navigation Co and renamed *Ocean King*. Reportedly, she has been since moved to the Philippines for use as a floating hotel.

### The DONIZETTI, VERDI and ROSSINI

The third of the Italian Line's long-haul passenger routes was to the west coast of South America via Panama. In the fifties, this service was maintained by three combination passenger-cargo liners, the 485ft *Amerigo Vespucci*, *Antoniotto Usodimare* and *Marco Polo*, known jointly as the Navigator class; they had accommodation for 90 passengers in cabin class and 436 in third class. Although launched in 1942, during the war, the ships were completed by the Ansaldo yards at Genoa in 1948–49. In 1963, in something of a Finmare fleet reshuffle, Lloyd Triestino (about to take delivery of their largest liners of all, the 27,900-ton *Guglielmo Marconi* and *Galileo Galilei*), transferred their three Australia-run sisterships, the *Australia*, *Oceania* and *Neptunia*, to the Italian Line. Following some alterations and improvements, they became the 'Three Musicians', the *Donizetti*, *Verdi* and *Rossini*, and were scheduled for the Pacific service to South America.

Originally designed to carry 135 in first class and 535 in tourist class, the accommodation was revised to carry 160 in first and 440 in tourist class. As a considerable improvement on the earlier ships, each class had its own lido deck, open-air pool, several modern public rooms and most of the cabins had private bathrooms (many of those in first class could be converted into daytime sitting rooms). There were sailings from Genoa every three weeks and they cut the passage time to Valparaiso by three days, making for a twenty-eight-day passage between the first and last port before reversing course. The ports of call following Genoa and Naples were Cannes, Barcelona, Tenerife, then across to La Guaira, Curaçao, Cartagena, Cristobal and a transit of the Panama Canal, Buenaventura (Colombia), Guayaquil (Ecuador), Callao (Peru), Arica, Antofagasta and Valparaiso (all in Chile).

This service, like most of the Italian Line passenger trade, began to decline by the late sixties. By the

*On 16 April 1964, outbound for South America,* Verdi *collided with the Liberian tanker* Pentelikon. *The Italian liner reversed course, and is shown with bow damage arriving at Gibraltar, en route for repairs at Genoa.*

Alex Duncan

mid-seventies, it was kept operative purely by pressures from the strong Italian seamen's unions. As Captain Narciso Fossati, the last commodore of the company's liner fleet, recalled, 'The ships were kept running to the last possible moment.' 1976 was the very end. Soon after the *Leonardo da Vinci* closed out the New York service and shortly before the run to Rio and Buenos Aires was terminated, the 'Three Musicians' finished their schedules. Although they were laid-up for a short time at Genoa in the summer and autumn of 1976, they were later towed to La Spezia, anchored in the outer harbour and then gradually taken in hand by the local scrappers. They too were among the last of the liners to fly the colours of the once mighty Italian Line.

*During a French maritime strike, on 28 May 1968, the French Line's* Antilles *(left) and the giant* France *terminated their sailings at Southampton's Ocean Dock rather than continue to Le Havre*

## The ANTILLES and FLANDRE

The French Line (Compagnie Generale Transatlantique) suffered particularly heavy war losses among its passenger fleets, a matter complicated further by the loss by fire of several other liners in the late thirties. Consequently, in postwar planning in the late forties, schemes were drawn up, with the assistance and financial support of the Government in Paris, for several new passenger ships. While some would run on the colonial North and West African trades, the biggest pair, at 20,000 tons each, were destined for the Atlantic. The initial idea was that these near-sisterships would ply the Caribbean route, along with the prewar *Colombie*, which had resumed sailings in the autumn of 1950. However, soon after the first keel plates were laid, the plans for the second ship were changed. She would sail only in the winter months to the Caribbean; for the remainder, she would trade to New York, on the prestigious North Atlantic run.

The first of the pair, named *Antilles*, was launched at the naval dockyard at Brest, on 26 April 1951. The second ship, to be called *Flandre*, came from Ateliers et Chantiers de France at Dunkirk and was launched six months later, on 31 October. Initial publicity material highlighted the advanced design of the two new liners: a single, tapered funnel (*Antilles* had a taller funnel), two masts, electric cranes rather than the customary kingposts and booms, and a level of first class accommodation that was said to 'rival first class on the Cunard 'Queens'. If the latter point was slightly exaggerated, if only in respect of their sheer size, the two French ships would certainly offer exceptionally attractive passenger quarters. The style appeared, in fact, to be something of a modernized, postwar art deco. There was noticeable use of stainless steel, indirect lighting and tubular furniture. If smaller in scale, the first class public rooms would be in keeping with the high standards noted for French Line passenger ships.

French Line

Because of a series of delays and other problems, the second of this pair, the *Flandre*, was actually completed first. Delivered in July 1952, she left Le Havre on the 23rd for what was to be her seven-day crossing to New York. It was just weeks after the record-breaking maiden voyage of the American super-ship *United States*. In the mid-thirties the French had their own Blue Riband holder, the *Normandie*, but they were now content with far more moderate tonnage. At her best, *Flandre* was intended to manage 22 knots at full-speed. The French début came to be the complete opposite of the American triumph. Due primarily to faults in her main electrical switchboard, the *Flandre* lost most of her power during the maiden sailing and limped into New York some 22 hours late. She needed tug assistance, even as the fireboats accorded her their welcome sprays. It was all terribly embarrassing, especially for the French, and this was compounded when New York dockers thereafter dubbed her as 'the Flounder'. She was expected to be a smaller assistant to the elegant *Ile de France*, which was returned to service in 1949, and also to the company's new flagship, the *Liberte*, which was the rebuilt *Europa* from the prewar North German Lloyd fleet. The humiliated *Flandre* had to be sent back to her builder's yard at Brest for a thorough examination and series of repairs that would last ten months. Sections of her electrical system had to be redesigned and then rebuilt to prevent a reoccurence. She did not resume sailing between Le Havre and New York, with a call at either Southampton or Plymouth, until April 1953.

The *Antilles*, commissioned in January 1953, fortunately suffered none of the woes that plagued her near-sister. First used for some 'show off' cruises to the Atlantic Isles and Mediterranean, she crossed to the Caribbean for the first time in May. While her overall routing often varied, she sailed between Le Havre and Southampton to Vigo, San Juan, Pointe a Pitre, Fort de France, La Guaira, Trinidad and Barbados. Periodically, she was sent on more extended cruises, which included calls at such ports as New Orleans, Galveston, Bermuda, Nassau, Kingston, Grand Cayman and Veracruz. Having the same high standard of accommodation as the *Flandre*, the *Antilles* had a three-class configuration: 404 berths in first class, 285 in cabin class and finally 89 in tourist class. After several changes in her early years, the *Flandre*'s arrangements were in two-class North Atlantic fashion, 212 berths in first class and 511 in tourist class.

A decade after her inauspicious first appearance at New York, the *Flandre* was reassigned, in the autumn

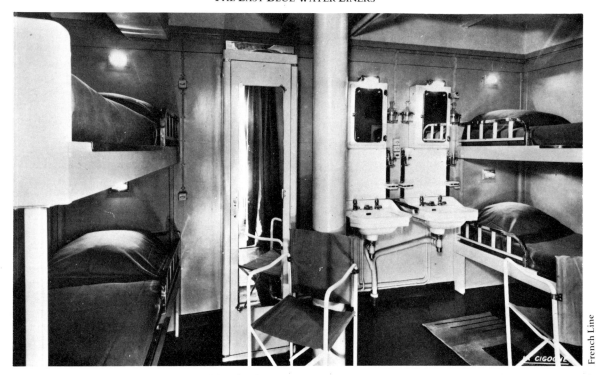

French Line

*A four-berth tourist class cabin aboard the* **Flandre**.

of 1962, to full time Caribbean service. Both the earlier *Ile de France* and *Liberte* had retired and been replaced by the superliner *France*, but the smaller, slower *Flandre* could hardly be expected to be a suitable running mate to the new national flagship. Furthermore, traffic demands on the transatlantic route had diminished to an extent wherein only the larger ship was required. Repainted like her sistership, with an all-white hull, the *Flandre* replaced the veteran *Colombie* and sailed to the Caribbean all the year round. The only notable detours for the ship seem to have been in 1967, when she crossed to the St Lawrence, to Quebec City and Montreal, for special cruises in conjunction with Canada's Expo '67.

At about the same time, the traditional two-class Caribbean liner trade began to decline, particularly in the face of competition from the airlines as well as specialized cruise ships in the United States. Seemingly in an effort to improve their operations, both the *Antilles* and *Flandre* began to be used for winter season cruises, mostly of a week's duration, out of San Juan or Guadeloupe to other nearby Caribbean islands. While these sailings were actively promoted, particularly with flight connections from major North American cities on Air France, neither ship was ideally competitive in the increasingly specialized

Caribbean cruise market. What they both really needed were full refits, giving them large stern lido decks, more modern public rooms and totally rebuilt cabin accommodation. The *Flandre* barely survived one more winter season (1967–68) before being placed on the international sales' lists.

The Costa Line of Italy was then actively expanding its cruise ship division, particularly for employment in North American waters. They were willing to spend millions on the fifteen-year-old *Flandre*, which would be renamed *Carla C.*, to make her a more competitive and successful ship. All cabins were rebuilt (for 754 one-class passengers only), the public rooms completely redecorated and a large lido area with two pools built in the stern area of the ship. Restyled at Genoa and delivered in December 1968, the ship might have gone directly into Costa cruise service if it had not been for a lucrative charter offer from the then new Princess Cruises of Los Angeles. They wanted a second ship to expand their American West Coast operations, sailing not only from Los Angeles southward to the Mexican Riviera but for a new dimension – two- and three-week cruises through the Panama Canal and into the Caribbean before turning back. Although never officially renamed, the *Carla C.* was advertised as the *Princess Carla*. The company's other cruise ship, the 12,000-ton Italian-flag *Italia*, was marketed as the *Princess Italia*. While both were chartered ships, they were very successful and soon led to the acqustion of two larger liners, the sistership *Sea Venture* and *Island Venture*, from Norwegian owners. They became the *Pacific Princess*, well known from her use in the television series 'The Love Boat', and the *Island Princess*. While the firm became a part of the P&O Group, they added, in 1984, their first brand-new luxury cruise ship, the 44,200-ton *Royal Princess*.

The former *Flandre* was returned to the Costa Line in 1970, and began what has since been almost her permanent employment: weekly seven-day cruises from San Juan to Curaçao, La Guaira, Grenada, Martinique and St Thomas. To date, she remains in this very popular service, although with little trace of her French Line heritage.

The *Antilles* sailed single-handedly on the French Caribbean trade until her sad demise by fire, on 8 January 1971. While homeward bound from San Juan to Le Havre, she struck an uncharted reef off the tiny island of Mustique. Leaking fuel erupted into a fire which then rapidly spread throughout the ship. Her 635 passengers and crew were evacuated and were later rescued by Cunard's *Queen Elizabeth 2* and two French Line freighters. A day later, the fire-ravaged *Antilles* began to sink. On the 18th, she broke in half and still later she broke into three pieces – the sad remains of a once handsome liner, she lies on that same reef off Mustique to date. Her rust-coloured bow points downward, her funnel and upper decks have collapsed within the midship section and the stern section is canted aft. Since scrapping her where she lies would be extremely difficult and expensive, it is likely that the remains of the *Antilles* may well be something of a 'Caribbean ruin' for years to come.

Immediately after the loss of the *Antilles*, the French Line searched desperately for a replacement ship. They approached the Norwegian America Line in Oslo, who were building a new ship, *Vistafjord*, for delivery in spring 1973, and offered a sizeable amount of money (in fact far more than the actual value), for the 18,700-ton *Bergensfjord*, her fifteen-year-old predecessor. Withdrawn two years earlier than planned, the *Bergensfjord* was refitted as the French *De Grasse* (originally the name *Louisiane* had been intended). Now a one-class cruise ship, she would make periodic

*The first class swimming pool aboard the* Flandre.

French Line

crossings to the Caribbean. The purchase of this ship was ill-timed; soon after her first appearance under the tricolor, fuel oil costs increased dramatically, and simultaneously passenger loads began to slump. In little over two years, the *De Grasse* was offered for sale. After sailing for other Norwegians owners in Eastern waters as the *Rasa Sayang*, going to Greek owners who renamed her as the *Golden Moon* and

finally to a long-term charter in which she would have reverted to *Rasa Sayang* for Australian cruising, she caught fire while undergoing a refit at Perama, Greece, on 27 August 1980. In flames from end to end, she had to be towed to the shallow waters of nearby Kynosoura Bay and deliberately sunk. Like the *Antilles*, her mangled remains still poke above local waters.

## CHARGEURS REUNIS/MESSAGERIES MARITIMES

### The Lavoisier and Claude Bernard

In another postwar scheme to replace well-worn, ageing prewar passenger ships, the French Government offered construction subsidies to a number of firms, including Chargeurs Reunis, which ran passenger and cargo services to three continents: to the east coast of South America, to colonial West Africa and to another strong colonial outpost, French Indo-China. The first of a series of combination passenger-cargo ships were designed soon after the end to hostilities. The orders for a pair, to be named after French scientists, were given in late 1945 to Ateliers et Chantiers de la Loire at St Nazaire. The plans called for two 11,900-tonners, with space for 94 passengers in first class and 230 in third class (in later years, this was changed to 147 in first class and 296 in third class). The *Lavoisier* was launched on 30 October 1948, and delivered in September 1950; the *Claude Bernard* came down the ways a day later, on 31 October, but was completed six months earlier, being handed over in March 1950. With the very slightest modifications, two near-sisters followed in 1952, but were assigned to a subsidiary company, Compagnie de Navigation Sud-Atlantique, as the *Laennec* and *Charles Tellier*.

As the first of a series the *Lavoisier* and *Claude Bernard* hinted at the fine standards to be found in most postwar French liners. Gone was the era of austere steerage and migrant accommodation, of cramped open-air deck spaces and of small, dark-coloured public rooms. The new ships were furnished in a delightful postwar contemporary styling and while all of the staterooms in first class had private bathrooms, most of those in third class had at least private toilets. There were fine separate restaurants, an outdoor terrace, partial air-conditioning and a deck swimming pool. Each ship also had six cargo holds, with about a third of their freight space being refrigerated for the important northbound Argentine beef.

Similar to other French ships on the South America east coast run, the *Lavoisier* and *Claude Bernard* sailed from Hamburg, Antwerp and Le Havre, then

continued to Vigo, Leixoes (in Portugal) and Madeira (to load migrants mostly), before continuing to Rio de Janeiro, Santos, Montevideo and Buenos Aires. By the early fifties, when there were three other combination liners on this route, the aforementioned *Laennec* and *Charles Tellier*, and also the *Louis Lumiere* of 1952, sailings for the eight-week round-trip voyages were offered at two-week intervals from Northern European ports.

Being the first of the series and then, years later, becoming the eldest, both the *Lavoisier* and *Claude Bernard* were the first selected for retirement as the South American passenger trade began in its gradual decline in the 1960s. They also began to lose some of their cargo, which went instead to newer, larger and faster freighters. The *Lavoisier* was withdrawn in 1961 and sold that August to little-known buyers, Commerciale Maritima Petroli SpA of Palermo, who had the ship gutted and then rebuilt at Genoa as the cruise ship *Riviera Prima*. A product of an extraordinary conversion, the ship emerged as a first-rate cruise ship, with all-first class accommodation (for 600 passengers), a new series of public rooms and a full lido deck built in the stern. Recommissioned in the fall of 1962, she was chartered mostly to American interests; the Caribbean Cruise Lines of New York ran a series of luxury sailings ranging from three-day weekends 'to nowhere', week-long runs to Bermuda or Nassau, and fortnights in the West Indies. Unfortunately, the operation was clouded by financial trouble and pressed by creditors, so that she was sold off to Berge Sigval Bergesen of Oslo. Refitted and upgraded further, she became the *Viking Princess* for a newly formed affiliate company, the Viking Cruise Lines. Once again, North American cruising was her mainstay, not only from New York and Port Everglades, Florida, but from Boston, Baltimore, Philadelphia and Norfolk.

During a cruise from Florida, on 8 April 1966, the *Viking Princess* became yet another victim to that problem faced by French-built ships: fire. An engine room fire spread quickly and later engulfed the entire

Roger Sherlock

*The former* Laennec, *renamed* Belle Abeto *for Panamanian owners, traded in her final years between Indonesia and Arabia carrying Muslim pilgrims between Singapore and the Far East. She was destroyed by fire at Sasebo, Japan, on 30 July 1976.*

ship. Her passengers and crew abandoned her and were sent to nearby rescue ships. Two passengers died of subsequent heart attacks. The Liberian freighter *Navigator* later towed the burnt-out wreck of the *Viking Princess* into Port Royal, Jamaica, but with the grim knowledge that she was not worth repairing. Later that year, she endured a gentle tow across the Atlantic to Bilbao in Spain, where she was dismantled.

A year or so after the former *Lavoisier* was sold to become a cruise ship, the *Claude Bernard* was put up for sale as well. She was sold to Deutsche Seereederei of Rostock, East Germany, for use as a merchant marine training ship. Renamed *J G Fichte*, she often appeared in Western ports and was a fascinating and most intriguing ship. Painted over in her East German colours and bearing a rather unknown name, she frequently confused even the best 'passenger ship watchers'. Retired in 1979, she was sold off to a Panamanian holding company and became the *Sunrise IV* and later *Pegancia*. Laid-up in her final months at Colombo on Sri Lanka, she was towed in April 1981 to Karachi for breaking-up.

## The LAENNEC and CHARLES TELLIER

Often thought to be part of the French Line fleet, because of their black hulls, white upper works and

red-and-black funnels, the sisterships *Laennec* and *Charles Tellier* were part of the Compagnie de Navigation Sud-Atlantique, a smaller affiliate of Chargeurs Reunis. Ordered several years after the *Lavoisier* and *Claude Bernard*, they came from the same yard at St Nazaire and were delivered in January and July of 1952 respectively. They had the same high standards of accommodation, for 110 first class and 326 third class passengers, and doubled their revenues with a six-hold cargo capacity that included substantial refrigerated space for northbound beef.

Both ships had nearly fifteen years on the South American run to Rio, Santos, Montevideo and Buenos Aires before the passenger trade all but disappeared and the once lucrative cargo went in faster new freighters. The *Laennec* was sold off during 1966, to Compania de Navigation Abeto SA of Panama for Eastern services. Becoming the *Belle Abeto*, she alternated at first between the Muslim pilgrim trade between Djakarta and Jeddah, and between Singapore, Hong Kong, Kobe and Yokohama. The *Charles Tellier*, which had been laid-up at Le Havre in December 1966, later went to the same Panamanian-flag buyers. Peter T Eisele, editor of the American shipping journal *Steamboat Bill*, in an article entitled 'Indonesian Pilgrim Ships', fully recorded the changes for the former French South American liners. 'The former *Laennec* was refitted to carry 100 cabin passengers and 1352 pilgrims. Her sistership *Charles Tellier*, which became the *Le Havre Abeto*, was altered for 415 cabin passengers and 610 pilgrims. The ships were eventually chartered to the Arafat Lines [an

Indonesian shipping company]'.

Little has been documented of the exact movements of these converted ships except that they were frequently seen in Djakarta harbour. The *Belle Abeto* (ex-*Laennec*) was destroyed by fire at Sasebo, Japan, on 30 July 1976. Ablaze from end to end, she had to be towed to the outer harbour and deliberately sunk. Soon afterwards, the *Le Havre Abeto* (ex-*Charles Tellier*) seems to have been laid-up off Tanjunk Priok, Djakarta's port. In the World Ship Society's *Marine News*, M H Pryce described her from a visit in May 1982. 'Lying close by [to the *Mei Abeto*, the former French *Louis Lumiere*] is the *Le Havre Abeto*, formerly the *Charles Tellier*. Both ships are in very poor condition, heavily rusted, windows smashed and with a general impression of neglect. The underwater hulls are so heavily fouled that it provides full-time employment for several fishermen, catching prawns amongst the weed. The easier transport of pilgrims by air combined with new stringent regulations for pilgrim ships, is likely to ensure that both ships' next voyages will be to the breakers.' Indeed, they were. The *Mei Abeto* was sold to Bangladesh breakers and arrived in tow at Chittagong on 20 May 1984; the *Le Havre Abeto* arrived at the same port a month later, on 17 June.

## The LOUIS LUMIERE

As the last of a series, known as the 'French savant' class, the *Louis Lumiere* was alone in being ordered from Chantiers et Ateliers of St Nazaire. She was also singular in having a streamlined funnel slightly tapered, and with a pronounced sloping top. Delivered in October 1952, she joined the twice-monthly service to South America, sailing from Hamburg, Antwerp and Le Havre to Vigo, Lisbon, Rio de Janeiro, Santos, Montevideo and Buenos Aires. She was also fitted with high standard accommodation, especially in first class; the berthing plan showed 109 berths in first class and 302 in third class.

During 1962, in a coordinated effort to strengthen and maximize the profit of French passenger ship services, Messageries Maritimes took over the combined passenger operations of both Chargeurs Reunis and Compagnie de Navigation Sud-Atlantique. All of the combination ships, including the *Louis Lumiere*, *Charles Tellier* and *Laennec*, were repainted in the all-white livery of Messageries Maritimes and the company logo appeared on all-white funnels which were capped by a thin black band. Five years later, the three remaining passenger ships on the South American trade were replaced by the brand-new *Pasteur*. The *Louis Lumiere*, like her earlier running-mates,

went to Compania de Navigacion Abeto of Panama. Chartered to the Indonesian-flag Arafat Lines mostly for the Muslim pilgrim trade to Jeddah, she sailed as the *Mei Abeto* with revised capacity for 415 cabin passengers and 622 prilgrims. On one of her earliest trips, reported in May 1968, she had mechanical problems, broke down and had to be towed into Djakarta. As with her other former French fleet-mates, her movements for the next decade or so are mostly unrecorded. In 1976, she was supposedly sold outright to the Arafat Lines, but then was resold in the following year to her earlier Abeto owners. She was laid-up at Djakarta in July 1977, and sold off seven years later to Bangladesh breakers. She was delivered at Chittagong in May 1984.

## The PASTEUR

Soon after the Messageries Maritimes took over all of the long-distance French liner services in 1962, the company considered developing at least one more new liner, another large combination type in fact, despite the first appearance of commercial jet aircraft. She was to be called *Australien*, and to sail from Marseilles to the Caribbean, the Panama Canal and then to the South Pacific and Australia. According to their plans, this 17,900-tonner would replace an earlier pair of combination liners, the *Caledonien* and *Tahitien*, which dated from the early fifties. The building order was signed with Ateliers et Chantiers de Dunkerque et Bordeaux at their Dunkirk yards in 1963, but then soon afterward, due to a sudden change in trade on the Pacific/Australian service, the plan was altered and the ship restyled for what was thought to be the more pressing South American trade. In fact, she proved to be one of the last two-class ships intended for the Latin American route.

Launched as the *Pasteur*, on 2 June 1966, she used the name given to an earlier liner, a 29,200-tonner that was built in 1939, but never used in commercial service. All of the old *Pasteur*'s French-flag days were spent as a large trooper. When she was sold off in 1957, she joined the North German Lloyd and became their last transatlantic flagship using another well-known name, *Bremen*. The new *Pasteur* was delivered in October 1966, and soon replaced all of the older French combination liners on the South American trade. Her sailings were, in fact, to be coordinated with an Argentine liner, the 11,400-ton *Rio Tunuyan*, which had been refitted with space for 372 tourist class passengers. The *Pasteur*, which had had exceptionally luxurious accommodation for 163 first class and 266 tourist class passengers, was the very finest ship of her time sailing from northern European

Roger Sherlock

*The **Pasteur** was the final new passenger ship in the Messageries Maritimes fleet. Having a very high standard of accommodation, she was very popular on the run to Rio, Santos, Montevideo and Buenos Aires.*

ports. Her routing, identical to her predecessors, took her from Hamburg, Antwerp and Le Havre to Vigo, Lisbon, Rio de Janeiro, Santos, Montevideo and Buenos Aires. A call at Southampton was introduced on 27 February 1969, just as the one-time rival Royal Mail Lines retired the last of its *Amazon* class of liners from the same trade. Shortly thereafter, the call at Southampton was included in both directions (at first, it was outbound only) as well as at Dunkirk. The freight calls at Antwerp were discontinued so that the overall routing took the ship on an inbound run to Dunkirk, Southampton, Le Havre and Hamburg.

Ocean liner enthusiast and sea traveller John Havers had a short run aboard the *Pasteur* in the early 1970s. 'One of the last long-distance liners, she carried from 114 up to 163 at full capacity in first class and 266 in tourist, and had five hatches for cargo. I travelled in her from Southampton to Le Havre (three days in port) and then on to Hamburg (three days in port) and then back to Southampton. A marvellous "coastal"

run with ample time in port. The outstanding memory of this voyage is of food that was truly out of this world, even despite the "between voyages" nature of the run and the crew taking leave where they could. With every lunch and dinner, one was given a litre of red and a litre of white wine in labelled bottles. A formidable challenge to one's thirst. The patisserie sweets were the tastiest delicacies I have ever consumed. Private facilities in all cabins [first class]. The public rooms were straightforward modern types, clean and comfortable. The most used and attractive place was the first class bar, which was long (sixteen stools), very well lit and nicely designed. I met a long-distance round-tripper from Germany, who made the whole voyage [to Buenos Aires and return] at least once a year and did not know what he would do if the *Pasteur* was withdrawn. My voyage was made in the summer of 1972.' It was only months later, in October, that the *Pasteur* was withdrawn, the last deep-sea passenger ship in the once large Messageries Maritimes fleet. She found a buyer immediately.

Her new owners, the Shipping Corporation of India, had her sent to the Amsterdam Drydock Company yards for a refit and alterations. Renamed the *Chidambaram*, she would be used, beginning in the following April, on the low-fare trade between Madras and Singapore with calls en route at Nagapattinam, Trincomalee and Penang. With part of her original cargo accommodation converted to dormitories, her passenger capacity was more than tripled, to 154 passengers in cabin class and 1526 in dormitory and deck classes. On 12 February 1985, in the Bay of Bengal, the *Chidambaram* was swept by fire; 50 people died. Damaged beyond economic repair, the ship was broken up.

## ——————YBARRA LINE——————

### The CABO SAN ROQUE and CABO SAN VICENTE

When Ybarra & Company, best known as the Ybarra Line, decided to build its two largest and finest passenger liners in the mid-fifties, they aroused considerable interest by staging a competition among young Spanish artists and decorators who might like to participate in the creation of Spain's largest passenger ships to date. The outcome was so pleasing, using a high degree of modern rather than traditional or more customarily 'heavy' Spanish interior themes, that an exhibition devoted to the ships was sent on a tour not only within Spain, but to South America where the ships would trade as well. The traditional designs of two funnels and two masts were dropped and replaced by a single funnel and with one mast placed above the bridge section. They were to be named *Cabo San Roque* and *Cabo San Vicente*, and would be serious rivals to ships such as Italian Line's *Augustus* and *Giulio Cesare*, Costa Line's brand-new *Federico C.* and the French *Bretagne* and *Provence*.

Ordered from Sociedad Espanola de Construccion Naval at Bilbao, the *Cabo San Roque* was launched on 23 April 1955, and completed in the late summer of 1957; the *Cabo San Vicente* went down the ways on 6 October 1956 and was delivered in April 1959. At nearly 15,000 tons, they used Sulzer diesels to reach top speeds of 22 knots if necessary. The high standard first-class accommodation, with 241 berths, included upper deck quarters, separate public rooms, private bathrooms for all cabins and an outdoor lido and swimming pool. Tourist class, with 582 berths, also had separate facilities, all cabins and no dormitories, and a separate lido and pool area. The ships were routed on a monthly basis between Genoa, Barcelona,

*Ybarra Line's* Cabo San Vicente *and her twin sister, the* Cabo San Roque, *were for many years the largest passenger liners under the Spanish flag.*

Roger Sherlock

Michael D J Lennon

Palma de Majorca, Cadiz, Lisbon and Tenerife, and then across to Rio de Janeiro, Santos, Montevideo and Buenos Aires. They were also used for a considerable amount of cruising, particularly in the summer months during the peak of Spain's holiday trade.

In the summer of 1967, for example, the *Cabo San Vicente* made a twenty-day cruise from Bilbao to Le Havre, Hamburg, Stockholm, Helsinki, Copenhagen, Bergen, Sognefjord, London, Le Havre and return to Bilbao. In that same summer, the *Cabo San Vicente* offered a fifteen-day voyage within the Mediterranean, from Barcelona to Genoa, Alexandria, Beirut, Haifa, Famagusta, Rhodes, Santorini, Genoa, Marseilles and return to Barcelona. A year later, in the summer of 1968, the *Cabo San Vicente* made two Mediterranean cruises, first from Barcelona to Cannes, Genoa, Capri, Messina, Piraeus, Varna, Constanza, Odessa, Yalta, Istanbul, Kuşadasi, Messina, Capri, Genoa and Barcelona; the second, also from Barcelona, to Dubrovnik, Corfu, Istanbul, Yalta, Odessa, Constanza, Thasos, Mount Athos, Piraeus and Heraklion. Cruises were also run from South America like the two sailings of the *Cabo San Vicente* in the winter of 1968–69. The first voyage, lasting nearly two months, took the ship around continental South America, from Buenos Aires to Punta Arenas, Puerto Montt, Valparaiso, Callao, the Galapagos, Balboa, the

*Within the large Elders & Fyffes 'banana boat' fleet, the* Camito *and the* Golfito, *were the only vessels to carry more than the customary dozen passengers. Both ships had over a hundred berths in very comfortable accommodation.*

Panama Canal, Kingston, Miami, St Thomas, Guadeloupe, Tobago, Trinidad, Bahia, Rio de Janeiro and Santos. Immediately after returning to Buenos Aires, she set off on a fifty-five-day run to Montevideo, Santos, Tenerife, Cadiz, Malaga, Barcelona, Palma de Majorca, Dubrovnik, Istanbul, Constanza, Haifa, Piraeus, Naples, Livorno, Barcelona, Las Palmas and then a return to Santos and Buenos Aires.

By the early seventies, despite the overall decline of two-class South American sailings, the ships might have been refitted for more extensive cruising had it not been for highly increased fuel oil costs. The *Cabo San Vicente* was offered for sale in the autumn of 1975 and went to the Mogul Line of India to become the pilgrim ship *Noor Jehan* for the Bombay–Jeddah trade. Laid-up in February 1984, she has since been broken-up at Bombay. The *Cabo San Roque* was sold on a less happy occasion. Badly damaged by a fire at a shipyard at Ferrol in Spain, on 24 January 1977, the damaged hulk was sold to Growth Maritime Investments Ltd of Cyprus and taken to Piraeus for repairs. Renamed

*Golden Moon*, there was some speculation that she would be rebuilt for the cruise trades, but this ended when, a year later, she was sold once again, this time to the Cuban Government. Registered to Empresa Navigacion Mambisa of Havana, she was renamed *Africa-Cuba* and fitted out as a troop transport and student ship. She was back on the mid-Atlantic route, but carrying far less jovial passenger than in her Ybarra days. However, in the summer of 1982, ill-kept, rusting and in need of considerable repair, she was sold to Barcelona scrappers. Although Ybarra continued in the ferry trades, they opted not to resume their liner operations after the *Cabo San Roque* and *Cabo San Vicente*.

## ———— FYFFES LINE ————

### The GOLFITO and CAMITO

The Fyffes Line, well known in Britain although a subsidiary of the American-owned United Fruit Company, who earlier ran passenger-carrying 'banana boats' of their own, had two post-war near-sisterships in Caribbean service. The *Golfito* was delivered by the Alexander Stephen yards at Glasgow in 1949. At 8700 tons, she had all-first class accommodation for 111 passengers and four holds for outbound general freight; on her homeward run she

carried as many as 140,000 stems (1750 tons) of bananas. A handsome ship, with a single raked funnel and twin masts, she was nearly duplicated seven years later, in 1956, with the *Camito*. She too came from Alexander Stephen and Sons. Passenger quarters were extended over three decks and included several public rooms, a restaurant and top-deck pool. There were two deluxe suites aboard each ship, with bedroom, sitting room and bathroom; most of the other cabins were either singles or doubles, many of which had private toilet facilities.

The ships plied a twenty-five-day round-trip itinerary, sailing from either Southampton or Avonmouth to Barbados, Trinidad and Kingston. After the spring of 1968, a homeward call at Bermuda was added. Round voyage cruise fares at that time were listed as £228. Unfortunately, soon afterward, Fyffes – like almost all other British-flag shippers – were faced with several decisive factors: greatly increased operational costs, competition from less expensive foreign-flag rivals and a decline in passengers who were deserting such freighter-like ships in favour of

*Built in the late thirties as freighters, the* Willemstad *and her sistership* Oranjestad *were both rebuilt in 1950 for the passenger service to Surinam. Both ships finished their sea-going lives as Saudi Arabian pilgrim ships.*

Roger Sherlock

*The prime passenger ships in the postwar Royal Netherlands fleet were the modern-looking sisters* Prins der Nederlanden, *shown above at Southampton, and the* Oranje Nassau – *they were longtime favourites on the Caribbean trade.*

larger, better-equipped cruise liners or speedy aircraft. In their final years, ships such as the *Golfito* and *Camito* were supported by an older but dwindling clientele. When the Fyffes Group, as the company had been retitled, began looking into foreign-flag and chartered tonnage, both of these combination passenger ships were retired. The *Golfito* went to breakers at Faslane in Scotland in 1971; the *Camito*, after being laid-up at Southampton in June 1972, sailed out to the East early in the following year and was broken-up at Kaohsiung.

## —ROYAL NETHERLANDS STEAMSHIP CO—

### The ORANJESTAD and WILLEMSTAD

The Dutch logically had an interest in the Caribbean and South American passenger trades because of their colonial holdings on such islands as Curaçao and Aruba, and in Surinam. With particularly heavy war losses, the Royal Netherlands Steamship Co, also well known as KNSM (an abbreviation for its full Dutch title, Kon. Nederlandsche Stoomboot Mij NV), took two prewar cargo ships, the four-masted *Pericles* and *Socrates* and had them rebuilt for passenger service. Sent to the Amsterdam Drydock Co, they were renamed as *Oranjestad* and *Willemstad* respectively and given enlarged superstructures with accommodation for ninety-four first class passengers and, if required, sixty-two in more austere 'group' quarters. Upon completion, they were introduced on the thirty-eight-day round-trip run from Amsterdam and Southampton to Madeira, Pointe a Pitre, Fort de France, Barbados, Trinidad, Paramaribo and Georgetown; then returning to Plymouth and Amsterdam.

Both ships remained on this trade for fifteen years, by which time both the passenger and cargo requirements had changed such that the newer and more modern *Oranje Nassau* was reassigned from the Caribbean trade to the Surinam route. The *Willemstad* was briefly shifted to a projected 'sunshine' cruise trade from Amsterdam and Southampton to Madeira, but this proved to be shortlived. Soon afterwards, in early 1967, the two little liners were sold to Saudi Arabian interests for the Muslim pilgrim trades. The *Oranjestad* became the *Miriam B*; the *Willemstad* changed to *Moor B*. Both served rather irregularly for several years more, but were finally dispatched to the scrappers' yards in 1973–74.

### The Oranje Nassau and Prins Der Nederlanden

Two very fine, well appointed combination liners were added to the Royal Netherlands fleet in 1957. At the time, the company, one of the largest under the Dutch flag, comprised over sixty ocean-going vessels. Honouring the Dutch Royal House of Orange, the *Oranje Nassau* came from NV Scheepsbouwerf Gebroeders Pot at Bolnes and her sistership, the *Prins der Nederlanden*, from the P Smit, Jr yards at Rotterdam. They were motor ships of 7200 tons and had all-first class accommodation for 116 passengers as well as special quarters for 68 'group' travellers. The first class quarters were contained on three-decks: Promenade, A and B decks, and included a forward lounge, two enclosed promenades, a writing room, smoking room, barber shop, beauty salon, restaurant and special children's facilities that included a playroom, separate dining area and play deck.

The ships were routed on thirty-four-day round-trip voyage from Amsterdam and Southampton to Barbados, Trinidad, La Guaira, Curaçao, Aruba, Puerto Limon, Kingston, Santiago de Cuba, Port-au-Prince and then a return to Plymouth and Amsterdam. Intended initially for one-way traffic, they later developed strong followings especially in the winter seasons from round-trip cruise passengers. In 1966, the five-week sailings were priced from £206. Soon afterwards however, in a reshuffling of the Royal Netherlands passenger fleet, the *Oranje Nassau* was transferred to the Surinam service, replacing the older sisters *Oranjestad* and *Willemstad*. However, in a matter of years, both the Caribbean and Surinam trades would undergo considerable changes because of the

transition to containerized cargo shipping, newer and faster freighters and the general intrusion of aircraft on such long-haul passenger runs. Because the company decided to abandon all of its passenger services, including the freighter voyages and later became absorbed in the giant Royal Nedlloyd Group, the *Oranje Nassau* and *Prins der Nederlanden* were retired. In the summer of 1972, they were moored together at Amsterdam awaiting their fates. Some months later, in January 1973, they were transferred to the Cuban Government for use as military transports and training ships, becoming the *XX Aniversario* and *Vietnam Heroico* respectively. They remain in service at the time of writing.

## ——— HOLLAND-AMERICA LINE ———

### The Dalerdyk and Dongedyk

While assuredly best known for its transatlantic passenger service to New York (terminated in 1971) and as a popular cruise company (their remaining operation to date, now based in Seattle rather than Rotterdam), the great Holland-America Line also ran a limited passenger service to the Caribbean and then through Panama to the North American West Coast.

Roger Sherlock

*Although she had what might be considered the profile of an ordinary twelve-passenger freighter, Holland-America's* Dongedyk *had exceptionally fine first class accommodation for as many as fifty-two passengers.*

Outbound from Bremen, Hamburg, Antwerp, Rotterdam and London, which were important cargo ports, the nine-week round voyages were routed across the mid-Atlantic to Bermuda and then to Curaçao and Cristobal before continuing in the Pacific to Los Angeles, San Francisco, Portland, Seattle, Victoria and Vancouver.

By the late fifties, the two eldest of the four combination ships on this run were the 10,900-ton sisters *Dalerdyk* and *Dongedyk*. Fitted with high standard postwar accommodation for 46 and 52 first class passengers respectively, they had been built in 1929–30 at the Wilton-Fijenoord yards at Schiedam as the *Damsterdijk* and *Delftdijk* for the same Caribbean-North American route. The latter survived the Second World War intact, only to be seriously

*Certainly one of the loveliest public rooms aboard a small combination passenger-cargo ship, the Smoking Room on board the* Dongedyk, *which was decorated in a postwar style similar to Holland-America's major liners on the North Atlantic trade.*

van Herk Collection

damaged by an undetonated mine in the Elbe, in January 1950. She returned to service, after full repairs and a refit, two years later as the *Dongedyk*. The *Damsterdijk* was seized by the Nazis in the summer of 1940 and outfitted for the projected invasion of Britain, but only to be found in very poor condition in the summer of 1945. Towed to Holland and gradually repaired, she was fully restored as the *Dalerdyk* in 1949.

As well-maintained prewar passenger-carrying freighters, these ships continued in service until the mid-sixties. The *Dalerdyk* was sold off in 1963 to a Panamanian holding company, who renamed her as the *Presvia*, before reselling her to Japanese ship-breakers. The *Dongedyk* remained in service until 1966, when she was acquired by a Liberian-flag intermediary, who renamed her *Tung Long*, for the re-sale to Taiwanese scrappers at Kaohsiung.

*Dongedyk's Library-Card Room – a pleasant place to spend a quiet afternoon or an evening after dinner.*

## The DIEMERDYK and DINTELDYK

Soon after the war, Holland-America decided to supplement its Caribbean/Pacific passenger-cargo services with two sixty-passenger vessels. Soon after they were laid down in 1949, the intended hulls of these 11,000-ton sisterships, ordered from Wilton-Fijenoord at Schiedam, were redesigned and altered for North Atlantic tourist class service. The proposed *Diemerdyk* became the *Ryndam*, the *Dinteldyk* the *Maasdam*. Shortly afterwards in an adjoining slip at the same builders yard, a third ship took shape. She would come off the ways as planned, a delayed *Diemerdyk*. Plans were, of course, that a sistership would follow, but then ideas changed and nearly seven years elapsed before a compatible ship was produced.

Soon after the *Diemerdyk* was delivered, in the late spring of 1950, she made one 'introductory' sailing to New York, but then was sent on runs to Los Angeles, San Francisco and Vancouver. Similar to her prewar fleet-mates, the *Dalerdyk* and *Dongedyk*, this new

Roger Sherlock

*When first commissioned, in the late spring of 1950, the Diemerdyk made an 'introductory' crossing on Holland-America's traditional run to New York. She was berthed in Brooklyn, just opposite Manhattan, for the occasion.*

vessel had high standard all-first class accommodation and every stateroom had private bathroom facilities. The *Dinteldyk*, built alongside the transatlantic *Statendam* at the Wilton yard in 1956–57, varied only slightly in design from her earlier near-sister. However there was one rather obvious difference: this new ship's hull was painted dove grey, a colour which was usually used by the Holland–America Line for its wintertime tropical cruise ships. Evidently, although this new combination ship had some air-conditioning in her passenger quarters, the Dutch were experimenting with the effects of such light colouring in warm weather areas. While the *Dinteldyk* retained the grey colouring scheme, the earlier *Diemerdyk* was never repainted.

When Holland-America gradually entered a freight consortium and then moved into containerized shipping (before turning completely to cruising from US ports), the *Diemerdyk* and even the later *Dinteldyk* became less economical. The former was sold off first, in 1968, to the ever-expanding CY Tung Group of Hong Kong. Registered to their Oriental Africa Lines of Monrovia, Liberia, she became the *Oriental Amiga* and, using her limited passenger spaces, was assigned to the round-the-world services of the affiliate Orient Overseas Lines. The *Dinteldyk* followed two years later, in 1970, and became the *Oriental Fantasia*. Both ships were later downgraded to pure freighter service before being scrapped in Taiwan in 1979.

---

## SIOSA LINES

### The IRPINIA

As an Italian firm interested mostly in low fare and migrant trades, the Grimaldi-Siosa Lines made do with several second-hand liners. The most notable and well served of these was the *Irpinia*, a ship with a career that spanned over fifty years.

The 13,204-ton *Irpinia* had been built in 1929, by Britain's Swan, Hunter & Wigham Richardson shipyards at Newcastle. Her owners were French, however, and she was christened *Campana* for Transports Maritimes. Her purpose was to sail the South Atlantic, from Marseilles to Rio de Janeiro, Santos, Montevideo and Buenos Aires. The nature of this trade was reflected by her berthing figures: 150 passengers in a comfortable first class, 200 or so in a limited second class and then 820 in an austere third class.

The *Campana* was laid-up at Buenos Aires in 1940, supposedly for safety from the war then raging in Europe. Three years later, she was seized by the Argentines and renamed *Rio Jachal*, although she seems never to have sailed as such. In 1946, she was returned to the French and, after a short spell on the

*The two-funnelled **Irpinia** made several special crossings to New York in the late fifties. She is shown here in the summer of 1959 being assisted into Pier 97, at the foot of West 57th Street.*

Antonio Scrimali

Latin American route, she was chartered out to another French passenger company, Chargeurs Reunis, and began sailing out through Suez to colonial Indochina.

She was sold to the Grimaldi-Siosa Lines in 1955, who renamed her *Irpinia* and had her rebuilt at Genoa. A new raked bow was fitted and the original accommodation rearranged to take 187 passengers in first class and 1034 in tourist class. Mostly, she sailed from Naples, Genoa, Cannes and Barcelona to Tenerife in the Canaries and then across the mid-Atlantic to Guadeloupe, Martinique, La Guaira and Trinidad. In 1959–60, she spent two summers on the North Atlantic, sailing between Genoa, Naples, Palermo, Gibraltar, the Azores, Quebec City and Montreal. Although shortlived, it was one of the very few direct links to the Mediterranean from Eastern Canada.

In 1962, she had another major refit. This time, her original two stacks were taken off and replaced by a single, tapered funnel; new Fiat diesels were fitted (replacing the original steam turbines), and the accommodation arrangements were again altered, this time to 209 first class and 972 tourist class cabins. Hereafter, she sailed mostly from Southampton to Vigo, Lisbon, Madeira, Antigua, St Kitts, Montserrat, Guadeloupe, Martinique, Dominica, St Lucia, St Vincent, Barbados, Grenada, Trinidad, La Guaira, Curaçao, Kingston, then returning to Madeira, Lisbon, Vigo and Southampton. She took Spanish and Portuguese migrants and workers westbound, and West Indians homeward to Britain. But, by 1970, she turned mostly to cruising, usually within the Mediterranean.

*The former* Vulcania *of the Italian Line, built in 1928, sailed for Siosa Lines as the* Caribia *from 1966–72. She is shown near the end of her long career, laid-up at La Spezia.*

In 1976, just as she had been finally withdrawn and supposedly sold for scrapping, she was chartered by an American film company for a starring role in 'Voyage of the Damned'. Two temporary 'dummy' funnels were put aboard for her portrayal of the German liner *St Louis*, making its 1939 voyage to Havana with 900 Jewish refugees. Afterwards, despite her increasing age and maintenance costs, her owners, by then simply retitled the Siosa Lines, obviously had some second thoughts. She resumed Mediterranean cruising for several more years until 1981, by which time she was fifty-two years old. Two years later, after a long spell at anchor, she was taken in hand by the scrappers at La Spezia, Italy.

## The Ascania

Another Grimaldi-Siosa liner, the 9500-ton *Ascania*, worked the Caribbean migrant trade. She too was a former French passenger ship, the *Florida* of Transports Maritimes. She sailed the east coast of South America trade as well. During the war, she was sunk by German bombers during an air attack on Bone, Algeria on 13 November 1942. Refloated two years later, she was towed to Toulon and restored (her original two funnels were changed at this time to a single stack). After the hostilities, she went back on the Latin American run until 1955, when she was sold to Grimaldi-Siosa and renamed. Her accommodation was modified to cater for 183 passengers in first class and two grades of 932 passengers in tourist class.

Like the *Irpinia*, initially she departed on her Caribbean voyages from Naples and Genoa, and later from Southampton, Vigo and Lisbon. In her final years, in the mid 1960s, she did considerable cruising, mostly in the form of one-week trips out of Genoa. She was scrapped at La Spezia in the spring of 1968.

## The CARIBIA

To supplement its Caribbean migrant services from England as well as Spain and Portugal, the Siosa Lines bought the Italian Line's *Vulcania*, a 24,500-ton motor liner that was completed in 1928. Despite nearly forty years of service, the ship was considered by Siosa engineers, even in 1965, to be a suitable investment. Once again, they had purchased an old ship, that with only slight modification, would be ideal for what was primarily a low-fare service. She was renamed *Caribia* and upgraded slightly with a revised accommodation arrangement for 337 passengers in first class, 368 in cabin class and 732 in tourist class. She retained her North Atlantic black hull colouring for her Caribbean voyages, which departed from Venice in January 1966 and from Southampton in February and thereafter.

As the Caribbean trade began its gradual decline and as the *Caribia* grew older, it seemed a wiser decision to keep her in more local waters. In the spring of 1968, she stopped her West Indies voyages and thereafter was used during the summer season only on weekly cruises from Genoa around the western Mediterranean and to North Africa. Repainted with a white hull, she was rather unusual among cruise ships in that she continued to carry three classes of passengers, with prices varying accordingly. The least expensive, former tourist-class quarters were advertised as 'youth specials'.

It was during one of these cruises, off Nice, in September 1972, that the *Caribia* grounded and flooded her engine room. Because of her extreme age, she was only temporarily patched, towed to La Spezia and laid-up. It was rumoured she was scrapped, but in fact, in the following January, she was sold for breaking-up to Spanish buyers. She reached Barcelona on 18 September, but then was resold to the voracious Taiwanese scrappers. On 15 March 1974, in a continuation of her final saga, she left Barcelona under tow for the East. On 20 July, in the approaches to Kaohsiung, she sprang some serious leaks and later sank. After a long, busy and mostly profitable career, the former *Vulcania* escaped the scrapper's torch but went instead to an underwater grave.

## SPANISH LINE

### The BEGONA and MONTSERRAT

Although the Spanish Line, the Compania Transatlantica Espanola, operated several passenger ships on the Atlantic route to the Caribbean, including the sisters *Covadonga* and *Guadalupe* on the New York trade and the smaller *Satrustegui* and *Virginia de Churruca*, their primary ships on the West Indies migrant routes were the converted near-sisterships *Begona* and *Montserrat*.

Built in 1945, at Baltimore and Los Angeles respectively, they were originally the *Victory* class freighters *Vassar Victory* and *Wooster Victory*. When cleared by the US Government for foreign-flag services in 1947, they were refitted and later rebuilt by the Sitmar Line as the migrant ships *Castel Bianco* and *Castel Verde*. The Spanish bought the pair in 1957 and, following extensive refits and improvements, they were introduced on the Caribbean run in the spring and summer of the following year. Running an all-tourist class service (taking Spanish and Portuguese migrants outwards to the Caribbean and then West Indian migrants to Britain), they sailed in

regular service from Southampton to Coruna, Vigo, Las Palmas and Tenerife, and then crossed to La Guaira, Trinidad, Barbados, St Kitts and Kingston, before returning to Tenerife, Vigo and Southampton. Some specially booked sailings departed only from Spanish ports.

The *Begona*, the slightly larger ship, at 10,100 tons, had a certificate for 830 passengers whereas the *Montserrat*, at 9000 tons, was certified for 708 passengers. The cabin accommodation ranged from two-berth rooms with private showers and toilets to lower deck eight-berth family cabins. John Havers, who recalled seeing both of these Spanish liners at the Southampton Docks and who travelled to Spain in the *Montserrat*, remembered both ships. 'The *Begona*'s public room walls had been painted with murals by a passenger-artist, which brightened her up considerably. What other shipping company would permit this? Otherwise, my only memory for the *Montserrat* is of the totally separate accommodation and eating facilities for the West Indian migrants.'

The twenty-five-year-old steam turbines aboard the *Montserrat* grew faulty by 1970, and on 13 August they failed and she was left adrift some 1400 miles off the

Canaries. It was very fortunate that the nearest suitable ship for a transfer of passengers and most of the crew was her running-mate, the *Begona*. The former ship endured another three years before being scrapped at Castellon in Spain early in 1973. The *Begona* continued in service until September 1974, when, on the 27th, she too was plagued by engine troubles and put into Tenerife with 800 passengers on board. After brief repairs, she attempted to continue her Atlantic crossing to the Caribbean, but broke down, drifted helplessly for several days and then was finally taken in tow to Barbados by the ocean-going tug *Oceanic*. Her sailing days were clearly over. She returned without passengers to Spain and arrived at Castellon on 24 December for scrapping. She was the last of the Spanish Line's Caribbean passenger ships.

*A converted wartime-built* Victory *class freighter, the* Begona *and her near-sistership, the* Montserrat, *had enormously high superstructures set on comparatively short 455-foot hulls.*

Spanish Line

# CHAPTER FIVE

# EAST OF SUEZ

## ANCHOR LINE

### The CIRCASSIA, CILICIA and CALEDONIA

After the Second World War, the Anchor Line of Glasgow did not reopen their North Atlantic liner service to New York. Instead, they concentrated on the Indian route with two surviving and one brand-new passenger ship. It later proved to be the last British liner service of its kind.

The *Circassia* and *Cilicia*, dating from 1937–38, were built at the Fairfield Shipyards at Glasgow. After the war, a third, identical ship was thought necessary and was ordered from the same builders. This was the *Caledonia* of 1948. Each ship was 11,100 tons and 506 feet long overall, and earned its revenue by carrying some 300 first class passengers and five holds of cargo. (Homebound, the freight manifests often included

the likes of cotton, hemp, manganese and tea.) Each of the ships had seven passenger decks and were fitted with partial air-conditioning. All of the cabins had either a porthole or a window; the accommodation was renowned for its high standard. The three sisters worked in rotation on the following route: Liverpool out to Gibraltar, Port Said, passage through the Suez Canal, Aden and then on to Karachi with turnaround at Bombay.

Author C M Squarey, in his observations of the *Circassia* in the early 1950s, wrote 'Although she is but

*The Anchor Line's* Caledonia *and her two sisters, the* Cilicia *and* Circassia, *were the last British-flag liners to run a regular service to India.*

Michael D J Lennon

Fred W Hawks

*The* Leicestershire, *photographed on 17 August 1951, with the British India funnel colouring, used during her four-year charter to that firm for their London–East Africa service. She later reverted to Bibby colouring and was returned to the Burmese run.*

twelve years old, this ship shows every symptom of having acquired the art of growing old gracefully – an art too seldom mastered. Throughout, there is nothing "flashy" about her furnishings. In the public rooms, the scheme of decoration is governed by a note of pleasant restraint, thereby producing rooms whose charm not merely endures, but likely enough increases the longer the voyage goes on.'

Mr Squarey continued, 'Another distinguishing feature of the ship is her superb cleanliness – what was made to be polished, was polished; what was supposed to shine, did shine; what should glisten, glistened; nor was there a speck of dust in any remote nook or corner. The atmosphere that pervades this ship and others of the Anchor Line fleet perhaps might best be described as "Scotland afloat".'

Eric Brown, presently a ship's accountant with Cunard, makes very similar observations. In the fifties he served aboard these final Anchor liners. 'Life on

board was like a great country house – everything was polished, waxed and made to last the ship's lifetime. No major refits or redecorations were then thought of. Everything was clearly marked with the company crest or initials – from linens and blankets to silverware and china.'

Travelling with the Anchor liners was like making a voyage in a different era. 'In the restaurant, everything was cooked to order. Of course, the curries were numerous and varied. Everyone always dressed for dinner.' The passengers reflected the strong British link to India. 'We carried government officials, rich traders, their families and even Indian royalty. Often, we had a maharaja aboard, who rented an entire deck and posted armed guards along the corridor. Even the staff weren't permitted beyond the guards without permission. I can recall the maharanjee arriving in the dining room with shoes laced with diamonds and other precious stones. Their own private train had brought them to the ship at Bombay. They travelled to Britain for several months of social engagements and then returned on the ship in the same high style.'

'On afternoons, between two and four, the ship was deserted. Everyone napped. Then, at four, there was a high tea, enhanced by two Swiss confectioners carried on each ship. ... Double canvas awnings provided breezy shelters on deck and there was also a small portable swimming pool.

'In the early 1960s, the Anchor Line had plans of and even put out tenders for two new passenger ships, much in the style of Lloyd Triestino's *Asia* and *Victoria* [11,500 tons, 500 passengers each]. However, the idea never came to pass. Anchor dropped its passenger operations [in 1966] due to long-range forecasts. The days of passenger ships to India were over.'

The three Anchor liners gave quite profitable service. Two of the ships nearly reached thirty years of age. The eldest, the *Circassia*, was broken up in Spain in 1966. In the same year, the *Cilicia* and *Caledonia* were sold. The *Cilicia* went to Dutch owners, who used her as a stevedores' training ship at Rotterdam under the name *Jan Backx*. She was finally scrapped in Spain during the summer of 1980. The *Caledonia* also went to the Dutch, to serve as a student accommodation ship at Amsterdam. She was broken up at Hamburg in 1970.

## BIBBY LINE

### The WORCESTERSHIRE and DERBYSHIRE

Britain's Bibby Line was rather unusual in providing a regular passenger service to distant Burma and also in building a series of four-masted passenger-cargo ships. The last of this class, converted after wartime service, sailed until the early sixties. Both came from the Fairfield yards at Glasgow: the *Worcestershire* in 1931 and the *Derbyshire* four years later. They were very similar in design and each was completed with space for nearly 300 first class passengers. During the Second World War they served first as armed merchant cruisers and then as troop transports. The *Worcestershire* was, in fact, torpedoed in the North Atlantic in April 1941, but managed to make port safely and was later fully repaired. Both ships were returned to their builders, rebuilt (the *Worcestershire* with a single forward mast, the *Derbyshire* with twin masts), and each given reduced accommodation for 115 first class passengers. They resumed their Burmese sailings, travelling from Liverpool via Port Said, Port Sudan, Aden and Colombo to Rangoon. They were, of course, well supported by those passengers typical to British-flag liners on eastern routes until the fifties and early sixties: the civil servants and their families, the business classes, the planters, traders and the occasional tourist.

*A superb harbourside view of Bibby Line's* Derbyshire *in dock at Birkenhead, Merseyside. She is loading cargo for another outward voyage to Rangoon via the Suez Canal.*

F Leonard Jackson

*Heraklion (ex-*Leicestershire*) sailing for Typaldos Lines, outward bound from Piraeus in August 1966.*

The *Worcestershire* remained in service until her thirtieth year, in 1961, and was then sold to the Japanese for scrapping. For her final voyage, a near-empty delivery trip to Osaka, she was renamed *Kannon Maru*. The *Derbyshire* followed her three years later, in February 1964, when she put into Hong Kong for scrapping.

### The WARWICKSHIRE and LEICESTERSHIRE

In their postwar rebuilding programme, Bibby added two cargo liners that appeared rather conventional – but were in fact fitted with seventy-six first class berths. They were built at the Fairfield yards at Glasgow, and were virtually identical to each other, except that the *Warwickshire* was also fitted with a mainmast whereas the *Leicestershire* had a forward mast only. Rather handsome ships, with particularly spacious accommodation that included two suites and an outdoor pool, they were designed especially for the Rangoon run. However, soon after delivery, the *Leicestershire* was time-chartered to British India for four years (until 1954), had her funnel repainted in their colours and traded on the East African run, later in conjunction with that firm's new *Kenya* and *Uganda*.

The decline of the once busy overseas British passenger ship services and the shift of cargo to newer and faster ships and nationalized fleets ended the profitability for ships such as the *Warwickshire* and *Leicestershire*. Briefly used as twelve-passenger freighters, the latter ship made the final Bibby passenger sailing in 1964. Being in rather fine condition and suitable for alteration, they passed into Greek hands, to the Typaldos Lines. Renamed *Hania* and *Heraklion* respectively, both were rebuilt as ferries, for service either among the Aegean islands or in the Adriatic between Italy and Greece. For a time, the former *Warwickshire*, which had been altered to carry 1450 passengers, 100 cars, 80 coaches and thus had her gross tonnage increased from 8900 to 11,300, was listed as the world's largest ferry. The Typaldos Lines' passenger fleet steadily grew through the acquisiton of additional second-hand tonnage, but the loss of the ex-*Leicestershire* spelled its end. On 8 December 1966, during a violent Aegean storm, she capsized and sank within fifteen minutes with 241 casualties: In the Greek Government inquiries that followed, she was found to be unsafely loaded and this prompted the seizure and then collapse of Typaldos Lines. The owners were sent to prison and the remaining ships, such as the *Hania* (ex-*Warwickshire*), were laid-up in the backwaters of Perama Bay. In 1971 she was auctioned off to another Greek shipping concern, the

Kavounides Shipping Company, only to be sold again a year later to Hellenic Cruises and renamed *Sirius*. Although unused and reportedly scrapped, she was not fully dismantled until 1980, at Skaramanga.

*Badly rusted and neglected, the former* Warwickshire, *as the Greek-owned* Sirius, *was spotted by the photographer during a visit to Perama Bay in Greece. Surrounded by dozens of other ships, the ex-Bibby Line ship is second on the left alongside, on her right, the little passenger ship* Esperos, *once owned by the Kavounides Lines.*

James L Shaw

## BRITISH INDIA LINE

### The RAJULA

Until the late 1960s, the London-based British India Steam Navigation Company Ltd retained an enormous network of passenger ship services. According to Captain Terry Russell, who served with British India and now sails with its parent, the P&O Company, 'British India had its own "foreign service", which meant 2½ years based in India. Every officer was given a Hindustani book and expected to acquire at least a working knowledge of Hindi. Actually, many of the officers became quite proficient. One often transferred between ships, which were based at Bombay or Calcutta, and which therefore meant a

long, often uncomfortable train ride across India. Travel home on leave to Britain included passage in an available company freighter. There were no crew flights in those days. Also, there were special British India clubs in Bombay and Calcutta, and even British India flats in places like Hong Kong and Singapore. Officers could bring out their families for their stints of "foreign service".'

The eldest passenger ship in the British India fleet was the *Rajula*, built by Barclay Curle & Co, Glasgow in 1926. For some years after delivery, she held one of the greatest peacetime passenger records for carrying over 5000 per sailing. An 8500-tonner, she was fitted

141

*Shown here, in Kowloon Bay, September 1957, one of the most beloved ships in the British India passenger fleet, the* Rajula. *She sailed for forty-eight years and was said to have earned in revenues over six times her original building costs in 1926.*

with steam triple expansion engines that provided a service speed of 12 knots. Listed in her final years as having accommodation for a more moderate 37 in first class, 133 in second class and 1600 deck passengers, she worked out of the Indian east coast, from Madras and Nagapattinam to Penang and Singapore. According to Neville Gordon, who served aboard many of the British India passenger ships, she remained one of the cheapest ways to travel, even in the early seventies. 'In deck class, passengers could

buy inexpensive tickets with meals, but even less expensive ones without food. These passengers brought their own bedding and slept below decks in large cabins, wards and along the alleyways. They were, of course, permitted to come on deck and even sleep there if the weather conditions were favourable. The *Rajula* was exceptionally popular, even to her very last days. There are many people in Malaya from southern India and therefore there is constant travel to and fro. Other Indians made the round-trip just for shopping in duty-free Singapore.'

When British India finally decided to retire the forty-eight-year-old *Rajula* in 1973, there were outcries from loyalists and sentimentalists to prolong her service. In fact, a group of officers joined together with the intention of buying the ship and keeping her

P&O Group

African trade, the three sisters of the *Santhia* class for the Far Eastern run, the four D Class sisterships for the Persian Gulf and finally the *Kenya* and *Uganda* for the London-East African route.

The 8300-ton *Amra* sailed between Bombay, the Seychelles, Mombasa, and Dar-es-Salaam in East Africa, with accommodation for 222 saloon class passengers and 737 in deck class. Neville Gordon served aboard the *Amra* and has fond recollections of her saloon class quarters. 'She was always very tidy in this, the cabin class. The brass always shined, the wood was polished, the bathrooms cleaned and the stateroom blowers always worked. In each cabin, there was always a thermos of iced cold water and towels hanging on little loops that were always starched and stiff. Ships such as the *Amra* had a virtual monopoly until the early sixties [when a large airport opened] on the trade to and from the Seychelles. There were tourists travelling to and from both East Africa and Bombay. Passenger ships were still the only means of transport. Of course, the *Amra* also carried large numbers of Indians to and from East Africa, and in her four cargo holds, she would carry spices, cotton, clothing and general goods out of Bombay and then return with more spices, cotton, clothing and general goods and more general freight. She was used, too, for the transhipment of freight coming from the Far East and bound for East Africa. This would be offloaded from freighters at Bombay and then loaded into ships such as the *Amra*.'

Although the *Aronda* sailed a different service, from Karachi to Chittagong via Colombo, both ships were victims of aircraft competition that began in the early sixties. The *Aronda* was broken-up at Kaohsiung in 1964; the *Amra* two years later.

### The Kampala and Karanja

Built by Alexander Stephen & Sons of Glasgow, in 1947–48, the sisters *Kampala* and *Karanja* were designed especially for the busy India–East Africa trade, with both European and Indian passengers in mind. Provided with accommodation for 60 first class, 180 second and over 800 third class passengers, these ships spent all their lives with British India, on the route from Bombay to Karachi, the Seychelles, Mombasa, Zanzibar, Dar-es-Salaam, Beira, Lourenço Marques and finally Durban before reversing course.

The accommodation and service in first class became well-known and was often booked-up in London months and sometimes years in advance. Neville Gordon served in these ships as well and remembered their '...excellent organization and efficiency. We catered for the civil servants, wealthy

as a museum. Surprisingly, despite her age, the *Rajula*, was sold to the Shipping Corporation of India and renamed *Rangat*, for 'government service' only. She survived for little more than a year. Mechanically exhausted and well-worn, she was scrapped locally at Bombay in 1975.

### The Amra and Aronda

The sisterships *Amra* and *Aronda*, built by Swan, Hunter & Wigham Richardson Ltd in 1938 and 1941 respectively, were two of a sizeable number of British India passenger ships that would continue to be built after the war and into the early fifties. They were all destined to become the final British-flag ships ferrying passengers in Eastern waters for a colonial-styled firm: the *Karanja* and *Kampala* for the East

British tourists, some students, visitors, the pakka sahib as we called them [an Indian term for gentlemen]. The restaurant, always in perfect order with the whitest linen and the most sparkling silver, served British food with an Indian accent. For example, every Sunday, there would be Country Capon and Kedgeree (spiced rice). There would also be the more traditional offerings, such as roast beef with Yorkshire pudding. The officers and passengers always dressed for dinner on these "K ships", as we called them.

'Of· course, it was entirely differnt to today's modern cruise ships. The entertainment, for example, was quite limited, but very adequate for the passengers' needs at the time. There would be enormous teas in the afternoon and with violin music. After dinner, there might be dancing on deck with music provided by an Indian band or a film showing in the lounge. There was no air-conditioning, but only forced-air ventilation, which actually wasn't very effective. A portable pool was sometimes used on one of the aft decks.'

Ships such as the *Kampala* and *Karanja* performed, aside from their important passenger service and lucrative cargo role (both ships had five holds with refrigerated as well as general cargo spaces), another important task. According to Captain Russell, 'In their final years [the 1960s] especially, the British India ships proved to be a marvellous training ground for today's maritime management of East Africa, Malaysia, Kuwait, the Gulf Arab States, Ceylon and India. Many of their port ministers and shipping superintendents began as cadets on "BI".' Neville Gordon added, 'British India was not just a huge training ground, but the only training ground in those years.'

The *Kampala* sailed for British India until 1971 and was later broken-up on Taiwan; the *Karanja*, after a life-extending refit at Singapore in 1969, was not retired until 1976, and then sold to the Shipping Corporation of India for whom she still sails as the *Nancowry*.

### The SANGOLA, SIRDHANA and SANTHIA

This trio of sisterships, built between 1947–50, were especially designed for the Far East route. They sailed from Calcutta to Rangoon, Penang, Singapore, Hong Kong, Yokohama and Kobe. In fact, in later years, only the *Sangola* and *Sirdhana* worked this trade while the *Santhia* was used on the Persian Gulf run out of Bombay along with the 'D class' quartet.

They were given large capacities for their 8600-ton size, carrying a maximum 25 in first class, about 70 in two grades of second class, some 300 in bunked third

class and as many as 1000 deck passengers. In addition, each ship had four cargo holds, which included some refrigerated space. Neville Gordon recalled the Far Eastern services of the *Sangola* and *Sirdhana*. 'These very busy ships carried not only Indian passengers, but Chinese passengers as well, through the Far East out of Singapore and, in later years, Bengalis out of Chittagong to and from Calcutta. In their holds, they carried bales and bales of cotton and other raw goods to Far Eastern ports and then returned to India with textiles and cheap manufactured goods. Of course, like almost all of the "BI" passenger ships, they too were killed off by the appearance of the aeroplane.

'It was a rather sad, reflective time by the late 1960s. In India, British India had been the most prestigious firm to work for and it was often said, in years past, that the second highest paid official in all of India, earning just a few rupees less than the Viceroy, was the managing director of MacKinnon MacKenzie & Co, the Indian agents for "BI".' British India had been linked to the giant P&O Company since 1914, but was fully integrated by 1971. Captain Russell recalls, 'This coincided with British India's rapid decline and subsequent demise. There was an enormous shift in trade and a general move to more and more charters [in the company's cargo division]. Container shipping was then spreading worldwide. There was also a rapid rise in national shipping, namely some African-flag firms and then the big Shipping Corporation of India. Our passenger trade disappeared as well. Initially, the traditional first-class clientele vanished, but then even the once lucrative third-class traffic turned to inexpensive air flights. Furthermore, there were swift political and social changes, particularly in "new" self-governing East Africa. The colonial days were indeed over and the last links being severed. All of this was compounded as our fleet grew older, more expensive and was complicated further by the sudden closure of the Suez Canal in 1967.'

The *Sangola* was scrapped in Japan in 1963; the *Sirdhana* went a decade later to breakers in Taiwan. The *Santhia* was sold in 1967, to the Shipping Corporation of India and became the *State of Haryana*. She continued sailing until 1976 when, after some serious mechanical problems, she was laid-up, damaged by fire and then finally scrapped at Bombay a year later.

### The DUMRA, DWARKA, DARA and DARESSA

When British India's *Dwarka* – a little 4800 tonner that had worked the Persian Gulf local trades for over three decades – went to the scrap-heap in the spring

KARANJA

*Noted for their very comfortable first class quarters, the*
Karanja *and her sister* Kampala *were the largest British
India liners to be based at Bombay. The* Karanja *shown
here at Kilindini in Kenya, in 1963, is still in service, sailing
for the Shipping Corporation of India as the* Nancowry.

of 1982, a curtain came down. She was the last
'working' British passenger ship, so different to the
luxurious cruise liners that still fly the Red Ensign.
Alone, she was something of a final link to a lost
empire – to the British Raj, a colonial India of high
commissioners and their entourages, and to an age of
travel that seems antique compared to today's jet-
plane standards. The demise of the *Dwarka* also
signalled the end of the British India firm, of a history
that spanned from 1862 and that included over 450

ships. (One further British India ship, the educational
cruise ship *Uganda*, was still in service at the time.
However, for some years she had been predominantly
under the management of P&O Cruises in London,
the parent of British India.)

The *Dwarka* – named after a small town on India's
northwest coast – was one of four 'D class' sisters. The
first, the *Dumra*, was launched in 1946 at Glasgow.
The *Dwarka* followed a year later, the only member of
the quartet to come from Newcastle. The *Dara* was
launched in 1948 and the series was completed in 1950
with the *Daressa*. Rather handsome vessels, they
measured 399 feet in length, and the single screw
diesel machinery gave a service speed of 14 knots
(though more often 12½). They were ships of transport, cargo plus passengers – comfortable but not
luxurious, dependable but not speedy – appropriately

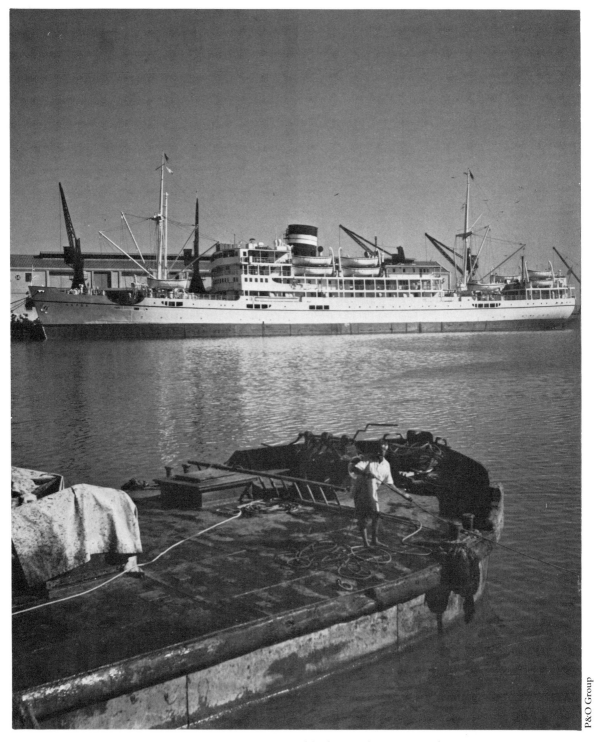

*British India's* Dumra, *one of the four 'D class' sisters used
on the Persian Gulf service, is shown loading cargo at
Bombay, her southernmost terminus.*

functional for their time.

The ships ran a set schedule that was known as the Fast Gulf Mail (fast only by local standards in comparison to other older ships). From Bombay, they went to Karachi and then on to Pasni, Gwadur (in what was Trucial Baluchistan), Muscat, Bandar Abbas, Shahjab, Dubai, Umm Said, Bahrain, Bushire, Kuwait, Abadan, Khorramshahr and Basrah, then returning to Karachi and Bombay. These ports of call were revised in later years.

The *Dwarka* and her sisters were originally designed to carry about a dozen passengers in first class, between forty and sixty in second class and approximately 1000 'deck' passengers (without berths, in what was a Middle Eastern version of steerage class). The range of clients was remarkable. Often, there were sheikhs and their parties occupying entire blocks of first class cabins, dishing out gold watches as tips. One of these Eastern royals once came aboard with enough cargo to fill an entire hold, personal cooks and servants, pet falcons and an entire string of hunting dogs. One former *Dwarka* crewman recalled, 'We played host to princes, cosetted kings and entertained regal entourages with all the pomp and circumstance of the era.'

But, there was another side to the passenger service of the *Dwarka* and her sisters. Over the years, she had endured several riots among those in the 'unberthed' spaces. Several passengers, somewhere computed at the rate of three per year, went over the side to grisly suicides; they were despondent after finding that their relocation in the Persian Gulf was not the promised land they expected. Others, deep in debt in their native lands could not face returning, after the guarantee of a new home or job had collapsed. These 'unberthed' areas, used almost exclusively by Indian and Pakistani passengers, were generally well booked. In these quarters passengers were allowed to bring along all their goods without paying excess charges thus avoiding using airfreight. Many travelled in this accommodation becasue their sponsors refused to pay for air tickets. The *Dwarka* and her sisters had been the executors of many official repatriation orders.

These 'huddled masses' of passengers were carried in the most austere conditions – often bringing their own food, utensils and bedding. There was no privacy, and little space. Within this class, there was even 'the virgin's cage', where unaccompanied women passengers were kept behind bars, away from the attentions of unaccompanied men.

The *Dwarka* sailed with a crew of 122, a figure somewhat higher than would be employed on board a similar-sized vessel in our contemporary, cost-conscious industry. Their duties ranged from supervising the Eastern kitchen, which among other accomplishments churned out 4000 chapatis (wholwheat breads baked in a special clay oven) a day to arranging for occasional films in the lounge for the first-class passengers.

Problems for the four 'D class' sisters began in the spring of 1961. The *Dara*, damaged by the explosion of a terrorist bomb, sank off Sharjah with the loss of 238 passengers and crew. One militant radio station was said to have reported the event a full four hours before the explosion.

The trade gradually declined and in 1964 *Daressa* was sold to the Greek-flag Chandris Cruises. Their plan was to convert the ship to a 600-passenger Mediterranean/Caribbean cruiser. Renamed *Favorita*, she was sent to Piraeus but then laid-up. Four years later, she was sold to Singapore's Guan Guan Shipping Company and was assigned to local Far Eastern passenger runs, mostly out of Singapore, as the *Kim Hwa*. She survived until serious mechanical problems signalled her end in 1974. The final blow was administered in a Hong Kong scrapyard. The number of once capacity-filled voyages continued to decrease – victims of aircraft competition and changing trade patterns. Some voyages averaged 500–600 passengers, but others dropped to a scant hundred. The third sister, the *Dumra*, was sold to Indian buyers in 1976, renamed *Daman* and then later scrapped. This left the *Dwarka* – singlehanded, aged, and sometimes unable to maintain her schedule.

Her engines had become museum pieces – one engineer referred to them as 'the old sewing machine'. Chief Engineer John Smith was questioned about what problems were experienced towards the end of the ship's career. He pondered and then responded, '... just one major problem: how to keep the damn thing going!' Another problem was that mechanical parts were simply unavailable. In the final years, everything had to be made by hand by a specialist British firm and then shipped to Bombay. A BBC television documentary on the *Dwarka*, made in 1979, stressed the ship's unique historic status, prompted hoards of journalists – from as far afield as Montreal and Tokyo – to make one last sentimental journey aboard the 'old girl'. Most of the crew were later reassigned within the P&O fleet.

When the *Dwarka* was sent to a scrapyard at Gadani Beach in Pakistan, the age of the British-flag passenger service in the far-off Middle East came to an end. Such British India names as *Mulbera* and *Nevasa*, *Kampala* and *Kenya*, *Sangola* and *Santhia*, *Chilka*, and *Carpentaria* are now part of another age.

### The ASIA and VICTORIA

As part of their seven-liner postwar rebuilding programme, Italy's Lloyd Triestino built two moderate sized 11,700-tonners for their well established Middle and Far East run. Ordered from the Cantieri Riuniti dell'Adriatico yards at Trieste, the twin sisters were delivered in spring 1953. Thereafter, they worked a monthly timetable, sailing from Genoa and Naples to Port Said, Suez, Aden, Karachi, Bombay, Colombo, Singapore, Hong Kong and back again. The extremely high standard first class facilities, with 286 berths included cabins with private bathrooms, several modern public rooms, a restaurant and outdoor pool; tourist class, limited to 141 berths, was equally as modern and included several public rooms, a separate pool and some cabins with private toilet and shower. The revenues of these ships were augmented cargo five holds.

John Havers, during his travels on the Union-Castle's Round Africa passenger run, which called at both Naples and Genoa, recalled seeing the *Asia* in the 1950s, '... a near-sister of the *Africa* [on the East African run], but with the accent on more passengers in first class. I was in a beautiful hilltop restaurant, eating in the open sun, at Camogli, on the eastern end of the Italian Riviera, when the *Asia* came out of Genoa and came in close to Camogli at full speed blowing her siren. A lone figure was seen waving a towel on the balcony of a house on the hillside. I guessed it was a captain's farewell to his wife. The ship then turned hard a starboard, to avoid the Portofino headland, and proceeded south. The gleaming white ship and her white backwash all in a brilliant blue sea was a magnificent sight to look down on.'

When the Suez was temporarily closed in 1967, the *Asia* and *Victoria* were re-routed via South Africa, terminating their sailings at Karachi and Bombay. Soon after this they began to lose money and often featured in the Italian Government's plans (they controlled Lloyd Triestino) for reorganization, for the

*Lloyd Triestino's* Asia *and her sister, the* Victoria, *were created for the Middle and Far Eastern express route. The* Asia *now sails as the livestock-carrier* Norleb; *the* Victoria *as the missionary ship* Anastasis.

Alex Duncan

two ships were frequently considered to be ideal candidates for conversion to Mediterranean cruise ships. They managed to remain in two-class service until the final decline of the state-owned Italian passenger fleet between 1974 and 1977. The *Victoria* was withdrawn in the late summer of 1974, and transferred within the Italian Finmare group, to the Adriatica Line. Retaining her original name, her new duties were divided: two-class voyages between either Genoa and Naples or Trieste and Venice to Beirut and Alexandria, or on Mediterranean cruises. She continued in Italian service for three more years until laid-up in June 1977. A year later, she was sold to the Youth-with-a-Mission Organization, registered under Cypriot colours and registered at Piraeus. As the *Anastasis*, she now serves as a worldwide missionary ship, particularly to underdeveloped and Third World nations, but has been re-registered, since 1982, to Maritime Mercy Ministries Ltd of Malta. Shortly after being laid-up at Trieste in April 1975, the *Asia* was sold to Rashid Fares Enterprises Ltd of Beirut, placed under the Lebanese flag and rebuilt as the livestock carrier *Persia*. She changed hands again, in 1984, going to another Lebanese concern, Norleb Shipping Enterprises Ltd, and has been renamed *Norleb*. She and her sister are the lone survivors of the postwar group of seven sisters and near-sisters built by Lloyd Triestino as postwar replacements.

*The* Viet-Nam *(shown here) and her sister, the* Laos *and* Cambodge, *were known as the 'Three Musketeers'. They ran the Messageries Maritimes service to the Far East via the Suez Canal. The* Viet-Nam, *later renamed* Pacifique, *finished her career ferrying Muslims to Jeddah as the* Malaysia Kita.

## MESSAGERIES MARITIMES

**The CAMBODGE, LAOS and VIET-NAM/PACIFIQUE**
France had, until the mid-1950s, maintained a sizeable fleet of passenger ships on Eastern runs, to the Middle East, East Africa and to the Far East, which included the vital link to the colonial outposts in Indo-China. The last ships to sail on the Far Eastern route were three handsome, well-decorated combination liners, the 13,200-ton sisters *Cambodge*, *Laos* and *Viet-Nam*. The *Viet-Nam* was delivered first, in the summer of 1952, by Chantiers Naval de la Ciotat; the *Cambodge* first arrived in the summer of 1953, having come from Ateliers et Chantiers de France at Dunkirk; the *Laos* completed the trio when she was commissioned in July 1954, from the same yard at La Ciotat. With 5 holds for cargo and accommodation for 347 passengers (117 in first class, 110 in tourist class and 120 in steerage third class), they ran a monthly schedule from Marseilles, sailing outbound to Port Said, Suez, Aden, Djibouti, Bombay, Colombo, Singapore,

Roger Sherlock

Saigon, Manila, Hong Kong, Kobe and Yokohama.

CM Squarey was quite delighted with the *Viet-Nam* during a visit to her shortly after she was commissioned. 'This all-white ship with her single funnel is indeed striking to look at. Her lines are elegant, making her both sleek and slick-looking, and, in point of fact, she averages between 21 and 22 knots to maintain her schedule. Her interior decoration gets right away from the old Messageries Maritimes manner. It portrays so well all that is best, without going to extremes, in modern French decoration. The forward first class lounge, for example, is a lovely room. The large murals feature Chinese dragons. The flooring in the centre is all inlaid woodwork whilst two delightfully designed carpets on the wings add tone to this room. Off this lounge on the starboard side is the Music Room, small but daintily decorated. Then comes the long bar which, in the tropics, can be opened up to the sea breezes. On the port side is a writing room notable for its lighting effects whilst at the stern comes a very pleasant verandah leading on to a lido area where there is a most enticing blue-tiled swimming pool, floodlit at night. The descent to the dining saloon is by a lovely stairway – the French are nearly always particularly good on that point – the

*The* Malaysia Raya, *the former* Laos, *was destroyed by fire while off Port Kelang, on 24 August 1976. She was taken in hand by Taiwanese breakers in the summer of 1977.*

room itself having distinct dignity about it, due mainly to the fact that it clings to simplicity of style.'

The operations of these ships, the 'Three Musketeers', went unchanged until 1967. When the Suez Canal was temporarily closed, they were routed via South Africa, which in due course cut deeply into their profits. Very shortly afterwards, prompted by the growing political turmoil in Southeast Asia, the *Viet-Nam* was renamed *Pacifique* (in September 1967). She was briefly used on a new round-the-world service, sailing outward via the Caribbean and South Pacific and then homeward with calls in South Africa, but soon after transferred to the Madagascar run. According to a master plan released by the financially-ailing Messageries Maritimes passenger department, in late 1968, the *Pacifique* was intended to close out the Madagascar route in 1971, while the *Cambodge* and *Laos* were to be shifted to the South Pacific/Australian run to replace two other company combination liners, the *Caledonien* and *Tahitien*. As costs continued to escalate and passenger loads

World Ship Society, Photo Library

dropped further still, this retirement plan was altered and speeded-up in the spring of 1969. The *Cambodge* and *Laos* were never moved to the Australian run, but were prematurely retired at the end of 1969; the *Pacifique* followed in less than a year.

The laid-up *Cambodge* was sold, in December 1969, to the Sun Line, a well known Greek islands cruise firm. Provisionally renamed *Stella V*, she was taken to La Spezia, partially gutted and then moved to Piraeus (February 1971) for complete rebuilding at a Perama shipyard. She reappeared in June 1973, vastly altered, as the cruise liner *Stella Solaris*, with a capacity for 765 all-first class passengers. She continues in service at the time of writing, spending her summers in the Aegean and Eastern Mediterranean, and her winters in the Caribbean and along the east coast of South America.

Both the *Pacifique* and *Laos* were far less fortunate, however. They were sold during 1970 to Compania de Navigacion Abeto SA, a Panamanian-flag firm with strong interests in the Muslim pilgrim trades as well as Far Eastern passenger services. The former, renamed *Princess Abeto*, was sent to Hong Kong and rebuilt with quarters for 1612 passengers, most of which were in the austere pilgrim sections of the ship. She was soon

*The overall design of Blue Funnel's* Peleus *and her sisters was capped by a tall stack, painted in the most distinctive blue and topped by a black band. Always recognizable, the ships were known as the 'Blue Flues'.*

leased to another Eastern shipper, the Fir Line, and renamed first the *Malaysia Baru* and then the *Malaysia Kita*, for sailings from Singapore to Jeddah as well as India. On 12 May 1974, she caught fire while undergoing repairs at Singapore. She was towed out of the harbour, abandoned, left to sink, and declared a total loss. It was not until nearly a year later, on 30 March, that serious salvage attempts began and still later, on 26 June, that she was actually raised. A burnt-out, twisted wreck, she sat in Singapore harbour for nearly another year before being towed to Kaohsiung in Taiwan for scrapping. Soon afterward, by 23 August 1976, the ex-*Pacifique* was broken-up.

The *Laos* had been sold to Compania Abeto as well, rebuilt at Hong Kong with a certificate for 1696 passengers and then renamed the *Empress Abeto*. She too was chartered to the Fir Line and then rechristened as the *Malaysia Raya* for both Singapore-Madras as well as Singapore–Jeddah services. She was lying at anchor at Port Kelang when a fire broke-out.

Wrecked totally and then beached, she was later towed to Singapore for inspection, but found to be beyond economic repair. She was delivered to Kaohsiung breakers on 7 July 1977.

*Unique in the world's passenger-ship fleet, Blue Funnel's* Centaur *was specially designed to carry sheep and cattle (as well as general cargo) forward and some 200 passengers aft. The last of the Blue Funnel passenger ships, she is now sailing for the Chinese in their coastal trades.*

## BLUE FUNNEL LINE

The PELEUS, PYRRHUS, PATROCLUS and PERSEUS
After their losses in the Second World War, the mighty Blue Funnel Line of Liverpool seemed to be content with twelve-passenger freighters. The only exceptions were two quartets of ships which could carry as many as thirty first class passengers each. In other respects, these ships, with their numerous kingposts and booms, singular blue and black stacks and limited white superstructures, could have been Blue Funnel cargo vessels. The first quartet, the 'P class' of sisterships, were designed for the Far Eastern run, sailing from Liverpool and then Rotterdam to Port Said, Singapore, Hong Kong, Kobe and Yokohama. The *Peleus* and *Pyrrhus*, both built in 1949, came from the Cammell Laird & Co yards at Birkenhead, while the *Patroclus* and *Perseus* were delivered a year later by Vickers-Armstrongs at Newcastle. In inspecting the *Peleus* soon after her

completion, in May 1949, C M Squarey wrote, 'Designed to carry thirty passengers, the cabins are notably spacious, and even down to the smallest fitting are very thoughtfully planned. The collapsible "morning tea" bedside table is a pleasant novelty. The lounge is charmingly decorated, and off it is a small bar with very comfortable settees – just the setting for good storytelling over long, cool drinks. I was impressed by the turn-out of the stewards, the goodness of lunch and not least, the manner of its serving; altogether, I left the ship delighted with everything about her, and methinks that she and her sisters will score very good marks from all those who put to sea in them.'

The *Pyrrhus* was badly damaged by fire while in Liverpool Docks, on 12 November 1964; her repair and then conversion to a twelve-passenger freighter were a prelude to the fate of the three other sisters.

They were similarly downgraded in 1967. All were scrapped on Taiwan in 1972–73.

### The HELENUS, JASON HECTOR and IXION

For their second quartet, begun with the completion of *Helenus* in October 1949, Blue Funnel had modified the basic 'P class' design by having one additional hatch forward. The passenger quarters were very similar, also designed to carry a maximum of thirty first class passengers. This class was used on another of Blue Funnel's routes, to Australia, sailing from Liverpool to Port Said, Aden, Albany or Fremantle, Melbourne and then turnaround at Sydney. They were fitted for carrying general cargo, largely homebound Australian wool, as well as some refrigerated areas (for meat especially) and a deep tank for liquid cargo. The *Jason* was alone in coming from the Swan, Hunter & Wigham Richardson yards at Newcastle; the other three were delivered by Harland & Wolff of Belfast.

Similar to their fleet-mates on the Far Eastern run, this class was finally reduced to all-freight sailings in 1964. In a vast reduction of the conventional Blue Funnel fleet, they were all sold for breaking in Taiwan in 1972.

### The CENTAUR

The name *Centaur* has been to the port of Singapore almost what the name *Queen Mary* was to Southampton or *Lurline* to San Francisco. Recently (1984), after nearly two decades of Singapore–Fremantle service and then a year's charter from the UK to South Africa, the *Centaur* was laid-up bereft of work and after some time sold to the Chinese for further service under their colours.

When the 7990-ton *Centaur* was under construction in 1963 at Scotland's John Brown shipyard, her owners –·the Blue Funnel Line of Liverpool – had one of the world's largest merchant fleets. Their ships were well known: classically beautiful and superbly proportioned, using names derived from Greek mythology (such as *Ajax*, *Hector* and *Perseus*) and with some of the most prominent funnels at sea, all of them painted in a distinctive blue with a black top. The company had deep interests in the Far and Middle East, and Singapore could well be considered their second home. The 480 foot *Centaur* was built for the firm's last passenger run, replacing the two little prewar running-mates, *Charon* and *Gorgon*.

Commissioned in January 1964, the *Centaur* sailed to the East, briefly served as an Australian Trade Fair Ship in Far Eastern waters and then took up her duties on the run to Fremantle. She could take 190 all-first class passengers (206 was the maximum), who were accommodated on three principal decks: Promenade, Bridge and Shelter. An outdoor pool, partially covered by a canvas awning, was fitted aft on the Promenade Deck and the surrounding lido area was occasionally used as an open-air night-time cinema. Also located on the Promenade Deck were the library (used also for afternoon taped concerts, church services, etc) and two suites, each with a bedroom, sitting room and full-size bath. A bar-lounge, gift shop and ten other cabins occupied the rest of this deck. The Bridge Deck included the Governor's Bar (also used as a meeting room), a laundrette, a hospital, the children's playroom and thirty-nine cabins (seventeen of which were without private facilities). A twenty-four-hour self-service 'cuppa tea' pantry proved a popular amenity. On the Shelter Deck, there was a dining room (which was used in the afternoons for children's films), poker machines and thirty-nine cabins (only three of which had a private shower and toilet).

The *Centaur* was of rather unusual design: her passenger areas were aft and the cargo holds forward. Among combination passenger-cargo liners, she was quite unique in being specially fitted to transport sheep and cattle from Australian ports to Singapore.

153

When she was completely withdrawn from that service, in September 1982, she had carried a total of 73,200 passengers, 1.1 million sheep, 17,700 cattle, 1100 horses and 390,000 tons of general cargo. She was so popular with sea travellers even near the end of her career, her owners ran $50 cruises 'to nowhere' out of Singapore. According to Jeremy Gray of Blue Funnel in Singapore, 'Some 65 per cent of her passengers in the end were loyalist repeaters.' Even the Australian dockers, familiarly known as 'wharfies', exempted her from their frequent strikes.

Dr David Kirkman served as surgeon on the *Centaur* and fondly recalled her. 'In her early days, the *Centaur* also sailed to the northwest of Western Australia to load cattle at the ports of Broome and Derby. Specially designed with a flat bottom, there were 20–25 foot tidal changes in those ports and the ship would be left high-and-dry until the next incoming tide. You could walk completely around the 480 foot long vessel, but then, quite suddenly, the inbound tide would come faster than you could run. Also, quite notably, two governors of Western Australia, one of whom was the former master of the royal yacht *Britannia*, were installed at ceremonies aboard the *Centaur*. They sailed from Singapore and then took the oath upon arrival at Fremantle. There was such a link to this ship that local Western Australian television company made a film of her last sailing from Fremantle. Everyone in Western Australia had at least heard of the *Centaur*.'

However, by the early eighties, the *Centaur*'s blend of passenger and cargo facilities had become impractical. The mere 200 passenger berths were simply not enough to pay her way (or justify her existence). The sheep trade had gone to a new generation of specialised carriers and the general freight business had shifted to container ships. Even her original owners, Blue Funnel Line of Liverpool, had shrunk to a mere fraction of their original size. In September 1982, after 303 voyages, the *Centaur* was withdrawn.

The *Centaur* had changed from British to Singaporean registry in 1973, when she was transferred to the China Mutual Steam Navigation Company, a division of the Blue Funnel Group. However, shortly thereafter, she was again shifted, to the Straits Steamship Company of Singapore. In February 1981, another local company, the Pacific International Lines, became a partner. This ever-changing saga continued when the Straits Company later reverted as full owners and still later (in November 1983) was bought out by the Keppel Shipyards, which is owned by the Government of Singapore. The well-known Blue Funnel name was retained, however, but as Blue Funnel Cruises, a division of Straits Steamship Company and, more recently (1983–84), as operators of the cruise ship *Princess Mahsuri*, the former West German *Berlin*, which has now reverted to her original name and owners.

Prompted by the sudden Falklands War and the requisitioning of its little passenger ship *St Helena*, Britain's Curnow Shipping Company chartered the laid-up *Centaur* in November 1982. Her important, but temporary routing was from Avonmouth to Ascension, St Helena and Capetown. This ended in January 1984, when the *St Helena* returned to her owners and resumed sailings. The *Centaur* made her nostalgic farewell run with passengers aboard, from Capetown to Fremantle and then to Singapore. According to Jeremy Gray, 'This was the end of an era, the end of a local institution.'

She was laid-up, left in the care of six crew and offered for sale at $2½ million, sitting for some time off Singapore's Sentosa Island. In remarkably tidy condition during my visit (July 1984) and with the enormous captain's day-room used to receive prospective buyers (and curious guests), there still seemed to be some life left aboard the otherwise silent *Centaur*. Fortunately, she has now taken up a new career with the Chinese, thus escaping the scrappers. She has been renamed *Hao Long*.

## ROYAL INTEROCEAN LINES

### The BOISSEVAIN, RUYS and TEGELBERG

According to Dr David Kirkman, who served aboard several of the Royal Interocean passenger ships as a surgeon, 'They were a huge Dutch firm, but never sailed their ships to Holland. In the 1950s and 1960s, they had over fifty ships. The company was created soon after Indonesian independence in the late forties through the merger of the local KPM Packet Company (Köninklijke Packet Vaart Maatschhappij) and the more extensive Java–China–Japan Line. The former KPM headquarters, served as Royal Interocean's main office in Singapore and then headquarters; The Royal Nedlloyd Group which absorbed the original Royal Interocean fleet now occupies the building.

'Royal Interocean passenger services were often abbreviated to "RIL", which was fondly known as "Relax in Luxury". Their three largest ships, the 14,300-ton sisters *Boissevain*, *Ruys* and *Tegelberg* [built in 1937–38] ran a three-class service [each ship carrying 400 passengers] that was one of the most extensive liner operations then available. It traded westbound from Yokohama and Kobe to Hong

*Built just prior to the outbreak of the Second World War, the
Tegelberg and her two sisters were created originally for the
KPM Packet Company. They later became the largest
vessels in the Royal Interocean Lines' three-continent service
from the Far East to South Africa to South America.*

Kong, Singapore, Port Swettenham, Penang, Mauritius, Lourenço Marques, Durban, Capetown and then
across the South Atlantic to Rio de Janeiro, Santos,
Montevideo and Buenos Aires. They carried all types
of passengers – from old colonials and rich tourists to
Chinese and Indian migrant settlers. The ships were
each named after prominent directors of the original
KPM Company. The artist-grandson of Mr Boissevain presently lives in western Australia, the heirs to
Mr Ruys still have huge holdings in Dutch tansport
and the son-in-law of Mr Tegelberg became one of
the directors of Royal Interocean.'

These three sisterships, noted not only for their high standard of passenger accommodation, but as being among the largest triple-screw passenger ships ever built, survived until 1968, when they each passed their thirtieth years. The combination liner *Straat Banka* [with space for fifty passengers] ran Royal Interocean's final South America–Far East passenger sailing on 17 August to 25 October 1968. The three older liners spent their final weeks in lay-up at either Kobe or Yokohama before being sold, at some $500,000 each, to Taiwanese breakers. Dr Kirkman added, 'A friend of mine was one of the crew of six that took the *Ruys* on her final voyage, a twenty-four-hour run from Hong Kong to the Kaohsiung scrap-yards. Even her kitchens had been closed down and the crew used pre-cooked food.'

### The TJITJALENGKA

Built a year after the earlier trio, in 1939 at Amsterdam, the smaller 10,900-ton *Tjitjalengka* served during the Second World War as a hospital ship and then later joined the long-haul Far East–South America

passenger run. She had space for 493 passengers in three classes, including an exceptionally comfortable first class section. According to Dr Kirkman, 'This ship had a special place in maritime history and has appeared on commemorative stamps issued from the island of Tristan da Cunha. She created a very strong bond with the locals there when she rescued the entire population after a volcanic eruption in the early 1960s.' Like the three earlier ships, she too was retired in 1968, and soon afterwards was sold to the Ming Hing Company of Hong Kong for breaking-up.

### The STRAAT BANKA and TJINEGARA

Constructed after the War, in 1951, at the P Smit yards of Rotterdam, the sisters *Straat Banka* and *Tjinegara* were designed as high-standard combination ships carrying no more than fifty first class passengers each. They were not given the more extensive quarters that were included aboard the prewar 'RIL' ships. The *Straat Banka* was used on a separate passenger-cargo run, between India and Australia, sailing in company only with smaller cargo ships, whereas the *Tjinegara*

worked the more distant trade between the Far East and South America. Dr Kirkman served aboard the *Straat Banka*. 'She worked the "Indian run", between Bombay, Cochin, Colombo, Penang, Singapore, Jakarta, Brisbane, Sydney and Melbourne. We'd take tallow and livestock to India, and then spices and tea outbound. These ships, like all the Royal Interocean vessels, had exceptional Dutch captains. So experienced and precise, it was said that these men could simply look over the side and know where they were just by the colour and quality of the water. One old commander taught himself Chinese and Japanese while at sea and did so well that now, in retirement, he is a professor of Asian languages at Sydney University. They raised their families in the East, but when their sons followed them to nautical colleges at Amsterdam and Rotterdam, Holland was a strange, foreign country to them. Royal Interocean usually hired only Dutch officers, with a handful of Chinese pursers.

'In the early 1960s, ships like the *Straat Banka* [and *Tjinegara*] faced the mandatory twenty-year refit prescribed by Dutch maritime law. Overcoming such a costly obstacle, Royal Interocean formed a "flag of convenience" subsidiary, the Mercury Shipping Company of Hong Kong, but which was really a one-room office with a typewriter. Like several other ships, the *Tjinegara* and *Straat Banka* changed hands as well as flags, and became the *Mercury Lake* and *Mercury Bay* respectively. They were put into straight freight service, mostly carrying second-hand cars to Indonesia. Near her end, I visited the former *Straat Banka* and was horrified to see automotive "heaps" stored even in the former lounge and restaurant. Both ships were broken-up by the late seventies.'

*The* Straat Banka *and her sistership, the* Tjinegara, *were the only combination passenger-cargo liners in the Royal Interocean fleet with as few as fifty passenger berths. Both finished their careers as 'tramp' cargo ships, carrying low-grade cargos.*

### The Tjiwangi and Tjiluwah

Two of Dr Kirkman's favourite passenger ships were the 8600-ton sisters *Tjiwangi* and *Tjiluwah*, built at the Van der Giessen shipyard at Krimpen in Holland, in 1951–52, with accommodation for 98 first class and 120 second class passengers (local deck passengers were also carried). 'Unfortunately, these very fine ships were designed a bit too late for the local Dutch colonial inter-island services. Instead, Royal Interocean created a new "Asean" service just for them – from Melbourne, Sydney and Brisbane on an eleven-day non-stop voyage to Yokkaichi (a Japanese port in Ise Bay, near Nagoya) to offload our biggest cargo: Australian wool. From there, we'd go to Nagoya, Yokohama and Kobe, then to Keelung and Kaohsiung, where I especially remember seeing those incredible scrapyards. Afterwards, we'd have a four-day stay at Hong Kong and then sail directly to Brisbane. Homeward, we carried much lighter cargo: tinned fruit, textiles, clothing and small manufactured goods from Taiwan mostly. In comparison, the Australian dockers at Melbourne took a full week to load the same cargo that the Japanese would handle in a single day at Yokkaichi. Beautifully decorated and superbly maintained, these ships were known as the "big white yachts". They had a two-month round-trip voyage that was very popular with wealthy, older Australians.

'In the early seventies, when the *Tjiwangi* and *Tjiluwah* turned twenty, they, too, were required to have huge refits and special surveys under Dutch

STRAAT BANKA

Vincent Messina Collection

maritime law. This appeared uneconomic to the accountants at Royal Interocean. Consequently, they were sold to the Singapore-registered Pacific International Lines and became the *Kota Bali* and *Kota Singapura* respectively. They were put on the shorter Singapore–Fremantle run, but purely as passenger ships. Cargo was no longer carried. They were quite successful for a time, but very much downgraded, aimed at a budget tourist market. They were also poorly maintained. I was saddened to visit them in later years and notice the dirty conditions, the cigarette burns and the greasy grime that prevailed in the passenger areas.

'Ironically, the aged *Kota Bali* (ex-*Tjiwangi*) finished her days on the very service for which she was first intended: the Indonesian inter-island trade out of Jakarta. Chartered to the locally-owned Pelni Line, but registered at Penang in Malaysia, she travelled to ports such as Surabaya and Makassar. Unfortunately, her general condition grew worse still. Now [1984], both ships have been scrapped.'

### The NIEUW HOLLAND

At the beginning of the 1970s, the Royal Interocean Line gradually reduced its passenger operations to one final ship, the 13,700-ton *Nieuw Holland*, the former *Randfontein*, built in 1958 for the Holland-Africa Line. Dr Kirkman recalled, 'The *Nieuw Holland* was berthed next to the retiring *Tjiluwah* at the Hong Kong Ocean Terminal, in the late summer of 1971. As crew, we walked across from one ship to the other, carrying our possessions and other necessary items. Unfortunately, the long-distance Australia–Hong Kong–Japan run continued to change. The passenger trade was declining and the freight shifting to container ships. The *Nieuw Holland* lasted but two years. She was soon sold to the Chinese Government, renamed as the *Yu Hua* [and later *Hai Xing*] and used to carry railway engineers and construction crews to East Africa.'

*Known affectionately by Australians as the 'big white yachts', the* Tjiwangi *and her sistership, the* Tjiluwah, *ran two-month round-trip sailings to Japan, Taiwan and Hong Kong that were very popular with older, wealthy passengers.* Tjiwangi *is seen here at Hong Kong.*

# CHAPTER SIX

# DOWN UNDER, TO AUSTRALIA & NEW ZEALAND

## SHAW SAVILL LINE

### The DOMINION MONARCH

Shaw Savill was one of the best known names, along with the larger P&O-Orient Lines, in Australia/New Zealand passenger shipping. Their prewar fleet contained diverse passenger ships: high-standard deepsea liners, low-fare migrant ships and cargo vessels with limited first class quarters. Certainly, one of the company's finest liners and one of the most superb

passenger ships ever to sail in the 'Down Under' trade was the 26,500-ton *Dominion Monarch*.

An individual ship within the Shaw Savill fleet, the *Dominion Monarch* was built by Swan, Hunter & Wigham Richardson Ltd at their Newcastle yards and delivered in January 1939. She was the highest powered motor ships in the world and the largest liner then on the Australian trade. Unfortunately her

commercial sailings were soon to be disrupted by the outbreak of the Second World War. Used as a troop transport, she was very nearly captured by the Japanese forces during the invasion. and fall of Singapore. While lying in drydock, with her engines dismantled for repairs, it was only due to the near superhuman efforts of her crew that she was urgently repaired and then slipped off to sea. Thereafter, she gave heroic, accident-free service until her release by the British Government in 1947. She was restored and resumed her Shaw Savill sailings in December 1948, on 3½-month round-trips between London, Southampton, Las Palmas, Capetown, Fremantle, Melbourne, Sydney and Wellington. Her accommodation was restored to its luxurious prewar standard, with only 508 first class berths, including a large cinema, a 300-seat restaurant, an outdoor pool, private bathrooms in many of her staterooms and among the largest open-air deck spaces. There were six hatches (including one positioned just aft of the bridge and

wheelhouse, and just forward of the first funnel), and the cargo space was divided between nearly 512,000 cubic feet for refrigerated goods (mostly for valuable meats from Australia and New Zealand) and 147,000 cubic feet for general cargo. Bob Cummins served as a steward and waiter aboard the *Dominion Monarch* and remembered her as one of the finest ships of her day. 'She was an exceptionally beautiful ship with a spacious promenade deck, deluxe staterooms and little lamps on each dinner table in the restaurant (the overhead lights were switched-off). We carried wealthy Australian farm and ranch owners and their families, theatre people, up-market tourists and retired round-trippers.'

Rather unfortunately, the *Dominion Monarch* was retired at the age of twenty-two in 1961. By then, she

*Shaw Savill's luxurious* Dominion Monarch, *at little more than twenty years of age, leaves the Glasgow Wharf at Wellington on her final trip to England.*

Shaw Savill Line

proved to be a rather uneconomic mix of too little freight space (compared to the new cargo ships on the Australia/New Zealand trades) and too few passenger spaces (especially as the Australian run turned more and more toward the lower priced tourist market). She was sold to the Mitsui Co of Japan for scrapping, but then was leased, in a final, rather inglorious spark of life, to serve as a moored hotel-ship at Seattle for the 1962 World's Fair. She was moored across from another former British liner, P&O's *Mongolia* (and later New Zealand Shipping's *Rimutaka*), which as the Mexican cruise ship *Acapulco* was chartered for dock-side hotel service. That autumn, the *Dominion Monarch*, which had been renamed *Dominion Monarch Maru*, completed her term at Seattle and sailed across the Pacific to Osaka for breaking-up. She reached her last port-of-call on 25 November.

### The SOUTHERN CROSS and NORTHERN STAR

Shaw Savill might have built a running-mate to the all-first class *Dominion Monarch* if the war had not erupted, but when the final construction and postwar replacement plans were drawn up, it was with a different view of the 'Down Under' passenger trade. Company directors and designers saw substantial growth not in the deluxe first class market, which would be the first to desert the liners in the face of aircraft competition, but instead in the tourist class trade, ranging from comfortable single- and double-berth rooms to family-style cabins with as many as six berths. Consequently, plans were drawn for one of the most outstanding passenger ships of the postwar decade.

Ordered from Harland & Wolff at Belfast, the new ship was given a royal baptism, being named by Queen Elizabeth II, who travelled especially for the occasion from her summer retreat at Balmoral, on 17 August 1954. Named *Southern Cross*, she broke almost all traditions and was a ship of superlatives. She was revolutionary for her time being the first big liner to have her engines and therefore her funnel placed aft (a design style copied frequently since, including the *Canberra* of 1961, built by Harland & Wolff for P&O). She was also the first major passenger ship to have absolutely no cargo space whatsoever (with the rather obvious exceptions of stores and passenger luggage and freight space) and the first to offer high-standard all-tourist class accommodation (with 1100 berths in all). Even her operating schedule was noteworthy: four annual round-the-world voyages, from Southampton to Las Palmas, Capetown, Durban, Fremantle, Melbourne, Sydney, Auckland, Wellington, Fiji, Tahiti, the Panama Canal, Curaçao, Trinidad and

*A rare meeting: the* **Northern Star** *(left) and the* **Southern Cross** *passing in the Panama Canal, in June 1965. The former was bound for England, the latter for Australia.*

return to Southampton. The full voyage took seventy-six days.

The *Southern Cross*, fitted with stabilizers, full air-conditioning, considerable open-air deck spaces (which included a top deck pool), a cinema, several public rooms and twin restaurants, proved to be a highly successful and profitable ship for nearly fifteen years. Her success led to the order of the slightly modified *Northern Star*, which was delivered by Vickers-Armstrongs in the summer of 1962. This second ship, again of the engines-aft design, was larger by nearly 5000 tons and had an increased

*The* **Southern Cross** *was the first major liner built with the funnel placed aft, thereby creating a large midship open-air deck space as well as undisturbed public areas below.*

162

Furness Withy Group

Shaw Savill Line

*The combination cinema-main lounge aboard the* Southern
Cross.

*Barely saved from the scrap-heap, in the early seventies, the former* Southern Cross *found new life with the Greeks, as the* Calypso *of the Ulysses Lines. She is shown departing from Lisbon, bound for a cruise in the eastern Atlantic.*

Luis Miguel Correia

capacity of as many as 1412 berths in all-tourist class quarters. Furthermore, in the annals of British shipping, they are similar to the famed Cunard Queens in that they were both launched by British Queens: the aforementioned *Southern Cross* having been launched by the Queen, while the *Northern Star* in a ceremony on 27 June 1961 was named by the Queen Mother. Both royal ladies were kept abreast of the careers of the ships they had launched.

After the *Northern Star*'s appearance, the *Southern Cross* was routed on the westabout world service, sailing outward via the Caribbean, Panama, etc. The newer ship ran the eastabout sailings. While both ships were popular with inter-port as well as one-way passenger traffic, they also developed a following among round-the-world travellers, who made the entire voyage, often at very reasonable tourist class fares. Minimum fares in a double-berth room aboard the *Northern Star* in 1966 began at £386.

Slumps in both the Australia/New Zealand and world voyage trades began by the late 1960s. In July 1968, the *Northern Star* sailed on the first of what

Shaw Savill Line

*One of the very few single-berth staterooms on board the* Southern Cross, *a ship aimed at the tourist, low-fare and migrant markets.*

Luis Miguel Correia

*The* Northern Star *arriving at Lisbon on one of her final cruises, in June 1975.*

would be many two-week cruise voyages, on this occasion from Southampton to the Mediterranean. The *Southern Cross* periodically joined her as well, sailing not only from Southampton but from Liverpool, while the *Northern Star* cruised from Sydney to the South Pacific islands. However, with dramatically increased fuel and staff costs, and new regulations for British passenger ships being enacted, the *Southern Cross* was laid-up permanently in November 1971, first at Southampton, nested alongside two other out-of-work British passenger ships, Cunard's *Carmania* and *Franconia*, then at a mooring in the River Fal in Cornwall. There were rumours at first that she might become a hotel and leisure centre, but instead passed into Greek hands in January 1973. Rebuilt at Perama with modernized accommodation for 1000 first class passengers, she reappeared in the spring of 1975, sailing as the *Calypso* for the Ulysses Lines Ltd. Trading mostly on two-week voyages to Scandinavia and within the Mediterranean, she also had an experimental stint on weekly New York–Bermuda cruises. In 1976, she was to have been time-chartered to the Monarch Cruise Lines, the Panamanian-flag

One of the two restaurants for the all-tourist class passengers on the Northern Star.

*Modern décor on the round-the-world tourist run: the Smoking Room aboard the* Northern Star, *a ship completed in 1962.*

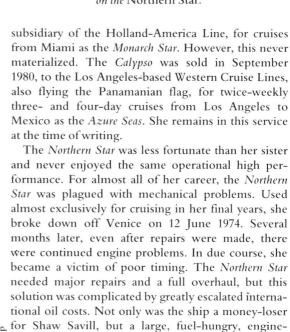

subsidiary of the Holland-America Line, for cruises from Miami as the *Monarch Star*. However, this never materialized. The *Calypso* was sold in September 1980, to the Los Angeles-based Western Cruise Lines, also flying the Panamanian flag, for twice-weekly three- and four-day cruises from Los Angeles to Mexico as the *Azure Seas*. She remains in this service at the time of writing.

The *Northern Star* was less fortunate than her sister and never enjoyed the same operational high performance. For almost all of her career, the *Northern Star* was plagued with mechanical problems. Used almost exclusively for cruising in her final years, she broke down off Venice on 12 June 1974. Several months later, even after repairs were made, there were continued engine problems. In due course, she became a victim of poor timing. The *Northern Star* needed major repairs and a full overhaul, but this solution was complicated by greatly escalated international oil costs. Not only was the ship a money-loser for Shaw Savill, but a large, fuel-hungry, engine-troubled liner, only a mere thirteen years of age, could hardly be expected to find a buyer in such a tense period for the trade. Even the usually keen Greeks seemed uninterested. Comparatively short-lived and with few years of full profit to her credit, the *Northern Star* was delivered to the Li Chong Steel &

*The* Gothic *at anchor at Aden, while serving as a royal yacht.*

Iron Works of Kaohsiung on 1 December 1974. At almost the same time, Shaw Savill was closing down all of its passenger-cruise operations.

**The ATHENIC, CORINTHIC, CERAMIC and GOTHIC**
Like some other British shipowners in the hard-pressed years immediately following the end of the war, Shaw Savill ordered several freighter hulls that could be modified to carry more than the traditional dozen passengers. Cunard was doing this for its transatlantic run between Liverpool and New York, using two redesigned Brocklebank Line freighters that would become the 250-passenger *Media* and *Parthia* of 1947–48. Others followed suit as well, like Blue Funnel, which had as many as thirty first class berths fitted to its new *Jason* and *Patroclus* classes.

The *Corinthic*, the first of the new Shaw Savill quartet, was launched on 30 May 1946, at the Cammell Laird yards at Birkenhead. The *Athenic* followed and came from Harland & Wolff at Belfast,

the *Gothic* from Swan, Hunter & Wigham Richardson at Newcastle and finally the *Ceramic*, also from Cammell Laird. They were intended for the extensive service from London to Auckland and Wellington via Curaçao and the Panama Canal. These round-trip voyages took four months and there was a four-week layover in European waters, divided between a long stay in the London Docks and then cargo calls at ports such as Hamburg, Rotterdam and Antwerp. The ships were fitted with exceptional cargo capacities, which were particularly useful for the northbound frozen meat trade. In six holds, provision was made for over 500,000 cubic feet of refrigerated goods and 158,000 cubic feet of general cargo.

The passenger accommodation, being of rather high standard, included a main lounge, verandah cafe, smoking room and dining salon. A portable pool was erected on deck as required. Among the staterooms, there were a suite, ten single and twelve double cabins with private bathroom facilities; the other cabins used public facilities located along the corridors.

Great honour befell the *Gothic* in 1951 when she was selected by the British Government to carry the Royal Family – King George VI, Princess Elizabeth and Princess Margaret – on a tour to Australia and New Zealand. The ship was sent to the Cammell Laird yards, refitted and specially painted with an all-white hull. Then, due to the King's poor health and later his sudden death, in February 1952, the tour was delayed and finally cancelled. However, in the autumn of 1953, the *Gothic* was again refitted as a royal yacht, this time to be used by Queen Elizabeth II and the Duke of Edinburgh for a round-the-world coronation tour. The Queen and her party joined the ship at Bermuda, in November 1953, and then continued aboard to Jamaica, the Panama Canal, Fiji, Tonga, New Zealand, Australia, Ceylon and East Africa. She left the ship at Aden and flew to Tobruk where she was greeted by the brand-new royal yacht *Britannia*. The *Gothic* was briefly moored alongside the new vessel and an exchange of goods and luggage was made. While the Queen sailed home to the Pool of London via Gibraltar in the *Britannia*, the *Gothic* was sent to drydock and restored to her Shaw Savill styling. Although always remembered thereafter for her special coronation cruise, the *Gothic* resumed her intended commercial service to New Zealand.

Both the *Corinthic* and *Athenic* were retired and then delivered to Taiwanese breakers at Kaohsiung two days apart in October 1968. The *Gothic* had been all but completely destroyed just two months prior. On 2 August, while sailing home from Wellington to Panama, a fire erupted in the superstructure, spread quickly and claimed seven lives. Badly damaged and blackened, the *Gothic* returned to Wellington and was temporarily repaired. She returned to London on 10 October, but on inspection was deemed to be beyond economic repair. After some additional repairs, she made a final sailing to Australia on loan to the Cairn Line, which was, like Shaw Savill, owned by the Furness Withy Group. On 13 August 1969, the *Gothic* was handed over to Kaohsiung scrappers. The *Ceramic*, having been downgraded to a freighter, was finally withdrawn in the spring of 1973 and sold to shipbreakers at Tamise in Belgium.

### The AKAROA, ARAWA and ARANDA

According to John Draffin, who served as a purser aboard both Royal Mail and Shaw Savill liners, 'While Furness Withy acquired Royal Mail in the mid 1960s, including their passenger fleet, they were always more interested in the Shaw Savill Line. After big losses in the Argentine beef trade, with delayed and near-empty sailings [in 1967–68], yet while attempting to maintain a passenger schedule, the three "A sisters" of Royal Mail were finally transferred to Shaw Savill. Unfortunately, it was a less than successful decision.

*Built for the Royal Mail Lines' service to South America, the former* Amazon *was renamed* Akaroa *and had rather a shortlived career with Shaw Savill.*

Alex Duncan

Leif Hoegh & Co

*The former* Akaroa, Arawa *(shown here as the* Hoegh Trotter)*, and* Aranda *were almost totally unrecognizable after being rebuilt as car carriers for global trading. Each ship had a capacity for some 3000 vehicles.*

The "A sisters" were made one-class ships, but, having been originally three-class in design and layout, seemed "chopped-up" with too few small lounges, etc. Furthermore, by this time, Shaw Savill's passenger division was no longer at its best.'

The *Amazon*, the first of the Royal Mail's South American trio from 1959–60, was transferred to Shaw Savill in February 1968. Renamed *Akaroa*, she was despatched on their round-the-world and Australia/ New Zealand services. The other two sisters were soon to follow. The *Aragon* was laid-up for a time in the River Fal, which was fast becoming something of a limbo for out-of-work British passenger ships. She passed to Shaw Savill in February 1969, and hoisted her new colours as the *Arawa*. The *Aragon*, the last to remain with Royal Mail, closed out the South American passenger trade from London on 21 February. She soon shifted to Shaw Savill and became the *Aranda*.

Shaw Savill abandoned the three-class system for this trio and listed them as having accommodation for 470 one-class passengers. Their rather large cargo capacity, particularly their extensive refrigerated space, was useful on the long-haul trades out to Australia and New Zealand. Mostly, they sailed on world voyages – from London, the usual itinerary being to the Azores, Barbados, Trinidad, Curaçao, the Panama Canal, Tahiti, Auckland, Wellington, Sydney, Melbourne, Fremantle, Durban, Capetown and Las Palmas, before returning to London. Sometimes, the sailings were reversed and at other times the ports of call were varied. There was even some occasional cruising, from Australia and New Zealand, on short runs in the South Pacific. But, unfortunately, more hard times were ahead.

The *Akaroa* (ex-*Amazon*) was seriously damaged by a fire at sea, while some 1000 miles southwest of the Azores, on 15 April 1970. She limped back to Britain for repairs. But, within a year, rumours hinted that the three ships were again unprofitable, left behind in ever-changing worldwide shipping patterns. One story, which emerged in the spring of 1971, suggested that the *Akaroa* would be converted to a floating hotel in the Seychelles. Nothing came to pass. Shortly thereafter, the threesome was abruptly withdrawn from service.

There was very little time spent in idleness, however. The trio were sold for $700,000 (just above their combined scrap value at the time) to Norwegian buyers: the *Akaroa* to A/S Uglands Rederi and the *Aranda* and *Arawa* to Leif Hoegh & Co. Their futures represented a joint project: for a total of $8 million, they would be converted to car carriers. The *Akaroa* was rechristened *Akarita* and sent to Grimstad in Norway for conversion. The *Aranda*, which became *Hoegh Traveller*, and the *Arawa*, which changed to *Hoegh Transit*, sailed to the Viktor Lenac Shipyard at Rijeka, Yugoslavia, for what then represented one of the biggest conversions to be contracted to a Yugoslav yard. Their task was increased when the *Akarita* had her transformation, which was commenced at Grimstad, completed at Rijeka.

It was surely the first time that deep-sea passenger ships had found new life as car carriers. All of the cargo holds were gutted and changed into vehicle stowage spaces. The passenger quarters were also removed and left the ships almost unrecognizable. However, some of the original first class cabins were retained as were the original single funnels. The bridge and wheelhouse sections were moved a long way forward, to a position above what had previously been the first cargo hold. Overall, the ships became high, floating sheds – undoubtedly 'working ships' with little hint of any sleekness in design. Each ships' tonnage dropped from 20,000 to 11,000 tons and their capacities were listed as 3000 cars per ship. Upon completion, they were assigned to the worldwide Hoegh-Ugland car-carrying trade. The author has seen at least two since their conversion at Port Newark, New Orleans, Yokohama and in the upper reaches of the Hudson River.

Their subsequent histories include some further changes. The *Hoegh Transit* (ex-*Arawa*, ex-*Arlanza*) became the *Hoegh Trotter* within a year following her sale to the Norwegians. All three ships changed hands in 1978. The *Akarita* (ex-*Akaroa*, ex-*Amazon*) went to Sagitta (Liberia) Ltd, under Liberian colours and became the *Hual Akarita*. The *Hoegh Traveller* (ex-*Aranda*, ex-*Aragon*) and the *Hoegh Trotter* both transferred to the Ace Navigation Co Ltd, also taking Liberian colours, and became the *Hual Traveller* and *Hual Trotter* respectively. In 1981, there were still further amendments. The *Hual Akarita* reverted to the name *Akarita* while the *Hual Traveller* became the *Traveller* and the *Hoegh Trotter* the *Trotter*.

In 1976, each of the ships passed their five-year surveys. But as the shipping scene continued to change, with fluctuations in trading requirements and the continued emphasis on operational efficiency, the three ships were given a quite different evaluation. Evidently, they were no longer needed. The *Traveller*

Michael Cassar

Ocean Monarch's shortlived service with Shaw Savill was most unprofitable. Little more than four years after a costly, long-delayed refit, she was sold off to Taiwanese breakers. She is shown outbound from Southampton, on 13 June 1975, stripped of all but one of her lifeboats on the port side, destined for the ship breakers at Kaohsiung.

departed from New Orleans in October 1981, bound for the scrapyards at Kaohsiung, Taiwan. The *Trotter* followed in December and the *Akarita*, last of the original trio, went her way in January.

### The OCEAN MONARCH

Shaw Savill's final passenger ship was perhaps the least successful in their fleet. The *Empress of England* was acquired from Canadian Pacific in February 1970, having been used in North Atlantic and cruise service. Renamed *Ocean Monarch*, she became the sixth liner in a sudden, but ill-timed expansion for Shaw Savill. After a single round-trip out to Australia, it was

intended that she would join the *Southern Cross* and *Northern Star* in cruise service while the *Akaroa*, *Arawa* and *Aranda* handled the remains of the round-the-world service.

The *Ocean Monarch*, built in 1957 at the Vickers-Armstrongs yard at Newcastle, was sent to Cammell Laird at Birkenhead for modernization and conversion to an all-tourist class cruise ship. Her passenger capacity, listed as 160 first class and 898 tourist class in her Canadian Pacific days, was rearranged to 1372 one-class. John Draffin recalled the acquisition of this ship and intended transformation. 'It was a big fiasco. There were endless costs, a year's delay at the yards, breakdowns, general unhappiness and poor planning.' Well behind her intended schedule, the *Ocean Monarch* left Birkenhead after fifteen months, in October 1971. By this time, Shaw Savill's plans had changed considerably: the *Southern Cross* had been withdrawn, the three 'A class' ships sold and the passenger division was slipping further into the red. While used for cruising from both Britain and Australia, the *Ocean Monarch* contributed very little to the company's treasury. Soon after the enormous oil price increases of 1973, the fate of this sixteen-year-old ship was sealed. Upon completing her 1974 schedules, she was offered for sale and, with no commercial possibilities appearing, she went to the Taiwanese for breaking up. She reached Kaohsiung, on 17 July 1975. It was the end of Shaw Savill's passenger fleet.

*Passage through Panama: New Zealand Shipping Company's* Rangitane *is to the right, Shaw Savill's* Southern Cross *is farther back, to the left.*

## — NEW ZEALAND SHIPPING COMPANY —

### The RANGITANE, RANGITOTO, RUAHINE and REMUERA

In the 1950s and 1960s, Britain maintained the largest passenger ship network in the world. There were few ports that British-flag liners did not visit, even if only occasionally. One of the more popular and noted firms was the London-based New Zealand Shipping Company. Dating from 1883, it was a corporate arm of the giant P&O Group, although always

maintaining separate colours, management, staffing and operations.

In its final passenger years, during the 1960s, the New Zealand Shipping Company ran four large combination passenger-cargo vessels. All of them had Maori names. The 21,800-ton sisterships *Rangitane* and *Rangitoto* of 1949 were, in fact, two of the largest combination passenger-cargo liners ever built. Each had space for 436 one-class passengers as well as six holds for cargo. A slightly smaller version of this pair, the 17,800-ton *Ruahine*, with accommodation for 267 passengers, was added in 1951. The fourth ship, the 13,600-ton *Remuera*, joined in 1962, but was, in fact, the former Cunard transatlantic liner *Parthia* of 1948. She was added temporarily, to assist with New Zealand passenger sailings. The purchase of a second-hand ship was then far more appropriate than building expensive, new tonnage. Certainly, aircraft competition was on the horizon. The *Remuera* was quite unsuccessful. She lasted but two years and then, in late 1964, was sold to the Eastern & Australian Steamship Company, another member of the P&O Group, for their Australia–Far East service. She sailed for them as the *Aramac* until scrapped on Taiwan in 1970.

The New Zealand Shipping Company passenger ships worked on a very extensive routing that took them from London to the Caribbean, through the Panama Canal, then southwards to Tahiti and finally onwards to Auckland or Wellington. Homewards, they included Kingston in Jamaica, Port Everglades and Bermuda, before continuing to Southampton and finally London. John Draffin, who served as an assistant purser on these ships and who is presently a purser with Commodore Cruises of Miami, recalled these extended sailing patterns. 'Outbound from London, it was ten days across to Curaçao, then two days to Panama, twelve days to Tahiti and a final eight days to Auckalnd. We would then have a six-week wait in New Zealand, since our loading had to coincide with the freshest kill of lamb. Homebound, with space for over 8000 tons of cargo on each ship, the bulk of our manifest was refrigerated lamb. We'd also have some wool and casin, the latter being a byproduct of milk used in making glue.'

John Draffin also recalled the passenger operations of these ships. 'Outbound passengers were mostly immigrants seeking new lives in New Zealand. Homeward, we carried earlier migrants, who were returning to Britain as tourists or for family visits. Most of the cabins were large – four-, six- and eight-berths – for family travel. We had an outdoor pool for daytime use, but otherwise all entertainment was created by the passengers. We would have some records for night-time dancing in the lounge. As a member of the purser's department, one of my tasks was to improvise various pastimes. For example, on one day, we would have a lei-making demonstration. Then, on the following day, we would have a competition of the results. We'd also have some of the older passengers making grass skirts and then we'd entice the young ladies to give a dance performance.

'At the conclusion of the homeward voyages, we would always land the passengers at Southampton rather than London. Mostly, it was an easier journey for them into London (as compared to the train runs from the London Docks and then into the City). Then, of course, there were the hazards of London fogs and therefore possible delays. Furthermore, we would discharge half of our crew at Southampton along with the disembarking passengers. When the ships continued onward to the London Docks, it was for cargo only.'

The entire New Zealand Shipping Company passenger run was eliminated in the late 1960s, with the usual reasons of a declining passenger and freight trade in the face of increasing competition from both aircraft and container ships. The *Rangitane* was withdrawn in May 1968, the *Ruahine* in the following July and the *Rangitoto* in July 1969.

All three ships were sold to the Hong Kong-based CY Tung Group, which had them refitted and improved for round-the-world passenger and cargo sailings with limited, but more luxurious first class accommodation. They were teamed under the banner of a Tung subsidiary, the Orient Overseas Line. The former *Rangitoto* sailed as the *Orient Carnaval*, the *Rangitane* as the *Oriental Esmeralda* and the *Ruahine* as the *Oriental Rio*. Several further, but steadily less profitable years of service followed. The former *Ruahine* was withdrawn and then scrapped in 1974 and the other two followed in 1976.

## SITMAR LINE

### The FAIRSEA

The Sitmar Line, which derived its name from its more official title, Societa Italiana Trasporti Maritti-mi, entered the low-fare Australian (and Latin American) migrant trades in the late forties, in the postwar boom when not only migrants but also refugees and displaced persons needed inexpensive transport. For some years, their largest ship on the Australian run was the 13,400-ton *Fairsea*.

The *Fairsea* dated from 1941, having been launched in March of that year by the Sun Shipbuilding &

Roger Sherlock

*Sitmar's* Fairsea *is shown here at Capetown, after the closure of the Suez Canal in 1967 and near to the end of her sailing days.*

Drydock Company at Chester, Pennsylvania. She was built as the *Rio de la Plata*, one of four combination passenger-cargo ships for the Moore McCormack Lines' run between New York and the east coast of South America. Soon afterwards, as America prepared for war, she was handed over to the US Navy and redesigned as the auxiliary aircraft carrier USS *Charger*. Completed in March 1942, she was given to Britain as part of the lend-lease programme and not returned to the Americans until 1946, at which time she was laid-up for three years, assuredly surplus to future Navy requirements.

The *Charger* was sold to Sitmar in 1949, and registered under their Panamanian subsidiary, the Alvion Steamship Corporation. Rebuilt from an aircraft carrier into a very functional, quite austere passenger ship, she was given berthing for 1440 tourist class travellers. Renamed *Fairsea*, she was routed mostly to Australia in those early years. Some years later, in 1957–58, in preparation for a long-term

charter to the British Government to carry outbound migrants to Australia, she underwent an extensive refit at Trieste. She was made fully-air conditioned, given remodelled public rooms, and the cabins were rearranged as 81 doubles, 124 four-berth, 35 six-berth, 23 eight-berth and 36 larger rooms. All but ten of these were without private facilities. She was placed under the Italian flag just prior to entering a new round-the-world service, from Southampton to Port Said, Suez, Aden, Fremantle, Melbourne, Sydney, Auckland, Papeete, Balboa, Cristobal, Curaçao and Lisbon before returning to the UK.

The *Fairsea* continued in her worldwide tourist and migrant service until she was seriously damaged by an engine room fire while some 900 miles west of the Panama Canal, on 29 January 1969. Immobilized, she was later taken in tow to Balboa by the American freighter *Louise Lykes*. Her owners' appraisal was almost expected: in view of her advanced years, she was beyond economic repair. That summer, she was towed gently across the Atlantic to La Spezia in Italy for scrapping.

### The CASTEL FELICE

The *Castel Felice*, Sitmar's eldest passenger ship, was one of those interesting cases of an older ship seeking renewed life. In all, she had had nine changes of name.

Built by Alexander Stephen & Sons of Glasgow in 1930, as the *Kenya* for the British India Line, she traded between India, the Seychelles and East Africa, with passengers divided between 66 in first class, 120 in second class and 1700 in deck steerage. In 1940, she was requisitioned as a wartime transport and then, in 1941, reclassified as a landing ship under the name HMS *Hydra*. Soon afterwards, the British Ministry of War Shipping changed this to HMS *Keren*.

Surviving the war intact, she was sold to the Ministry of Transport and within two years, by 1948, was laid-up in Scotland's Holy Loch. However, the

*The former wartime auxiliary aircraft carrier* Fairsky *was bought by Sitmar in 1950, but was not completed for passenger service until 1958. She finished her career at Manila, serving as a permanently-berthed gambling casino.*

changes that followed were coupled with complications. She was stranded after breaking adrift in a gale, in February 1949, but was subsequently refloated and towed to Glasgow for repairs. At the repair yards, she reverted to the name *Kenya*, but then soon afterwards was sold to the Alva Steamship Co, another Sitmar subsidiary, who renamed her *Keren*, then back to *Kenya* and finally as *Fairstone*. During 1950, again renamed *Kenya*, she went back to lay-up in the Holy Loch, later followed by a series of voyages under tow: first to Falmouth, then to Antwerp and finally to Genoa (in August 1951). She was again briefly renamed *Keren*, and finally rechristened as *Castel Felice*, and began flying the Italian colours.

Extensively rebuilt with 596 first class and 944 tourist class berths, she began sailing for Sitmar in October 1952, first to Australia, then to the Caribbean and finally to the east coast of South America. Her mainstay was, as always in her commercial career, the migrant trades. During 1955, she underwent more extensive alterations at Genoa, during which her tonnage reached 12,478 (from 9890 in her British India

days) and her berthing plans were rearranged to accommodate a mere 28 passengers in first class and 1173 in tourist class. She entered regular Australian service three years later, in April 1958, and began sailings from Bremerhaven, Rotterdam and Southampton to Port Said, Suez, Aden, Fremantle, Melbourne, Sydney, Auckland returning to Europe either via Singapore, Colombo, Aden, Suez, Port Said and Naples or Papeete, Balboa, the Panama Canal, Curaçao and Lisbon. Her capacity was later adjusted to accommodate 1405 passengers, all of them in tourist class. Soon after the *Castel Felice* was re-registered in Panama, in 1968, Sitmar lost its Australian migrant contract given by the British Government and therefore much of its earlier passenger trade disappeared. At forty years of age, the veteran *Castel Felice* was delivered to Taiwanese breakers, in October 1970, after completing her last trip out to Melbourne at Sydney.

## The FAIRSKY

Another wartime ship that was later converted for passenger service, the 12,400-ton *Fairsky* was ordered from the Western Pipe & Steel Co of San Francisco in 1941, by the American-flag Isthmian Lines. She was launched as the C3-type freighter *Steel Artisan*, but soon afterwards was taken over by the US Navy and redesigned and outfitted as the auxiliary aircraft carrier USS *Barnes*. Upon completion, however, much like the *Fairsea*, she was transferred to the Royal Navy under lend-lease and renamed HMS *Attacker*. With an accident-free record, she was returned to the US Navy in January 1946, and thereafter laid-up pending disposal. A year later, she was sold to National Bulk Carriers Incorporated for intended conversion to an oil tanker, but plans never materialized and the vessel was resold, in 1950, to Sitmar. She remained untouched until 1952, when, as the *Castel Forte*, she was moved to the Newport News Shipyards in Virginia for conversion to a freighter. Once again, very little actually took place and the ship remained untouched for another five years.

In 1957, the hull was taken to the Bethlehem Steel Shipyards on Staten Island, in New York Harbor, and therein began her rebuilding to a passenger ship, a job completed in Genoa. She entered service as the *Fairsky*, in June 1958, sailing on the Australian run from Southampton. Fully air-conditioned and with contemporary decorations, she had a maximum capacity of 1461 passengers. Operated by Sitmar, her registered owners were the Fairline Shipping Corporation of Panama.

The *Fairsky* remained on the Australian migrant and tourist runs until March 1972, when she began a twenty-month lay-up at Southampton. With her original role now superseded by the airlines and remaining migrant contract left to the Chandris Lines, the *Fairsky* was used thereafter for Australian and Southeast Asian cruising. It was during one of these voyages, on 23 June 1977, while in Djakarta Bay during a cruise from Sydney to Bali, that she struck the sunken wreck of the 2100-ton Indonesian passenger ship *Klingi* and was holed, began to flood and had to be beached. With all of her passengers and most of her crew sent home, she was, within six days, patched and then sailed to Singapore for temporary repairs. In December, she was sold to Hong Kong shipbreakers and delivered in Junk Bay, only to be resold, in the following March, to the Peninsular Tourist Shipping Corporation and taken to Manila to become a floating hotel, leisure centre and casino. Renamed *Philippine Tourist*, she was berthed in the Manila docks for over two years. I recall seeing her, with green stripes painted on her single funnel, while inbound aboard the container ship *President Taft* in July 1978. Once on board, it was quite evident that she was not in the best possible condition. She later burnt out completely at her berth, on 3 November 1979. The wreck was towed across to Hong Kong in the following May for demolition which proceeded swiftly.

## The FAIRSTAR

Sitmar saw nothing but a bright future ahead for the Australian migrant trade and the low-fare tourist market when they bought the 20,500-ton *Oxfordshire* from Britain's Bibby Line. Actually, the former troop ship was to have been converted into an all-tourist class liner and then leased to Sitmar, but near to completion, in the spring of 1964, she was bought outright and became the *Fairstar*.

The ship had been completed in early 1957, by Fairfields of Glasgow, as Britain's last peacetime trooper, with accommodation for 220 in first class, 100 in second class, 180 in third class and 1000 troops. Built as a joint project between Bibby and the British Government, she was commercially managed for her government troop voyages, sailing out to Cyprus, the Middle East, the Far East, etc. Then, when the Government abruptly terminated their charter, in late 1962, and thereafter decided to airlift all military personnel, the *Oxfordshire* was offered for sale or charter.

Sitmar had her converted at the Wilton-Fijenoord yards at Schiedam in the Netherlands and then completed, because of a Dutch strike, by Harland &

*Sitmar's* Fairstar *anchored off Savu Savu in the Fiji Islands, in the late 1970s.*

Wolff at Southampton. Given a major reconstruction, she was made into a contemporary passenger ship with 1910 berths and such amenities as two large restaurants – one specially for children, an outdoor lido with pool, closed circuit television, a nursery as well as separate children's and teenagers' facilities, a 360-seat cinema, no less than eight bars, a passenger garage and private showers and toilets for nearly half of the cabins.

Introduced in May 1964, she joined the *Fairsea*, *Castel Felice* and *Fairsky* on the Australian trade and brought Sitmar's total passenger capacity to over 5000 berths. Like the other ships, she alternated her homeward runs via either the Suez Canal or the Panama Canal. When the trade had vanished almost entirely and all of the other Sitmar passenger ships had been withdrawn, the *Fairstar* made her final line voyage, in the summer of 1973. Thereafter, she has been used solely for cruising from Australia, a role which she continues most successfully and profitably to this day.

## LLOYD TRIESTINO

### The GALILEO GALILEI and GUGLIELMO MARCONI

In the boom years of the late fifties and early sixties, just prior to the first appearance of the jet in regions east of the Suez, Italy's Lloyd Triestino ordered their biggest liners of all, the 27,900-ton sisters *Galileo Galilei* and *Guglielmo Marconi*. Built in a highly productive era for Italian shipbuilders, between the completion of the luxurious *Leonardo da Vinci* of 1960 and the superliners *Michelangelo* and *Raffaello* in 1965, these new Australian liners were among the very finest ever to sail in that service. They were both built by Cantieri Riuniti dell'Adriatico at Monfalcone – the *Galileo*, as she was called, was commissioned in April 1963, the *Marconi* in the following November. Stabilizer-equipped and fully-air conditioned, they had very modern accommodation for 156 first class and 1594 tourist class passengers. Replacing a much smaller and slower trio, the *Australia, Neptunia* and *Oceania*, which were transferred to the Italian Line, the new twins were placed on a monthly schedule sailing between Genoa, Naples and Messina out to Port Said, Suez, Aden, Fremantle, Melbourne and Sydney. The passage from Genoa to Sydney was made in twenty-three days. In later years, they were occasionally sent home via the Pacific, Panama and the Caribbean.

Like almost all other state-owned passenger ships in the Italian fleet, these ships proved to be increasingly expensive, especially as much of their migrant and tourist trade began to wither. In January 1976, as the *Augustus* was retired, the *Marconi* was transferred to the Italian Line and used for about a year on the run to Rio, Santos, Montevideo and Buenos Aires with the *Cristoforo Colombo*. In 1977, both of the Lloyd Triestino liners were withdrawn and terminated that historic company's passenger operations. The *Marconi* was reactivated in December 1978, for cruising from New York under the banner of the newly-formed Italian Line Cruises International. Far less than the expected success, it was abruptly ended in the following summer and the ship kept in uncertainty, first at Port Canaveral, Florida and then at Naples. Years later, in 1983, she was sold to the Costa Line and has undergone a $50 million transformation into the cruise ship *Costa Riviera*, sailing from Port Everglades, Florida on weekly runs to the Caribbean.

The *Galileo*, while briefly laid-up at Palermo between 1977–79, was later reactivated for European cruising, first for Italian Line Cruises International and then under charter to Chandris Cruises. She has since been bought outright by that firm and re-registered in Panama, but has retained the name *Galileo*. Presently, she is kept in American waters, sailing from New York in the summer months and from Florida for most of the remainder, on one to seven day cruises.

*The* Guglielmo Marconi, *after nearly fifteen years on the Australian trade, was used for several months as a Caribbean cruise ship, sailing from New York, under the banner of Italian Line Cruises International; withdrawn within six months, she was sold years later to the Costa Line.*

Italian Line Cruises International

Antonio Scrimali

## CHANDRIS LINES

### The PATRIS

The Greek-flag Chandris Group of Companies, which would become one of the largest and most profitable liner companies of all, first began deep-sea passenger services, in December 1959, under the banner of the Europe-Australia Line. The first of several second-hand passenger ships, the company bought Union-Castle's superfluous *Bloemfontein Castle*, built at Belfast in 1950, and had her refitted for the Australian migrant trade. Built originally with just over 700 berths, she was refitted for 36 in first class and 1000 in tourist (later altered to 1400, all one-class). She was renamed *Patris*; carrying migrants outbound from Piraeus and Limassol to Port Said, Aden, Fremantle, Melbourne and Sydney, and returning with general tourist traffic and large quantities of refrigerated beef.

Highly profitable for well over a decade, she was later assigned, in 1972, to cruise service from Australia and on the run up to Singapore. Between February and November 1975, she performed a noble duty, serving as a temporary accommodation ship for residents of the Australian city of Darwin, which had been nearly destroyed by a tropical storm. In the following year, she returned to the Mediterranean and was assigned to tourist and ferry services on the Adriatic, sailing between Ancona, Patras and Piraeus. Refitted, she was rearranged to carry 1000 passengers and 300 cars. She changed hands three years later, going to the Karageorgis Lines and becoming their *Mediterranean Island* and then, in 1981, the *Mediterranean Star*.

*The* Ellinis, *a popular ship on the Australian route for ten years, 1963–73, subsequently used as a cruise ship, is shown laid-up, in June 1984, after nearly four years at Perama in Greece. The aft funnel of the former* Australis *can be seen to the right.*

### The ELLINIS

The enormous success of the *Patris* soon led to a whole fleet of Chandris migrant and tourist liners. The French *Bretagne*, chartered from 1960, was bought outright in September 1961 and refitted as the *Brittany*. Unfortunately, her career was quite short-lived; she was totally destroyed while undergoing engine repairs, in a shipyard fire at Skaramanga in Greece in April 1963 and had to be scrapped. Almost immediately thereafter, the US-flag Matson Lines announced that *Lurline*, built in 1932 and a longtime favourite on the California-Hawaiian cruise trade, was for sale. It would be the first of several American acquisitions by the Chandris Group. The *Lurline*, renamed *Ellinis* ('Greek Lady'), was refitted on the Tyne with a capacity increased from 761 first class to 1642 tourist class berths. She began sailing on the Australian route, from Southampton through the Mediterranean and via the Suez Canal out to Australia (in later years, she would return home by the Pacific and Caribbean routes); she also would put into Port Everglades in Florida and occasionally at New York for some eastbound transatlantic traffic. Fares on these Atlantic passages began at $175 in the late sixties.

The *Ellinis* ran her final Australian trips in 1973 and then was transferred almost exclusively to cruising –

*The* Australis *arriving at Lisbon, in November 1977, on her final 'line voyage' to Australia.*

from Southampton, Amsterdam, Genoa and Piraeus. There was even a stint of charter cruising from Capetown. Finally decommissioned in the autumn of 1980, after nearly fifty years of continuous service, she and her sister *Britanis* (the former *Monterey*, later renamed *Lurline* as well), are tremendous credits to their original builders, the Bethlehem Steel Company of Quincy, Massachusetts. Moored at an anchorage in Perama Bay, near Piraeus, the *Ellinis* has been alongside several other old, out-of-work passenger ships. In early 1985, she was secured to the former *Australis*, *Regina Prima* and *Ariane*, all retired Chandris passenger ships. With little hope of ever returning to sea, the *Ellinis* is now providing parts that are shipped to the US for use aboard the ageing *Britanis*.

Luis Miguel Correia

*A close-up view of the bridge area and forward funnel aboard the* Britanis.

## The AUSTRALIS

The one-time running-mate to the *United States*, the fastest liner ever built, the *America* of 1940 was laid up in the autumn of 1964, following the jet invasion, increased operation costs and some labour problems. Once again, the Chandris organisation saw great potential. Rebuilt at Piraeus as the *Australis*, her original 1046-berth capacity was converted to 2258 berths, all of them in tourist class. After her entry in the Australian trade, in the late summer of 1965, John Havers recalled paying a visit to the ship at Southampton. 'She still had some similarity to the Grand Hotels of the past, with the large doors and two-deck high public rooms. She was, of course, another long lasting tribute to American ship-building. My overall impression was of tremendous passenger carrying capacity. Deck after deck of cabins, giving a feeling of a 50,000 tonner and not the 34,500 tons she was credited with.' She was flagship to the booming, highly profitable Chandris Australian liner trade. Leonard Weir, an entertainments officer aboard her and several other Chandris liners, also had recollections. 'Outbound, we were usually full-up to the very last berth, which meant nearly 2300 passengers on the *Australis*. Most of the passengers were migrants, travelling on a £10 fare all the way to Melbourne or Sydney. We'd have three sittings for every meal: one

just for children and then two for adults. To the company accountants, the outward trip had already paid for the homeward run. Returning to Europe with fewer passengers, we usually had three types of passenger: the Australians as tourists, the "wool people" and the unhappy migrants who would not stay.'

The *Australis* closed out the Chandris Australian service in the autumn of 1977, the last of the Government contract ships carrying migrants. Thereafter, new settlers would travel by air. After a very short, unsuccessful stint as a New York-based cruise ship, ironically under her former name *America*, she was sent to the Mediterranean for further cruise voyages, but as the *Italis* and with her forward 'dummy' funnel removed. In November 1979, she was laid-up permanently at Perama, but with continual rumour that she would become a West African hotel ship. In preparation, she was even renamed *Noga*, but little else has taken place.

## The BRITANIS

When the Matson Lines of San Francisco offered another of their famed prewar liners, the *Monterey* of

Antonio Scrimali

*The* Achille Lauro, *the former Dutch* Willem Ruys, *has now resumed cruise sailings after the bankruptcy of the Lauro Line in 1982. She returned to service, under charter to Chandris Cruises, in the spring of 1985.*

1932 (which had been called *Matsonia* and then *Lurline*), for sale in 1970, little time was wasted in agreeing on a sale price. A near-sister to the earlier *Ellinis*, this vessel had even more modern accommodation and would be ideal for conversion for both the Australian trade and cruising. Her capacity was radically enlarged as well, from 761 berths in first class to 1632 in all-tourist class cabins. She entered service, after a thorough refit at Piraeus, in February 1971 as the *Britanis*.

As the Australian migrant trade and the lucrative Australian Government contract began to dwindle, the *Britanis* was re-routed to full-time cruising by 1975. She has, since 1981, been employed almost exclusively in US waters, sailing under the banner of a Chandris affiliate company, Fantasy Cruises. Enjoying yet more great success, even past her fiftieth year, she is used for one- to seven-cruises and even occasionally for some 'day trips', voyages that leave port in early morning and then return by later afternoon.

## LAURO LINE

### The ACHILLE LAURO and ANGELINA LAURO

When the Dutch-flag Nederland Line and Royal Rotterdam Lloyd closed out their final round-the-world passenger services in the autumn of 1964, they promptly sought buyers for their two liners, the 20,500-ton *Oranje* of 1939 and the 23,100-ton *Willem Ruys* of 1947. Italy's Lauro Line, long interested in the Australian trade, were contemplating two new 27,000-tonners to replace the small, converted aircraft carriers *Roma* and *Sydney*. In the two Dutch liners, both of them in superb condition, the Lauro Line saw a bright future. The orders for new tonnage were cancelled and the older ships sent to separate Italian yards for drastic facelifts and alterations. In an extraordinary coincidence, the *Oranje*, renamed as the *Angelina Lauro*, was seriously damaged by a fire while being refitted at Genoa, on 24 August 1965, while five days later, at a Palermo shipyard, the *Achille Lauro*, ex-*Willem Ruys*, was badly burnt as well. Although their deliveries were delayed considerably, they finally reappeared as exceptional modern tourist liners, with lido decks, pools, contemporary public rooms and cabins, closed circuit television and tall, eye-catching tapered funnels with smoke-deflecting tops. The

*Angelina Lauro* was listed as having a capacity for 189 first class and 1427 tourist class passengers; the *Achille Lauro* had 152 first class berths and some 1500 in tourist class. The ships were routed from Bremerhaven and Southampton out to Australia via the Suez Canal (or South African Cape) and then often returned via the Caribbean or, in a most unusual itinerary, via the southern tip of South America.

Both ships were withdrawn from 'line voyage' services in 1973 and thereafter used solely for cruising. While under charter to the Costa Line, the *Angelina*

*Lauro* burnt out at St Thomas in the West Indies, on 31 March 1979. Later salvaged, she left there, bound for the scrappers at Kaohsiung, in late July, only to sink in the Pacific while under tow, on 24 September. When the Lauro Line declared bankruptcy in early 1982, the *Achille Lauro* was impounded for debt, and for a time kept at Tenerife before being moved to Genoa. Three years later, in a reorganization plan and with a Chandris charter for Mediterranean cruising from Genoa, Lauro Line resumed services with the former *Willem Ruys*.

*The* Angelina Lauro, *another former Dutch liner, the* Oranje, *met her end while docked at St Thomas in the Caribbean. Destroyed by fire, she partially capsized and was later raised, but sank in the Pacific while under tow to the Taiwanese scrapyards.*

## MESSAGERIES MARITIMES

The CALEDONIEN and TAHITIEN

Another of the many Messageries Maritimes passenger services was a long-haul run from Marseilles

Luis Miguel Correia

Structurally altered and with her aft mast and kingposts
removed, the Atalante, the former Tahitien, now sails as a
Mediterranean cruise ship.

*Alex Duncan*

across to the Caribbean and through Panama before
steaming south in the Pacific to several islands and a
turnaround at Sydney. The last ships used on this run
were another pair of combination passenger-cargo
liners, the *Caledonien* and *Tahitien*. The former was
built by Ateliers et Chantiers de France at Dunkirk
and delivered in September 1952; the latter came from
the naval dockyard at Brest and was commissioned in
May 1953. At 12,700 tons, they had provision for
considerable cargo as well as 74 first class, 84 tourist
and 208 third class passengers.

Both ships continued for some years in their
intended service, carrying Government passengers,
the mail and important cargo to several island
outposts. However, just as Messageries Maritimes
were reviewing their passenger fleet and intending to
eventually withdraw this pair, the *Tahitien* suffered
an engine room fire, in the Pacific, on 2 May 1969.
Disabled, she had to be towed to Balboa and
temporarily repaired, finally returning to Marseilles
on 31 August. Following major repairs, she did not
resume her schedules until 27 December. She was

withdrawn in 1971 and laid-up for a time. Both ships
went to Greek owners; the *Caledonien* transferred to
the Efthymiadis Lines, was registered in Cyprus,
renamed *Nisos Kypros* and shortly afterwards *Island of
Cyprus*. Used in eastern Mediterranean passenger
service, she was broken-up in 1975. The *Tahitien*,
having been sold to Aphrodite Cruises, was refitted as
the cruise ship *Atalante*. She remains in the Mediterranean service at the time of writing.

# CHAPTER SEVEN

# FAR EASTERN WATERS

## NIPPON YUSEN KAISHA

### The HIKAWA MARU

Prior to the Second World War, the Japanese maintained passenger ship services across the Pacific to the United States, to South America and Northern Europe via the Suez Canal and even an extensive run that went completely around the world. But the great majority of the liners on these routes were lost in combat. Even the nation's biggest liners yet, the 27,700-ton *Kashiwara Maru* and *Izumo Maru*, were converted to aircraft carriers and then lost in 1944. At the time of the surrender, in the summer of 1945, the only survivor was one 11,600-tonner, the *Hikawa Maru*.

The *Hikawa Maru* had been built in 1930, at the Yokohama Dock Company yard. She sailed from Kobe on the 13 May that year, on her maiden crossing to Seattle. She and her two sisters, the *Hiye Maru* and *Heian Maru* (both also lost during the war), were certainly moderate by international standards. They were each 536 feet in length and fitted with accommodation for 76 in first class, 69 in tourist and 186 in third class. They provided a regular service where there was little need for great speed and high luxury. The *Hikawa Maru* and her sisters, capable of 17 knots, were powered by Danish-built Burmeister & Wain diesels.

From 1941 onwards, the *Hikawa Maru* served as a hospital ship, painted overall in white and with bold Red Cross markings. Most probably, this was the reason for her freedom from Allied attack and thus her survival. She was taken by the American invasion forces in August 1945, and used for trooping duty across the Pacific. Two years later, she was thoughtfully returned to her original Japanese owners, the Nippon Yusen Kaisha, the NYK Line, who were still very much depleted of practically all deep-sea tonnage. The *Hikawa Maru* was assuredly the largest survivor in the Japanese merchant fleet.

Like the defeated Germans, the Japanese were not in a position to reconstruct their passenger fleets. In fact, following the gradual recommencement of shipbuilding efforts, the greatest attention was placed on freighters that would help replenish their badly damaged economy. Consequently, the *Hikawa Maru* was to be NYK Line's only postwar liner. She was restored in 1947, and refitted to carry 80 in first class and the remainder in a third class that was divided between 69 in third class 'A' and 127 in third class 'B'. The style of her passenger quarters made no attempt at the modern, but instead copied much of her original 1930 arrangement. Because of shortages and labour difficulties, the *Hikawa Maru* did not resume sailing until 1950. Again, her trade route was trans-Pacific – between Kobe, Yokohama, Vancouver and Seattle, with an occasional call at Honolulu.

NYK's transpacific passenger services were never quite rekindled with the same sense of activity as in prewar days. The American President Lines, particularly with their new *President Cleveland* and *President Wilson*, dominated the luxury run to the Orient. Alternative travel (for migrants, refugees, the military, etc) was provided by a large fleet of American troop ships. Britain's P&O-Orient Lines extended their passenger routes in 1958 to include Pacific operations from North America and excitedly saw the Pacific as the 'last frontier' of ocean travel. At best, they enjoyed several good years as a round-trip cruise operator. There were, however, some periods of peaked interest in reviving 'big liner' Pacific services. In the very fine *Damned by Destiny*, published in 1982, authors David L Williams and Richard P De Kerbrech refer quite extensively to projected large liners for the NYK Line, as well as a 50,000-tonner for American President Lines, which it is generally believed would be named *President Washington*. None of these projects ever came to pass.

When the *Hikawa Maru* reached thirty in 1960, there was little attempt to replace her. Alone, the directorate at NYK felt that the aircraft industry had made sufficient inroads on long-haul Pacific passenger services to discourage any new liners with the obvious exception of cruise ships. However, the old liner had

Hisashi Noma Collection

*The only survivor of Japan's large prewar passenger fleet, the* Hikawa Maru *of the NYK Line sailed until 1960 and has since served as a hotel and museum ship at Yokohama.*

a very special place in the hearts of many Japanese maritime enthusiasts. Instead of proceeding to the dreaded scrap-heap, she was converted to a floating museum, dormitory ship and restaurant. She was opened to the public in 1961, permanently docked at Yokohama at a special berth adjacent to that port's large Ocean Terminal and in the shadows of the Port Tower.

In the summer of 1978, during a Pacific cruise aboard the container ship *President Taft*, I visited Japan's only surviving prewar liner. The notes in my diary from that time read, 'The *Hikawa Maru* is like some steam engine of a bygone era, an antique glider or motor car – the perfect gimmick for a tourist attraction. I seemed to be the only visitor on this

otherwise sweltering afternoon (10 July). 300 yen bought a ticket, a small photo of the ship and permission to walk along the narrow jetty and up the wooden staircase to the Main Deck entrance. Some Japanese women in white kimonos and aprons hovered about, fussing over nothing, it seemed. Not a flicker of air on board. A floating steambath. I followed tourist arrows. The saloon was done in dark woods, chocolate coloured chairs in some ancient velour fabric, stained glass skylights and old world globe lighting fixtures. The mood was of yesteryear. It was certainly transpacific, the 1930s, the way it must have been. Very quiet, not very elegant, but comfortable. A gentle comfort, in fact. Japanese designers and decorators were obviously not opting for high modernity. Well-heeled merchants, company officials and even the Crown Prince once sat here.

'Onward to some staterooms, gazed at over a black velvet rope, a sitting room, a cramped first class bedroom, faded curtains, poor lighting, a big porcelain tub, foot stools, huge separate wardrobes – how it must have been.

'Along the lower deck corridors, there were endless strands of well-painted wires overhead. Dark and hot. More cabins, all growing smaller. Public lavatories, all original, stuffed with the most oversized fixtures in heavy porcelain and with very limited privacy.

'There was an outdoor theatre over the aft cargo hatch. Peeling paint on the bridge wings. Tarnished brass in the wheelhouse. Very old-fashioned lifeboats. The funnel colours had faded. Here she sat – motionless – almost without any sparks of life as the city-port of Yokohama around her hummed and drummed in high activity.'

Now at over fifty-five years of age, the *Hikawa Maru* remains an interesting attraction at the port of Yokohama. For the liner enthusiast, she is well worth a visit.

## MITSUI–OSK LINES

### The BRAZIL MARU and ARGENTINA MARU

In July 1954 *Brazil Maru*, the first of two transpacific liners built by the OSK Line (Oska Shosen Kaisha), specifically for the migrant trade to South America, entered service. A 10,100-tonner, she was built by the Mitsubishi Shipyards at Kobe with a basic freighter hull that was designed also to handle 12 passengers in cabin class, 68 in tourist and 902 in third class. The first class section was normal high-standard freighter-style quarters with dining room, smoking room-lounge and six double cabins. Tourist class was less fancy, with 17 four-berth rooms. The third class

*Built especially for the migrant trade to South America, the* Brazil Maru *(1954), in the foreground, and the* Argentina Maru *(1958) are shown in a rare occasion together, at the Yokohama Ocean Terminal.*

Hisashi Noma Collection

consisted of all dormitory accommodation. Powered by Mitsubishi diesels, the *Brazil Maru* had a single screw and a service speed of 16 knots. Her routing was quite extensive: from Kobe and Yokohama across the Pacific to Los Angeles and then down to Cristobal and the Panama Canal, and onto La Guaira, Salvador (Brazil), Santos, Rio de Janeiro, Montevideo and Buenos Aires, before reversing course and heading home.

The migrant business obviously prospered. In 1958, an improved version of this ship was added. She too came from the Mitsubishi yards at Kobe, but was fitted instead with American-made Westinghouse turbines. Slightly larger, at 10,864 tons, her basic freighter design was fitted for twelve cabin passengers, ten in tourist 'A', 72 in tourist 'B', and 960 in third class. Named *Argentina Maru*, she sailed from Kobe on her maiden sailing to South America on 2 June of that year.

In December 1963, the Mitsui Line merged with the OSK Line, and these ships began sailing for the Mitsui–OSK Lines, but at a time when the Latin American migrant trade was steadily declining. Two years later, both ships were extensively refitted, primarily to cater more and more for North American passengers. The *Brazil Maru*'s accommodation was restyled to take twelve passengers in cabin class and 348 in tourist, with most of the earlier dormitories disappearing in the refit. The *Argentina Maru* was adjusted to take 23 in cabin class and 352 in tourist class. For a time, their services continued.

The *Argentina Maru* was withdrawn first, in February 1972. Renamed *Nippon Maru*, she was thereafter used for student and budget cruising, often to the North American west coast. She survived in this role until late 1976. She reached Kaohsiung on Taiwan, on 20 December, and was soon scrapped.

*Large crowds, in festive, cheering mood, are 'sending off' family and friends to South America aboard the* Argentina Maru. *The ships often returned with their third class accommodation practically empty.*

Hisashi Noma Collection

The *Brazil Maru* was laid-up in March 1973. In September, she made a special goodwill cruise to China, but then was sold to the Toba (Japan) Marine Cultural Council. Like her earlier predecessor, the *Hikawa Maru*, she was selected for conversion to a museum, recreation centre and restaurant. She was rebuilt for this role at the Mitsubishi yards at Kobe and then later moved to her permanent berth at Toba in Ise Bay, near Nagoya, being officially opened to the public on 5 July 1974. Now, rather ironically, two of Japan's three noted deep-sea postwar liners survive to date as museum ships.

At the time of writing, Japanese passenger shipping is restricted to cruise ships that sail mostly in Far Eastern waters. To cross the Pacific by passenger ship is now a rare opportunity.

## HAMBURG AMERICAN LINE/NORTH GERMAN LLOYD

The FRANKFURT, HAMBURG and HANNOVER, and the BAYERNSTEIN, HESSENSTEIN and SCHWABENSTEIN
At the end of the Second World War, in 1945, both the once mighty Hamburg American Line and North German Lloyd were depleted of almost all deep-sea tonnage and were left with little more than some coastal ships and harbour-craft. Gradually, they would rebuild their fleets, but under strict Allied supervision and only with small cargo ships at first. The first passenger ships were not planned until 1953–54, and surprisingly not for the prestige North Atlantic trade to New York, but for the more extensive route to the Far East. Six modified cargo liners, three for each firm, were ordered from the Bremer Vulkan shipyards at Bremen: the *Frankfurt*, *Hamburg* and *Hannover* for the Hamburg American Line and the *Bayernstein*, *Hessenstein* and *Schwabenstein* for the North German Lloyd.

At 9000 tons each, they were fitted with M.A.N. type diesels that rendered a service speed of 16½ knots. The fully-air conditioned passenger spaces were of the highest possible standard and were

*Rather strangely, the first new postwar passenger ships to be built for both the Hamburg American Line and the North German Lloyd were not for the prestige Atlantic trade to New York, but for the Far Eastern run via Suez. The Hamburg (shown here) and five sisterships maintained a weekly service together with six twelve-passenger freighters until the mid 1960s.*

Roger Sherlock

arranged on four decks; there was a maximum of eighty-six berths, all of them appropriately listed as first class. All of the staterooms had private bathroom facilities, individually controlled thermostats and extra sofa beds if required. The public rooms, all of them elegantly decorated in contemporary styles, included a main lounge, reading-writing room, cocktail bar, glass-enclosed promenade space, winter garden and restaurant. There was also an open-air swimming pool on deck.

The six ships were routed on a ninety-five-day round-trip schedule, sailing from Hamburg, Bremerhaven, Antwerp, Rotterdam and Southampton to Genoa, Port Said, Djibouti, Penang, Singapore, Hong Kong, Yokohama, Shimizu, Nagoya and Kobe before reversing course and repeating the itinerary. Captain Heinz-Dieter Schmidt, whose father was a master of the *Hessenstein*, states, 'Each of these ships, the first of the so-called "combo liners", had very deluxe accommodation. Fifty per cent of their travellers were Germans; the others were various Europeans and many British military and civil servants, who preferred the superior standard of these ships. They worked on a 3½-month schedule, with one sailing each week from Northern Europe, rotating between one of the eighty-six-passenger ships and a twelve-passenger freighter. Of course, cargo was very much a part of the livelihood of a ship like the *Bayernstein*. There were six holds for 10,000 tons of freight: general cargo outwards and items such as rubber, coconut oil (there was special tank space for 1500 tons), latex, textiles and the beginnings of the mass-produced goods from Japan and Hong Kong carried homewards.'

'However, ships like the 16-knot *Bayernstein* class were outmoded by the mid-sixties. They were sold off, to the giant CY Tung group. A new 22-knot *Westphalia* class of freighters took over the Far Eastern service. My father, who had also commanded the previous *Hessenstein*, was then at the helm of the new *Hessenstein*, built in 1967.'

Placed under the Liberian flag, for Tung's Orient Overseas Line, the ships were renamed respectively the *Oriental Hero*, *Oriental Inventor*, *Oriental Warrior*, *Oriental Lady*, *Oriental Musician* and *Oriental Ruler*. They were assigned to 120-day round voyages, with their passenger quarters in use, from New York, Baltimore, Charleston, New Orleans, Houston, Galveston and then a transit of the Panama Canal before calling at Los Angeles, and then continuing across the Pacific to Yokohama, Nagoya, Kobe, Pusan, Yosu and/or Inchon (in Korea), Keelung, Kaohsiung and Hong Kong. Passenger operations continued in full force until 1973, when high oil prices suddenly curtailed much of Tung's liner services. By 1976, all of these former German ships were downgraded and used in the tramp trades. The *Oriental Warrior* (ex-*Hamburg*) were lost by fire off Florida in 1972, and the other five were subsequently broken-up at either Hong Kong or Kaohsiung in 1978–79.

*The* Kananga, *one of the two combination passenger-cargo liners that still sail on the Antwerp–Zaire run. There is space for seventy-one first class passengers in her aft superstructure.*

# THE LAST LINE VOYAGES

## COMPAGNIE MARITIME BELGE

The FABIOLAVILLE and KANANGA
Although almost all of the once very common 'blue water' routes to places like South America, Africa and Australia had withered and then disappeared completely by the 1970s, it is, quite ironically, one of the

earlier colonial runs that survives at the time of writing. It is the run between Belgium and Zaire, the former Belgian Congo. The exact itinerary is between Antwerp and Matadi, with sailings every three weeks in each direction and calls en route at Tenerife, Dakar

and Abidjan. The two ships used, the *Fabiolaville* and *Kananga*, are among the very last of their kind, the once ubiquitous traditional passenger-cargo combination.

Built at the Cockerill shipyards at Hoboken in Belgium, the two ships, while identical sisters, are in fact owned by separate firms. The *Fabiolaville* is registered to the Compagnie Maritime Belge, the Belgian Line, at Antwerp while the *Kananga*, as her name suggests, is owned by an African firm, the Compagnie Maritime Zairoise of Kinshasa and Matadi. The ships, designed as engines-aft replacements for the earlier *Leopoldville* and her sisters of the late 1940s and early 1950s, were delivered in June 1972 and January 1973 respectively. They have been on the West African route ever since, running a service that is one of the very few non-cruise type operations still in existence.

At 13,481 tons and with space for seventy-one first class passengers only, their accommodation is arranged on three decks. The saloon, bar, verandah, outdoor pool, children's playroom and several larger staterooms are located on the uppermost A Deck. More cabins, all of which have private facilities, are on B and C decks. The restaurant is on this lower deck and there is also a small gift shop and hairdressers. Both ships have five cargo holds with a capacity for 200 containers. They usually carry conventional manufactured items on the southbound runs and then return with goods like cocoa, rubber, coffee, copper and cobalt. The passenger berthing scheme can accommodate fifty-eight adults and thirteen children and the ships are run by a crew of sixty-three.

It is quite amazing that this type of ship with somewhat limited accommodation and a rather select run, have survived well into the 1980s.

## CURNOW SHIPPING CO

### The St Helena

When the Union Castle-Safmarine liner run ended in October 1977, there were no longer passenger sailings to the South African Cape. Even more importantly, the little South Atlantic isle of St Helena (population 5000) was left without a link. The Curnow Shipping Company of Porthleven, Helston in Cornwall, then involved in the short sea-coaster cargo trades, decided to join with the Government of St Helena and jointly form the St Helena Shipping Company. Together, they would supply a small passenger ship if the British Government would grant its passenger and supply contract for service to St Helena. Agreement was reached and in September 1978 the little *St Helena*

commenced service between Avonmouth, Las Palmas, Ascension, Jamestown on St Helena, and Capetown.

The 3150-ton *St Helena* was built in 1963 at the Burrard Drydock Company at Vancouver for a Canadian firm, the Northland Navigation Company. As the *Northland Prince*, she plied a weekly year-round service to British Columbia and Alaska sailing from Vancouver to Bella Coola, Ocean Falls, Kitimat, Prince Rupert and Stewart. The round-trip took six days. Eventually displaced by changes in local cargo shipping and shifts in the passenger trade, mostly in the form of an ever-increasing generation of far larger cruise ships, she was withdrawn and sold to Curnow during 1977. She was refitted and given improved accommodation for 88 one-class passengers (originally, she had a maximum of 110 berths), and a new small funnel was added. Now flying the British flag, she has proved to be a popular passenger ship, in fact the last to offer regular sailings to the Cape.

John Dimmock, following nearly thirty years of service with the old Union-Castle Line, served as purser aboard the *St Helena*. 'She is an ideal little vessel for people who enjoy being aboard a ship, but for those not expecting push-button service. Our passengers have been mostly St Helenans, who have priority in bookings for all sailings. We also carry Government personnel as well as passengers on family visits to Ascension. There are also the occasional tourists. Life on board is somewhat different and certainly less active than on board the big cruise ships. There are tapes for after-dinner dancing, games, quizzes, considerable officer participation and one bar. There is one forward lounge and another aft. All cabins, which include private facilities, are adequate and there is a suite with its own mini-refrigerator. There is a large open-air deck aft and a small portable steel pool is placed on the forward deck over one of the hatches. Almost all of the officers are former Union-Castle staff while the hotel staff tends to be from St Helena.

'The *St Helena* is a particularly sturdy little sea boat [321ft long overall]. She carries mostly general cargo, in fact, almost anything, and of course, important consignments of mail.'

In the spring of 1982, like so many British merchant ships, the *St Helena* was called to duty in the Falklands War. John Dimmock was on board at the time. 'In the first phase of that South Atlantic military campaign, she served as a mother ship to minesweepers for the Royal Navy. Afterward, she was chartered to the British Ministry of Defence for trooping between Ascension and Port Stanley and then to South

*The little* St Helena *at Grytviken on South Georgia during her charter to the British Ministry of Defence, from May 1982 until June 1983.*

Georgia. We had a capacity for seventy-two troops, but were run entirely like a commercial passenger ship. The troops were allowed to wear their civilian clothes, were treated as passengers and made to feel as comfortable as possible. There were quizzes every night, movies and videos as well as deck games during the daytime. Many have fond memories of the *St Helena* during this period [she resumed normal trading between Avonmouth and St Helena in the autumn of 1983].'

John Dimmock was recalled to the UK by Curnow Shipping for two temporary assignments, both of them on the South Atlantic run to Ascension, St Helena and Capetown. 'In 1983, I made two voyages in the 8262-ton *Centaur*, formerly of the Blue Funnel Line of Liverpool and then owned by the Straits Steamship Company of Singapore. She was chartered by Curnow as a temporary replacement for the *St Helena*. She was the ideal type of ship, one of the very few passenger-cargo ships still available, that also had the right sort of derricks, hatches and could work her

own cargo. She also had very comfortable passenger spaces which I seem to recall were limited to 120 berths [190 was maximum capacity on the *Centaur*]. There were St Helenans in the hotel department, while the captain and his officers were from the Straits Company. We were almost always full-up with passengers. Curnow would have liked to have kept this vessel, but her engines were run-down and then there was the delicate matter of a Singapore-registered ship working a British Government contract service. She was returned to the Straits Company in January 1984.' ·

Curnow was briefly involved in another passenger venture, in the autumn of 1983, using the 11,724-ton *World Renaissance* of the Greek-flag Epirotiki Lines. John Dimmock served once again as purser. 'Curnow had a rush of blood and, together with TFC, the big South African tour firm, they chartered this 516-passenger cruise ship. I was aboard for the first sailing, from Plymouth to Las Palmas, Freetown, St Helena and Capetown, sailing at the end of November. There were 150 passengers on board, but it was far from a happy sailing. There were delays, docking problems, difficulties with the Venezuelan stewards and waiters, and even the rationing of water. We reached Cape-town just in time to make some scheduled Christmas–

New Year holiday cruises to Mauritius. The return voyage to Plymouth was even more difficult. The crew so hated the voyage through the Bay of Biscay that they threatened to leave the ship in the Canaries and the captain would only sail as far north as Lisbon. Curnow thereafter withdrew from the charter agreement and therein ended their brief service with the *World Renaissance*.'

Used in regular service since her Falklands duty, the *St Helena* suffered an electrical fire in her engine room while sailing off West Africa in November 1984. She had to be towed to Dakar, where repairs were made. She then continued onward to Capetown and fortunately was able to resume her normal schedule. Curnow have, of course, looked into the future of its passenger service to the South Atlantic. There have been some ideas of converting a suitable cargo ship with prefabricated passenger quarters or possibly using a small ship only between Ascension and St Helena, and thereby relying on air connections to and from Ascension Airport. It seems likely that the *St Helena* has some years of service ahead. She is unique, being the only passenger vessel to travel on the once busy Cape run.

## SAFMARINE LINES

### The ASTOR

When she was delivered, in December 1981, West Germany's *Astor* was soon appraised as one of the finest and most beautifully decorated new cruise liners of the early eighties. With a capacity limited to 638 passengers for her 18,835 tons, she was intended to offer very spacious accommodation on very luxurious cruises, mostly for Europeans and in particular the West Germans. Built at the HDW Shipyards Company at Hamburg and originally thought to be called *Hammonia*, she was owned by a relatively unfamiliar company to ocean cruising, the Hamburg-based HADAG (which should not be confused with Hapag-Lloyd, owners of the cruiseship *Europa*, which is often referred to more simply as Hapag). HADAG's previous experience had been in harbour ferries and excursion boats.

After a fire at her shipyard berth which caused a six-month delay (and additional unforeseen costs),

*Safmarine Lines'* Astor *restored passenger service to the South African Cape in spring 1984 and is shown departing from Southampton on her maiden voyage to Capetown and Durban. She was purchased by the East Germans in 1985 and renamed* Arcona.

Safmarine Lines.

the *Astor* set off on her first cruise, on 14 December, from Hamburg to the Mediterranean. She was named after tycoon John Jacob Astor, whose ancestry was North German, and also after Astor cigarettes, an up-market brand that is well know in Germany. This was part of a bid to capture more of an international following and to emphasize the luxuries of the new liner. The *Astor* set off, with moderate success, on mostly two- and three-week cruises to the North Cape, Baltic, the Mediterranean and West Africa. One special longer cruise, made in the autumn of 1982, included calls at Halifax, Boston, New York, Philadelphia and Baltimore. Captain Rainer Blotenberg, marine superintendent of the German-West Africa Line, a company which would later be involved in the *Astor*'s sale to East Germany, remembered the circumstances of the ship's original creation. 'The majority of the shares in HADAG were owned by the city-state of Hamburg. At the time, work in Hamburg shipyards was very scarce and so the local government offered a special construction loan, one which ensured the employment of 1500 shipyard workers for at least eighteen months. It was all a matter of employment.

'The initial plan was to match the *Astor* with Hapag-Lloyd's new *Europa*, a 33,800-ton luxury cruise ship commissioned a month later, in January 1982. In fact, there was no match. HADAG had no experience beyond day excursions to the island of Heligoland whereas Hapag-Lloyd had 150 years of experience in deep-sea passenger shipping and consequently a vast reputation and popularity. Combined with the delays in construction and subsequent cost overruns, the *Astor* was averaging a mere 200–300 passengers on her cruise voyages. Even a special programme on West German television did little to help the ship's problems. By late 1983, she was losing $3½ million annually. The Hamburg Government decided to sell its share in the liner and so the HADAG Company began to look for a partner. This came to be the Safmarine Lines, the South African Marine Corporation, who wanted to enter the luxury cruise trades through its Safleisure subsidiary.

'The South Africans soon bought the ship outright with the intention of partially reviving the old Cape Mail run between Southampton, Las Palmas, Capetown and Durban, which had been closed out since the final Union-Castle–Safmarine passenger sailings in the fall of 1977. These voyages were to be linked with cruises: from Durban to Mauritius and the Seychelles, from Capetown to the Antarctic, to Rio and even a special trip along the Amazon, and from Southampton as well as Hamburg to the Baltic,

Norwegian fjords, and (in July 1985) a unique three-week sailing to Greenland. Drydocked at first, the *Astor* – which retained her original name – was altered slightly and given some additional suites, which altered her capacity slightly and increased her tonnage to over 19,000. She began sailing under the South African colours in April 1984.'

According to Len Wilton, the passenger manager for Safmarine Lines in London, 'The *Astor* was purchased by South Africa because of the prestige of owning a passenger ship, to re-establish the old mail run and to show the flag. It was also to be an extended arm for Safleisure, which already owned hotels, clubs, airlines and travel agencies. In two years, 1984–85, the *Astor* established a 70 per cent occupancy rate on the long-haul voyages to and from South Africa. Outbound from Southampton, we had lots of high profile passengers and many former Union-Castle passengers. Northbound, there were far more younger and more budget types, many of them being South Africans seeking new life in the UK and in Europe. We also had special package tours of twenty-one days, "fly out and cruise home" operating from both ends. On the South African cruises, we tended also to have much younger passengers, in fact very similar to the Australian cruise market. In European waters, we tended to concentrate more on adventure cruising, seeking out unusual itineraries and ports of call. The *Astor* has an exceptionally shallow draught [approximately 18ft] and carries Zodiacs [motorized rubber rafts] for special landings. For example, she was the largest passenger ship since the 1930s to call at Greenwich and therefore come as close to London as possible. We had actually hoped to go alongside the HMS *Belfast*, moored in the Pool of London, but the *Astor* was 17ft too long. Extensions will be made and we plan such a visit with our new cruiseship in 1987.'

In the winter of 1985, after less than a year with the South Africans, it was announced, to the considerable surprise and interest of the passenger ship industry, that the *Astor* was to be sold once again, this time for delivery in the following August to Deutsche Seereederei, the German Sea Shipping Company of Rostock in East Germany. Captain Blotenberg was involved indirectly in the sale of the liner: 'My firm, the German-West Africa Line, agreed to act as something of an intermediary. The sale of the ship is actually part of a special trade arrangement between East and West Germany. Since, for rather obvious political reasons, the East Germans cannot buy directly from the South Africans, the ship is being briefly transferred to our company. East German monies are then transferred to the Germam-West

Africa Line, but go only "on paper" to Safmarine. Instead, the actual monies will be passed directly to the HDW Shipyards at Kiel, where a second *Astor* will be built. Ideally, the older ship could have `been transferred at a later date, but then East Germany's cruise ship *Volkerfreundschaft*, the former Swedish-American *Stockholm* of 1948 is worn out and already retired [sold to a Norwegian firm in July 1985].'

The author was aboard the *Astor*'s penultimate cruise, a twenty-day run from Hamburg, returning to Cuxhaven, visiting Leith; the Faeroe Islands; Godthaab, Jakobshavn, Narssaq and Igaliko in Greenland; the Westman Islands and Reykjavik in Iceland; and a return call at Leith for Edinburgh. The intended calls at Holsteinborg in Greenland were cancelled because of serious ice floes and at the Shetland Islands because of heavy seas and fog. There were 450 passengers on board, a mixture mostly of Germans, British, Americans and South Africans. A month before, in June, the ship had been transferred to Bahamian registry, primarily to avoid political difficulties with dockers in Norway during the ship's early summer Fjordlands cruise.

The *Astor* was handed over to the East Germans on 28 August and, after some modifications at the HDW yards at Hamburg, she was renamed *Arcona* for trade union cruising with industrial managers, workers and their families, sailing mostly out of Rostock. Earlier, rumours were that the ship would be renamed as *Volkerfreundschaft* and then as *Our Happy Country*, and that she would be resold to the Cuban Government.

The new *Astor* will be delivered in the spring of 1987. Len Wilton is quite excited about the project. 'We envisage considerable expansion ahead, in fact some joint ventures in our cruising operations. There will be three or four voyages each year between Europe and South Africa, but more winter cruising from Durban and Capetown, and summers out of European ports. There is a very bright future in adventure cruising; voyages that call at remote and select ports. For example, in the Mediterranean, we would like to consider Corsica, for example. We hope to build a strong following for the new ship, in fact something similar to the club-like atmosphere of the illustrious Royal Mail liner *Andes* in the 1960s.

'The new ship will be slightly larger, with a maximum of 650 berths, and will be more economical and sophisticated [from a Generation One liner to a Generation Five design]. There will be more suites and super-suites on board as well as larger and improved crew quarters. We also plan to add a full casino and larger conference ˙facilities. Overall, however, the new *Astor* will be quite similar in design to the previous *Astor*.'

With the exception of the aforementioned *Fabiola-ville*, *Kananga*, *St Helena* and possibly the new *Astor*, (due for delivery in 1987), the once busy sealanes of the 'Last Blue Water Liners' are now empty and desolate – most of the ships mentioned in these pages have gone to the scrap-heap and even their owners vanished. This book has been created – even at this distance in time – as a nostalgic glance back at a wonderful final generation of passenger ships.

# SPECIFICATIONS OF THE LAST
# BLUE WATER LINERS

*Accra* (Elder Dempster Lines)
Built by Vickers-Armstrongs Shipbuilders Limited, Barrow-in-Furness, England, 1947. 11,644 gross tons; 471 feet long; 66 feet wide. Doxford diesels, twin screw. Service speed 15½ knots. 313 passengers (289 first class, 24 third class).

*Achille Lauro* (Lauro Line) ex-*Willem Ruys*
Built by the De Schelde Shipyards, Flushing, Netherlands, 1939–47. 23,629 gross tons; 631 feet long; 82 feet wide. Sulzer diesels, twin screw. Service speed 22 knots. Approximately 1652 passengers (152 first class, approximately 1500 tourist class).

*Africa* (Lloyd Triestino)
Built by Cantieri Riuniti dell'Adriatico, Monfalcone, Italy, 1952. 11,434 gross tons; 523 feet long; 68 feet wide. Fiat diesels, twin screw. Service speed 19½ knots. 446 passengers (148 first class, 298 tourist class).

*Akaroa* (Shaw Savill Line) – see *Amazon*

*Albertville* (Compagnie Maritime Belge)
Built by John Cockerill S/A, Hoboken, Belgium, 1948. 10,877 gross tons; 505 feet long; 65 feet wide. Burmeister & Wain type diesel, single screw. Service speed 16½ knots. 207 one-class passengers.

*Amazon* (Royal Mail Lines)
Built by Harland & Wolff Limited, Belfast, Northern Ireland, 1959. 20,368 gross tons; 584 feet long; 78 feet wide. Turbo-charged diesels, twin screw. Service speed 17½ knots. 449 passengers (91 first class, 82 cabin class and 275 third class).

*Amra* (British India Line)
Built by Swan, Hunter & Wigham Richardson Limited, Newcastle, England, 1938. 8314 gross tons; 461 feet long; 61 feet wide. Steam turbines, twin screw. Service speed 16½ knots. 958 passengers (221 saloon class, 737 third class).

*Andrea C.* (Costa Line)
Built by Todd-California Shipbuilding Corporation, Richmond, California, 1942. 8604 gross tons; 467 feet long; 57 feet wide. Fiat diesel, single screw. Service speed 16 knots. 482 passengers (variable from 122 first class and 354 tourist class or 234 first class and 248 in tourist class).

*Angelina Lauro* (Lauro Line)
Built by Netherlands Shipbuilding Company, Amsterdam, Netherlands, 1939. 24,377 gross tons; 672 feet long; 83 feet wide. Sulzer diesels, triple screw. Service speed 21½ knots. 1616 passengers (189 first class, 1427 tourist class).

*Angola* (Companhia Nacional)
Built by Hawthorn Leslie & Company Limited, Newcastle, England, 1948. 13,078 gross tons; 550 feet long; 67 feet wide. Doxford diesels, twin screw. Service speed 17 knots. 546 passengers (105 first class, 141 tourist class, 300 third class).

*Anna C.* (Costa Line)
Built by Lithgows Limited, Glasgow, Scotland, 1929. 12,030 gross tons; 524 feet long; 65 feet wide. Fiat diesels, twin screw. Service speed 20 knots. 1066 passengers (202 first class, 864 tourist class).

*Antilles* (French Line)
Built by the Naval Dockyard, Brest, France, 1952. 19,828 gross tons; 599 feet long; 80 feet wide. Steam turbines, twin screw. Service speed 22 knots. 778 passengers (404 first class, 285 cabin class, 89 tourist class).

*Apapa* (Elder Dempster Lines)
Built by Vickers-Armstrongs Limited, Barrow-in-Furness, England, 1948. 11,651 gross tons; 471 feet long; 66 feet wide. Doxford diesels, twin screw. Service speed 15½ knots. 313 passengers (289 first class, 24 third class).

*Aragon* (Royal Mail Lines)
Built by Harland & Wolff Limited, Belfast, Northern Ireland, 1960. 20,362 gross tons; 584 feet long; 78 feet wide. Turbo-charged diesels, twin screw. Service speed 17½ knots. 449 passengers (91 first class, 82 cabin class, 275 third class).

*Aranda* (Shaw Savill Line) – see *Aragon*

*Arawa* (Shaw Savill Line) – see *Arlanza*

*Arcadia* (P&O-Orient Lines)
Built by John Brown & Company Limited, Clydebank, Scotland, 1954. 29,734 gross tons; 721 feet long; 91 feet wide. Steam turbines, twin screw. Service speed 22 knots. 1382 passengers (647 first class, 735 tourist class).

*Argentina Maru* (Mitsui- OSK Lines)
Built by Mitsubishi Heavy Industries Limited, Kobe, Japan,

*The* Athenic *at the Royal Albert Docks, London, a few days before her maiden voyage to New Zealand on 31 August 1947.*

Conway Picture Library

1958. 10,864 gross tons; 513 feet long; 67 feet wide. Steam turbines, single screw. Service speed 16½ knots. 1054 passengers (12 cabin class, 82 tourist class, 960 third class).

### Argentina Star (Blue Star Line)

Built by Cammell Laird & Company Limited, Birkenhead, England, 1947. 10,716 gross tons; 503 feet long; 68 feet wide. Steam turbines, single screw. Service speed 16 knots. 50 first class passengers.

### Arlanza (Royal Mail Lines)

Built by Harland & Wolff Limited, Belfast, Northern Ireland, 1960. 20,362 gross tons; 584 feet long; 78 feet wide. Turbo-charged diesels, twin screw. Service speed 17½ knots. 449 passengers (91 first class, 82 cabin class, 275 third class).

### Aronda (British India Line)

Built by Swan, Hunter & Wigham Richardson Limited, Newcastle-upon-Tyne, England, 1941. 8396 gross tons; 461 feet long; 61 feet wide. Steam turbines, twin screw. 1954 passengers (44 first class, 22 second class, 28 interchangeable, 60 intermediate, 1800 deck class).

### Arundel Castle (Union-Castle Line)

Built by Harland & Wolff Limited, Belfast, Northern Ireland, 1921. 19,216 gross tons; 686 feet long; 72 feet wide. Steam turbines, twin screw. Service speed 20 knots. 535 passengers (164 first class, 371 tourist class).

### Ascania (Grimaldi-Siosa Lines)

Built by Ateliers et Chantiers de la Loire, St Nazaire, France, 1926. 9536 gross tons; 490 feet long; 60 feet wide. Steam turbines, twin screw. Service speed 16 knots. 1247 passengers (87 first class, 1160 tourist class).

### Asia (Lloyd Triestino)

Built by Cantieri Riuniti dell'Adriatico, Monfalcone, Italy, 1953. 11,693 gross tons; 522 feet long; 68 feet wide. Fiat diesels, twin screw. Service speed 19½ knots. 431 passengers (290 first class, 141 tourist class).

### Astor (Safmarine Lines)

Built by HDW Shipyards, Hamburg, West Germany, 1981. 18,835 gross tons; 535 feet long; 73 feet wide. M.A.N. type diesels, twin screw. Service speed 18 knots. Approximately 500 one-class passengers.

### Athenic (Shaw Savill Line)

Built by Harland & Wolff Limited, Belfast, Northern Ireland, 1947. 15,187 gross tons; 560 feet long; 71 feet wide. Steam

*The* Canton, *following a thirteen month refit, is shown here on 8 October 1947, ready to reopen P&O's Far Eastern service.*

turbines, twin screw. Service speed 17 knots. 85 one-class passengers.

### Athlone Castle (Union-Castle Line)

Built by Harland & Wolff Limited, Belfast, Northern Ireland, 1936. 25,567 gross tons; 725 feet wide; 82 feet wide. Burmeister & Wain diesels, twin screw. Service speed 20 knots. 783 passengers (245 first class, 538 tourist class).

### Augustus (Italian Line)

Built by Cantieri Riuniti dell'Adriatico, Trieste, Italy, 1952. 27,090 gross tons; 680 feet long; 87 feet wide. Fiat diesels, twin screw. Service speed 21 knots. 1180 passengers (180 first, 1000 tourist class).

### Aureol (Elder Dempster Lines)

Built by Alexander Stephen & Sons Limited, Glasgow, Scotland, 1951. 14,083 gross tons; 537 feet long; 70 feet wide. Doxford diesels, twin screw. Service speed 16 knots. 353 passengers (253 first class, 76 cabin class, 24 interchangeable).

### Baudouinville (Compagnie Maritime Belge) – see also Cathay

Built by Cockerill-Ougree Shipyards, Hoboken, Belgium, 1957. 13,922 gross tons; 559 feet long; 70 feet wide. Steam turbines, single screw. Service speed 16½ knots. 301 one-class passengers.

### Bayernstein (North German Lloyd)

Built by Bremer Vulkan Shipyards, Bremen, West Germany, 1954. 8999 gross tons; 538 feet long; 64 feet wide. M.A.N. type diesel, single screw. Service speed 16½ knots. 86 first class passengers.

### Begona (Spanish Line)

Built by Bethlehem-Fairfield Shipyards, Baltimore, Maryland, 1945. 10,139 gross tons; 455 feet long; 62 feet wide. Steam turbines, single screw. Service speed 16 knots. 941 passengers (111 special tourist class, 830 tourist class).

### Bianca C. (Costa Line)

Built by Constructions Navales, La Ciotat, France, 1939–49. 18,427 gross tons; 594 feet long; 75 feet wide. Sulzer diesels, triple screw. Service speed 21 knots. 1232 passengers (202 first class, 1030 tourist class).

### Bloemfontein Castle (Union-Castle Line)

Built by Harland & Wolff Limited, Belfast, Northern Ireland, 1950. 18,400 gross tons; 595 feet long; 76 feet wide. Burmeister & Wain diesels, twin screw. Service speed 18½ knots. 739 tourist class passengers.

### Boissevain (Royal Interocean Lines)

Built by Blohm & Voss AG, Hamburg, West Germany, 1937. 14,285 gross tons; 559 feet long; 72 feet wide. Sulzer diesels, triple screw. Service speed 16 knots. 386 passengers in three classes.

### Braemar Castle (Union-Castle Line)

Built by Harland & Wolff Limited, Belfast, Northern Ireland, 1952. 17,024 gross tons; 576 feet long; 74 feet wide. Steam turbines, twin screw. Service speed 17½ knots. 453 cabin class passengers.

### Brazil Maru (Mitsui-OSK Lines)

Built by Mitsubishi Heavy Industries Limited, Kobe, Japan, 1954. 10,100 gross tons; 512 feet long; 64 feet wide. Mitsubishi diesel, single screw. Service speed 16 knots. 982 passengers (12 cabin class, 68 tourist class, 902 third class).

### Brasil Star (Blue Star Line)

Built by Cammell Laird & Company Limited, Birkenhead, England, 1947. 10,716 gross tons; 503 feet long; 68 feet wide. Steam turbines, single screw. Service speed 16 knots. 52 first class passengers.

### Britanis (Chandris Lines)

Built by Bethlehem Steel Corporation, Quincy, Massachusetts, USA, 1932. 18,254 gross tons; 638 feet long; 79 feet wide. Steam turbines, twin screw. Service speed 20 knots. 1632 all-tourist class passengers.

*Cabo San Roque* (Ybarra Line)
Built by Societa Espanola de Construccion Naval, Bilbao, Spain, 1957. 14,491 gross tons; 556 feet long; 69 feet wide. Sulzer diesels, twin screw. Service speed 20 knots. 823 passengers (241 first class, 582 tourist class).

*Cabo San Vicente* (Ybarra Line)
Built by Societa Espanola de Construccion Naval, Bilbao, Spain, 1959. 14,569 gross tons; 556 feet long; 69 feet wide. Sulzer diesels, twin screw. Service speed 20 knots. 823 passengers (241 first class, 582 tourist class).

*Caledonia* (Anchor Line)
Built by Fairfield Shipbuilding & Engineering Company Limited, Glasgow, Scotland, 1948. 11,255 gross tons; 506 feet long; 66 feet wide. Doxford diesels, twin screw. Service speed 16 knots. 304 first class passengers.

*Caledonien* (Messageries Maritimes)
Built by the Naval Dockyard, Brest, France, 1953, 12,614 gross tons; 549 feet long; 68 feet wide. Burmeister & Wain diesels, twin screw. Service speed 17 knots. 366 passengers (74 first class, 84 tourist class, 208 third class).

*Cambodge* (Messageries Maritimes)
Built by Ateliers et Chantiers de France, Dunkirk, France, 1953. 13,520 gross tons; 532 feet long; 72 feet wide. Steam turbines, twin screw. Service speed 21 knots. 347 passengers (117 first class, 110 tourist class, 120 steerage third class).

*Camito* (Elders & Fyffes Limited)
Built by Alexander Stephen & Sons Limited, Glasgow, Scotland, 1956. 8687 gross tons; 448 feet long; 62 feet wide. Steam turbines, twin screw. Service speed 17½ knots. 113 first class passengers.

*Canberra* (P&O-Orient Lines)
Built by Harland & Wolff Limited, Belfast, Northern Ireland, 1961. 45,733 gross tons; 818 feet long; 102 feet wide. Steam turbo-electric, twin screw. Service speed 27½ knots. 2272 passengers (556 or 596 first class, 1616 or 1716 tourist class).

*Canton* (P&O-Orient Lines)
Built by Alexander Stephen & Sons Limited, Glasgow, Scotland, 1938, 16,033 gross tons; 563 feet long; 73 feet wide. Steam turbines, twin screw. Service speed 18 knots. 542 passengers (298 first class, 244 tourist class).

*Capetown Castle* (Union-Castle Line)
Built by Harland & Wolff Limited, Belfast, Northern Ireland, 1938. 27,002 gross tons; 734 feet long; 82 feet wide. Burmeister & Wain diesels, twin screw. Service speed 20 knots. 796 passengers (243 first class, 553 tourist class).

*Caribia* (Grimaldi-Siosa Lines)
Built by Cantieri Navale Triestino, Monfalcone, Italy, 1928. 24,496 gross tons; 631 feet long; 80 feet wide. Fiat diesels, twin screw. Service speed 21 knots. 1437 passengers (337 first class, 368 cabin class, 732 tourist class).

*Carnarvon Castle* (Union-Castle Line)
Built by Harland & Wolff Limited, Belfast, Northern Ireland, 1926. 20,148 gross tons; 686 feet long; 73 feet wide. Burmeister & Wain diesels, twin screw. Service speed 20 knots. 584 passengers (134 first class, 450 tourist class).

*Carthage* (P&O-Orient Lines)
Built by Alexander Stephen & Sons Limited, Glasgow, Scotland, 1931. 14,280 gross tons; 543 feet long; 71 feet wide. Steam turbines, twin screw. 394 passengers (181 first class, 234 tourist class).

*Castel Felice* (Sitmar Line)
Built by Alexander Stephen & Sons Limited, Glasgow, Scotland, 1930. 12,478 gross tons; 493 feet long; 64 feet wide. Steam turbines, twin screw. Service speed 17 knots. 1405 tourist class passengers.

*Cathay* (P&O-Orient Lines)
Built by Cockerill-Ougree Shipyards, Hoboken, Belgium, 1957. 13,809 gross tons; 558 feet long; 70 feet wide. Steam turbines, twin screw. Service speed 16½ knots. 240 first class passengers only.

*Centaur* (Blue Funnel Line)
Built by John Brown & Company Limited, Clydebank, Scotland, 1963. 8262 gross tons; 480 feet long; 66 feet wide. Burmeister & Wain diesels, twin screw. Service speed 20 knots. 190 first class passengers only.

*Ceramic* (Shaw Savill Line)
Built by Cammell Laird & Company Limited, Birkenhead, England, 1948. 15,896 gross tons; 560 feet long; 71 feet wide. Steam turbines, twin screw. Service speed 17 knots. 85 first class passengers only.

*Charles Tellier* (Messageries Maritimes)
Built by Chantiers et Ateliers de la Loire, St Nazaire, France, 1952. 12,006 gross tons; 538 feet long; 64 feet wide. Sulzer diesels, twin screw. Service speed 16 knots. 411 passengers (109 first class, 302 third class).

*Charlesville* (Compagnie Maritime Belge)
Built by John Cockerill S/A, Hoboken, Belgium, 1951. 10,946 gross tons; 505 feet long; 65 feet wide. Burmeister & Wain type diesel, single screw. Service speed 16½ knots. 248 one-class passengers.

*Chitral* (P&O-Orient Lines)
Built by Chantiers de L'Atlantique, St Nazaire, France, 1956. 13,821 gross tons; 558 feet long; 70 feet wide. Steam turbines, twin screw. Service speed 16½ knots. 240 first class passengers only.

*Chusan* (P&O-Orient Lines)
Built by Vickers-Armstrongs Shipbuilders Limited, Barrow-in-Furness, England, 1950. 24,215 gross tons; 672 feet long; 85 feet wide. Steam turbines, twin screw. Service speed 22 knots. 1026 passengers (475 first class, 551 tourist class).

**Cilicia** (Anchor Line)
Built by Fairfield Shipbuiding & Engineering Company, Glasgow, Scotland, 1938. 11,172 gross tons; 506 feet long; 66 feet wide. Doxford diesels, twin screw. Service speed 16 knots. 298 first class passengers.

**Circassia** (Anchor Line)
Built by Fairfield Shipbuiding & Engineering Company, Glasgow, Scotland, 1937. 11,170 gross tons; 506 feet long; 66 feet wide. Doxford diesels, twin screw. Service speed 16 knots. 298 first class passengers.

**Claude Bernard** (Chargeurs Reunis)
Built by Ateliers et Chantiers de la Loire, St Nazaire, France, 1950. 12,021 gross tons; 537 feet long; 64 feet wide. Sulzer diesels, twin screw. Service speed 17 knots. 324 passengers (94 first class, 230 third class).

**City of Durban** (Ellerman & Bucknall Lines)
Built by Vickers-Armstrongs Shipbuilders Limited, Newcastle, England, 1954. 13,345 gross tons; 541 feet long; 71 feet wide. Doxford diesels, twin screw. Service speed 16½ knots. 107 first class passengers.

**City of Exeter** (Ellerman & Bucknall Lines)
Built by Vickers-Armstrongs Shipbuilders Limited, Newcastle, England, 1953. 13,345 gross tons; 541 feet long; 71 feet wide. Doxford diesels, twin screw. Service speed 16½ knots. 107 first class passengers.

**City of Port Elizabeth** (Ellerman & Bucknall Lines)
Built by Vickers-Armstrongs Shipbuilders Limited, Newcastle, England, 1952. 13,363 gross tons; 541 feet long; 71 feet wide. Doxford diesels, twin screw. Service speed 16½ knots. 107 first class passengers.

**City of York** (Ellerman & Bucknall Lines)
Built by Vickers-Armstrongs Shipbuilders Limited, Newcastle, England, 1953. 13,345 gross tons; 541 feet long; 71 feet wide. Doxford diesels, twin screw. Service speed 16½ knots. 107 first class passengers.

**Conte Biancamano** (Italian Line)
Built by William Beardmore & Company, Glasgow, Scotland, 1925. 23,842 gross tons; 665 feet long; 76 feet wide. Steam turbines, twin screw. Service speed 18 knots. 1578 passengers (215 first class, 333 cabin class, 1030 tourist class).

**Conte Grande** (Italian Line)
Built by Stablimento Tecnico, Trieste, Italy, 1928. 23,562 gross tons; 667 feet long; 78 feet wide. Steam turbines, twin screw. Service speed 18 knots. 1379 passengers (261 first class, 338 cabin class, 780 tourist class).

**Corfu** (P&O-Orient Lines)
Built by Alexander Stephen & Sons Limited, Glasgow, Scotland, 1931. 14,280 gross tons; 543 feet long; 71 feet wide. Steam turbines, twin screw. Service speed 17 knots. 394 passengers (181 first class, 213 tourist class).

*Shaw Savill Line's Ceramic at the Royal Albert Docks, London, in November 1964.*

204

Conway Picture Library

*Corinthic* (Shaw Savill Line)
Built by Cammell Laird & Company Limited, Birkenhead, England, 1947. 15,682 gross tons; 560 feet long; 71 feet wide. Steam turbines, twin screw. Service speed 17 knots. 85 first class passengers only.

*Dalerdyk* (Holland-America Line)
Built by Wilton Fijenoord Shipyard, Schiedam, Holland, 1930. 10,820 gross tons; 509 feet long; 65 feet wide. Sulzer diesels, twin screw. Service speed 15 knots. 46 first class passengers only.

*Dara* (British India Line)
Built by Barclay Curle & Company Limited, Glasgow, Scotland, 1948. 5030 gross tons; 399 feet long; 55 feet wide. Doxford diesel, single screw. Service speed 14 knots. 1028 passengers (13 first class, 65 second class, 950 deck class).

*Daressa* (British India Line)
Built by Barclay Curle & Company Limited, Glasgow, Scotland, 1950. 4180 gross tons; 399 feet long; 55 feet wide. Doxford diesel, single screw. Service speed 13½ knots. 586 passengers (26 first class, 60 second class, 500 deck class).

*Derbyshire* (Bibby Line)
Built by Fairfield Shipbuilding & Engineering Company, Glasgow, Scotland, 1935. 10,641 gross tons; 501 feet long; 66 feet wide. Sulzer diesels, twin screw. Service speed 14½ knots. 115 first class passengers.

*Diemerdyk* (Holland-America Line)
Built by Wilton Fijenoord Shipyard, Schiedam, Holland, 1950. 11,195 gross tons; 494 feet long; 69 feet wide. Steam turbines, twin screw. Service speed 16½ knots. 61 first class passengers only.

*The* Jadotville *in 1961. Compagnie Maritime Belge sold her and her sister, the* Baudouinville *to P&O-Orient when they became superfluous on the Antwerp–Congo trade after the Congo was granted independence in 1960.*

*Dinteldyk* (Holland-America Line)
Built by Wilton Fijenoord Shipyard, Schiedam, Holland, 1957. 11,366 gross tons; 504 feet long; 69 feet wide. Steam turbines, twin screw. Service speed 16½ knots. 60 first class passengers only.

*Dominion Monarch* (Shaw Savill Line)
Built by Swan, Hunter & Wigham Richardson Limited, Newcastle, England, 1939. 26,463 gross tons; 682 feet long; 85 feet wide. Doxford diesels, quadruple screw. Service speed 19½ knots. 508 first class passengers.

*Dongedyk* (Holland-America Line)
Built by Wilton Fijenoord Shipyard, Schiedam, Holland, 1929. 10,942 gross tons; 529 feet long; 65 feet wide. M.A.N. diesels, twin screw. Service speed 16 knots. 52 first class passengers.

*Donizetti*
Built by Cantieri Riuniti dell'Adriatico, Trieste, Italy, 1951, 13,226 gross tons; 528 feet long; 69 feet wide. Sulzer diesels, twin screw. Service speed 17½ knots. 600 passengers (160 first class, 440 tourist class).

*Dumra* (British India Line)
Built by Barclay Curle & Company Limited, Glasgow, Scotland, 1946. 4867 gross tons; 399 feet long; 55 feet wide. Doxford diesel, single screw. Service speed 14 knots. 1154

passengers (13 first class, 41 second class, 1100 deck class).

### Dwarka (British India Line)
Built by Swan, Hunter & Wigham Richardson Limited, Newcastle-upon-Tyne, England 1947. 4851 gross tons; 399 feet long; 55 feet wide. Doxford diesel, single screw. Service speed 13½ knots. 1104 passengers (13 first class, 41 second class, 1050 deck class).

### Edinburgh Castle (Union-Castle Line)
Built by Harland & Wolff Limited, Belfast, Northern Ireland, 1948. 28,705 gross tons; 747 feet long; 84 feet wide. Steam turbines, twin screw. Service speed 22 knots. 755 passengers (214 first class, 541 tourist class).

### Elisabethville (Compagnie Maritime Belge)
Built by John Cockerill S/A, Hoboken, Belgium, 1948. 10,877 gross tons; 505 feet long; 65 feet wide. Burmeister & Wain type diesel, single screw. Service speed 16½ knots. 207 one-class passengers.

### Ellinis (Chandris Line)
Built by Bethlehem Steel Corporation, Quincy, Massachusetts, USA, 1932. 24,351 gross tons; 642 feet long; 79 feet wide. Steam turbines, twin screw. Service speed 20 knots. 1642 tourist class passengers.

### Enrico C. (Costa Line)
Built by Swan, Hunter & Wigham Richardson Limited, Newcastle, England, 1951. 13,607 gross tons; 580 feet long; 73 feet wide. Steam turbines, twin screw. Service speed 18 knots. 1198 passengers (218 first class, 980 tourist class).

### Eugenio C. (Costa Line)
Built by Cantieri Riuniti dell'Adriatico, Monfalcone, Italy, 1966. 30,567 gross tons; 712 feet long; 96 feet wide. Steam turbines, twin screw. Service speed 27 knots. 1636 passengers (178 first class, 356 cabin class, 1102 tourist class).

### Europa (Lloyd Triestino)
Built by Ansaldo Shipyards, Genoa, Italy, 1952. 11,440 gross tons; 522 feet long; 68 feet wide. Fiat diesels, twin screw. Service speed 19½ knots. 446 passengers (148 first class, 298 tourist class).

### Fabiolaville (Compagnie Maritime Belge)
Built by Cockerill-Ougree Shipyards, Hoboken, Belgium, 1972. 13,303 gross tons; 529 feet long; 75 feet wide. Burmeister & Wain type diesel, single screw. Service speed 20 knots. 71 one-class passengers.

### Fairsea (Sitmar Line)
Built by Sun Shipbuilding & Drydock Company, Chester, Pennsylvania, USA, 1941. 13,432 gross tons; 492 feet long; 69 feet wide. Doxford diesel, single screw. Service speed 16 knots. 1460 tourist class passengers.

### Fairsky (Stimar Line)
Built by Western Pipe & Steel Company, San Francisco, California, USA, 1941. 12,464 gross tons; 502 feet long; 69 feet wide. Steam turbines, twin screw. Service speed 18 knots. 1461 tourist class passengers.

### Fairstar (Sitmar Line)
Built by Fairfield Shipbuilding & Engineering Company, Glasgow, Scotland, 1957. 23,764 gross tons; 609 feet long; 78 feet wide. Steam turbines, twin screw. Service speed 20 knots. 1910 tourist class passengers.

### Federico C. (Costa Line)
Built by the Ansaldo Shipyard, Genoa, Italy, 1958. 20,416 gross tons; 606 feet long; 79 feet wide. Steam turbines, twin screw. Service speed 21 knots. 1279 passengers (243 first class, 300 cabin class, 736 tourist class).

### Ferdinand de Lesseps (Messageries Martimes)
Built by Forges et Chantiers de la Gironde, Gironde, France, 1952. 10,882 gross tons; 492 feet long; 64 feet wide. Burmeister & Wain diesels, twin screw. Service speed 17 knots. 400 passengers (88 first class, 112 tourist class, 40 third class, 160 steerage).

### Flandre (French Line)
Built by Ateliers et Chantiers de France, Dunkirk, France, 1952. 20,477 gross tons; 600 feet long; 80 feet wide. Steam turbines, twin screw. Service speed 22 knots. 743 passengers (232 first class, 511 tourist class).

### Frankfurt (North German Lloyd)
Built by Bremer-Vulkan Shipyards, Bremen, West Germany, 1954. 8959 gross tons; 538 feet long; 64 feet wide. M.A.N. diesel, single screw. Service speed 16½ knots. 86 first class passengers.

### Galileo Galilei (Lloyd Triestino)
Built by Cantieri Riuniti dell'Adriatico, Monfalcone, Italy, 1963. 27,907 gross tons; 702 feet long; 94 feet wide. Steam turbines, twin screw. Service speed 24 knots. 1750 passengers (156 first class, 1594 tourist class).

### Giulio Cesare (Italian Line)
Built by Cantieri Riuniti dell'Adriatico, Monfalcone, Italy, 1951. 27,078 gross tons; 681 feet long; 87 feet wide. Fiat diesels, twin screw. Service speed 21 knots. 1183 passengers (181 first class, 288 cabin class, 714 tourist class).

### Golfito (Elder & Fyffes Limited)
Built by Alexander Stephen & Sons Limited, Glasgow, Scotland, 1949. 8740 gross tons; 447 feet long; 62 feet wide. Steam turbines, twin screw. Service speed 17½ knots. 111 first class passengers.

### Gothic (Shaw Savill Line)
Built by Swan, Hunter & Wigham Richardson Limited, Newcastle, England, 1948. 15,911 gross tons; 560 feet long; 71 feet wide. Steam turbines, twin screw. Service speed 17 knots. 85 first class passengers only.

### Guglielmo Marconi (Lloyd Triestino)
27,905 gross tons – otherwise see Galileo Galilei.

*The arrival of the Oriana on 30 December 1960 at Sydney
on her maiden voyage.*

Conway Picture Library

*The* Sirdhana *in December 1947. She was one of three sisterships built between 1947 and 50 by the British India Company for the Far East route.*

**Hamburg** (Hamburg American Line)
9008 gross tons – otherwise see *Frankfurt.*

**Hannover** (Hamburg American Line)
8974 gross tons – otherwise see *Frankfurt.*

**Hector** (Blue Funnel Line)
Built by Harland & Wolff Limited, Belfast, Northern Ireland, 1949. 10,125 gross tons; 523 feet long; 69 feet wide. Steam turbines, single screw. Service speed 18½ knots. 30 first class passengers.

**Helenus** (Blue Funnel Line)
10,129 gross tons – otherwise see Hector.

**Hessenstein** (North German Lloyd)
Built by Bremer-Vulkan Shipyards, Bremen, West Germany, 1954. 8929 gross tons; 538 feet long; 64 feet wide. M.A.N. diesel, single screw. Service speed 16½ knots. 86 first class passengers.

**Hikawa Maru** (Nippon Yusen Kaisha)
Built by Yokohama Dock Company, Yokohama, Japan, 1930. 11,625 gross tons; 536 feet long; 66 feet wide. Burmeister & Wain diesels, twin screw. Service speed 16 knots. 276 passengers (80 first class, 69 third class A, 127 third class B).

**Himalaya** (P&O-Orient Lines)
Built by Vickers-Armstrongs Shipbuilders Limited, Barrow-in-Furness, England, 1949. 27,955 gross tons; 709 feet long; 91 feet wide. Steam turbines, twin screw. Service speed 22 knots. 1159 passengers (758 first class, 401 tourist class).

**Iberia** (P&O-Orient Lines)
Built by Hartland & Wolff Limited, Belfast, Northern Ireland, 1954. 29,614 gross tons; 719 feet long; 91 feet wide. Steam turbines, twin screw. Service speed 22 knots. 1406 passengers (673 first class, 733 tourist class).

**Imperio** (Companhia Colonial)
Built by John Brown & Company Limited, Clydebank, Scotland, 1948. 13,186 gross tons; 532 feet long; 68 feet wide. Steam turbines, twin screw. Service speed 17 knots. 590 passengers (114 first class, 156 tourist class, 120 third class).

**Infante dom Henrique** (Companhia Colonial)
Built by Cockerill-Ougree Shipyards, Hoboken, Belgium, 1961. 23,306 gross tons; 642 feet long; 84 feet wide. Steam turbines, twin screw. Service speed 20 knots. 974 passengers (148 first class, 826 tourist class).

**Irpinia** (Grimaldi-Siosa Lines)
Built by Swan, Hunter & Wigham Richardson Limited, Newcastle, England, 1929. 13,204 gross tons; 537 feet long; 67 feet wide. Fiat diesels, twin screw. Service speed 16 knots. 1181 passengers (209 first class, 972 tourist class).

**Ixion** (Blue Funnel Line)
10,125 gross tons – otherwise see *Hector.*

**Jadotville** (Compagnie Maritime Belge)
Built by Chantiers de L'Atlantique, St Nazaire, France, 1956. 13,790 gross tons; 558 feet long; 70 feet wide. Steam turbines, twin screw. Service speed 16½ knots. 300 one-class passengers.

**Jagersfontein** (Holland-Africa Line)
Built by De Schelde Shipyards, Flushing, Holland, 1940–50. 10,574 gross tons; 528 feet long; 63 feet wide. Sulzer diesels, twin screw. Service speed 17 knots. 160 passengers (100 first

class, 60 tourist class).

## Jason (Blue Funnel Line)
Built by Swan, Hunter & Wigham Richardson Limited, Newcastle-upon-Tyne, England, 1949, 10,160 gross tons; 523 feet long; 69 feet wide. Steam turbines, single screw. Service speed 18½ knots. 30 first class passengers.

## Jean Laborde (Messageries Martimes)
10,902 gross tons – otherwise see *Ferdinand de Lesseps*.

## Kampala (British India Line)
Built by Alexander Stephen & Sons Limited, Glasgow, Scotland, 1947. 10,304 gross tons; 507 feet long; 66 feet wide. Steam turbines, twin screw. Service speed 16 knots. 1065 passengers (60 first class, 180 second class, 825 third class).

## Karanja (British India Line)
10,294 gross tons – otherwise see *Kampala*.

## Kenya (British India Line)
Built by Barclay Curle & Company Limited, Glasgow, Scotland, 1951. 14,464 gross tons; 540 feet long; 71 feet wide. Steam turbines, twin screw. Service speed 16 knots. 297 passengers (194 first class, 103 tourist class).

## Kenya Castle (Union-Castle Line)
17,041 gross tons – otherwise see *Braemar Castle*.

## La Bourdonnais (Messageries Maritimes)
Built by Lorient Naval Shipyard, Lorient, France, 1953. 10,886 gross tons – otherwise see *Ferdinand de Lesseps*.

## Laennec (Messageries Maritimes)
See *Charles Tellier*.

## Laos (Messageries Maritimes)
13,212 gross tons – otherwise see *Cambodge*.

## Lavoisier (Messageries Maritimes)
11,969 gross tons – otherwise see *Claude Bernard*.

## Leicestershire (Bibby Line)
Built by Fairfield Shipbuilding & Engineering Company, Glasgow, Scotland, 1949. 8922 gross tons; 498 feet long; 60 feet wide. Steam turbines, single screw. Service speed 14½ knots. 76 first class passengers.

## Leopoldville (Compagnie Maritime Belge)
See *Albertville*.

*The* Stratheden *on 23 December 1963 on her way to help the liner* Lakonia *which was ablaze about 180 miles north of Madeira.*

Conway Picture Library

*Libertad* (ELMA Lines)
Built by Vickers-Armstrongs Shipbuilders Limited, Barrow-in-Furness, England, 1950. 12,653 gross tons; 530 feet long; 71 feet wide. Steam turbines, twin screw. Service speed 18 knots. 96 first class passengers.

*Louis Lumiere* (Messageries Maritimes)
Built by Chantiers et Ateliers de France, St Nazaire, France, 1952. 12,358 gross tons; 537 feet long; 64 feet wide. Sulzer diesels, twin screw. Service speed 16 knots. 436 passengers (110 first class, 326 third class).

*Melanesien* (Messageries Maritimes)
Built by De Schelde Shipyards, Flushing, Holland, 1925. 9905 gross tons; 507 feet long; 60 feet wide. Sulzer diesels, twin screw. Service speed 15 knots. 180 passengers (100 first class, 80 third class).

*Mocambique* (Companhia Nacional)
12,976 gross tons – otherwise see *Angola*.

*Montserrat* (Spanish Line)
Built by California Shipbuilding Corporation, Los Angeles, California, 1945. 9001 gross tons; 455 feet long; 62 feet wide. Steam turbines, single screw. Service speed 16 knots. 708 tourist class passengers.

*Niassa* (Companhia Nacional)
Built by Cockerill-Ougree Shipyards, Hoboken, Belgium, 1955. 10,742 gross tons; 497 feet long; 64 feet wide. Doxford diesel, single screw. Service speed 16 knots. 306 passengers (22 first class, 284 tourist class).

*Nieuw Holland* (Royal Interocean Lines)
Built by Wilton-Fijenoord Shipyard, Schiedam, Holland, 1958. 13,568 gross tons; 584 feet long; 70 feet wide. M.A.N. diesels, twin screw. Service speed 18 knots. 289 passengers.

*Northern Star* (Shaw Savill Line)
Built by Vickers-Armstrongs Shipbuilders Limited, Newcastle, England, 1962. 24,731 gross tons; 650 feet long; 83 feet wide. Steam turbines, twin screw. Service speed 20 knots. 1437 tourist class passengers.

*Ocean Monarch* (Shaw Savill Line)
Built by Vickers-Armstrongs Shipbuilders Limited, Newcastle-upon-Tyne, England, 1957. 25,971 gross tons; 640 feet long; 85 feet wide. Steam turbines, twin screw. Service speed 20 knots. 1372 one-class passengers.

*Oranje Nassau* (Royal Netherlands Steamship Company)
Built by N V Scheepsbouwerf Gebroeders Pot, Bolnes, Holland, 1957. 7214 gross tons; 432 feet long; 57 feet wide. Stork diesel, single screw. Service speed 15½ knots. 184 one-class passengers.

*Oranjefontein* (Holland-Africa Line)
Built by P Smit Jr, Rotterdam, Holland, 1950. 10,549 gross tons; 527 feet long; 63 feet wide. Burmeister & Wain diesels, twin screw. Service speed 17 knots. 160 passengers (100 first class, 60 tourist class).

*Oranjestad* (Royal Netherlands Steamship Company)
Built by van der Giessen Shipyard, Krimpen, Holland, 1938. 5091 gross tons; 378 feet long; 50 feet wide. Stork diesel, single screw. Service speed 14½ knots. 156 one-class passengers.

*Orcades* (P&O-Orient Lines)
Built by Vickers-Armstrongs Shipbuilders Limited, Barrow-in-Furness, England, 1948. 28,396 gross tons; 709 feet long; 90 feet wide. Steam turbines, twin screw. Service speed 22 knots. 1365 passengers (631 first class, 734 tourist class).

*Oriana* (P&O-Orient Lines)
Built by Vickers-Armstrongs Shipbuilders Limited, Barrow-in-Furness, England, 1960. 41,923 gross tons; 804 feet long; 97 feet wide. Steam turbines, twin screw. Service speed 27½ knots. 2134 passengers (638 first class, 1496 tourist class).

*Orion* (P&O-Orient Lines)
Built by Vickers-Armstrongs Shipbuilders Limited, Barrow-in-Furness, England, 1935. 23,696 gross tons; 665 feet long; 82 feet wide. Steam turbines, twin screw. Service speed 19 knots. 1691 tourist class passengers.

*Oronsay* (P&O-Orient Lines)
Built by Vickers-Armstrongs Shipbuilders Limited, Barrow-in-Furness, England, 1951. 27,632 gross tons; 709 feet long; 90 feet wide. Steam turbines, twin screw. Service speed 22 knots. 1416 passengers (612 first class, 804 tourist class).

*Orontes* (P&O-Orient Lines)
Built by Vickers-Armstrongs Shipbuilders Limited, Barrow-in-Furness, England, 1929. 20,186 gross tons; 664 feet long; 75 feet wide. Steam turbines, twin screw. Service speed 18 knots. 1370 tourist class passengers.

*Orsova* (P&O-Orient Lines)
Built by Vickers-Armstrongs Shipbuilders Limited, Barrow-in-Furness, England, 1954. 28,790 gross tons; 723 feet long; 90 feet wide. Steam turbines, twin screw. Service speed 22 knots. 1503 passengers (694 first class, 809 tourist class).

*Pacifique* (Messageries Maritimes)
Built by Chantiers de la Ciotat, La Ciotat, France, 1952. 13,162 gross tons – otherwise see *Cambodge*.

*Paraguay Star* (Blue Star Line)
see *Argentina Star*.

*Pasteur* (Messageries Maritimes)
Built by Ateliers et Chantiers de Dunkirk et Bordeaux, Dunkirk, France, 1966. 17,986 gross tons; 571 feet long; 78 feet wide. Sulzer diesels, twin screw. Service speed 20 knots. 429 passengers (163 first class, 266 tourist class).

*Patroclus* (Blue Funnel Line)
Built by Vickers-Armstrongs Shipbuilders Limited, Newcastle, England, 1950. 10,109 gross tons; 516 feet long; 68

Conway Picture Library

*In November 1948* Strathnaver, *after war service, arrives at the Harland and Wolff yard in Belfast for reconversion to a passenger ship.*

feet wide. Steam turbines, single screw. Service speed 18½ knots. 30 first class passengers.

*Patria* (Companhia Colonial)
13,196 gross tons – otherwise see *Imperio.*

*Patris* (Chandris Lines)
Built by Harland & Wolff Limited, Belfast, Northern Ireland, 1950. 18,400 gross tons; 595 feet long; 76 feet wide. Burmeister & Wain diesels, twin screw. Service speed 18½ knots. 1036 passengers (36 first class, 1000 tourist class).

*Peleus* (Blue Funnel Line)
Built by Cammell Laird & Company Limited, Birkenhead, England, 1949. 10,093 gross tons; 516 feet long; 68 feet wide. Steam turbines, single screw. Service speed 18½ knots. 30 first class passengers.

*Pendennis Castle* (Union-Castle Line)
Built by Harland & Wolff Limited, Belfast, Northern Ireland, 1958. 28,582 gross tons; 763 feet long; 84 feet wide. Steam turbines, twin screw. Service speed 22 knots. 736 passengers (197 first class, 473 tourist class, 66 interchangeable).

*Perseus* (Blue Funnel Line) – see *Patroclus.*

*Pierre Loti* (Messageries Maritimes)
Built by Brest Naval Dockyard, Brest, France, 1952. 10,945 gross tons – otherwise see *Ferdinand de Lesseps.*

*Pretoria Castle* (Union-Castle Line) – see *Edinburgh Castle.*

*Principe Perfeito* (Companhia Nacional)
Built by Swan, Hunter & Wigham Richardson Limited, Newcastle, England, 1961. 19,393 gross tons; 625 feet long; 79 feet wide. Steam turbines, twin screw. Service speed 20 knots. 1000 passengers (200 first class, 800 tourist class).

*Prins der Nederlanden* (Royal Netherlands Steamship Company)
Built by P Smit Jr, Rotterdam, Holland, 1957. 7221 gross tons; otherwise see *Oranje Nassau.*

*Provence* (Transports Maritimes)
15,719 gross tons – otherwise see *Enrico C.*

*Pyrrhus* (Blue Funnel Line) – see *Peleus.*

*Rajula* (British India Line)
Built by Barclay Curle & Company Limited, Glasgow, Scotland, 1926. 8496 gross tons; 477 feet long; 62 feet wide. Steam turbine expansion engines, twin screw. Service speed 12 knots. 1770 passengers (37 first class, 133 second class, 1600 deck class).

*Randfontein* (Holland-Africa Line) – see *Nieuw Holland.*

*Rangitane* (New Zealand Shipping Company)
Built by John Brown & Company Limited, Clydebank, Scotland, 1949. 21,867 gross tons; 609 feet long; 78 feet wide.

*Conway Picture Library*

*The* Uganda *in July 1952 having just completed her trials in readiness for the British India Company's East African service.*

Doxford diesels, twin screw. Service speed 16½ knots. 436 one-class passengers.

**Rangitoto** (New Zealand Shipping Company)
Built by Vickers-Armstrongs Shipbuilders Limited, Newcastle, England, 1949. 21,809 gross tons; otherwise see *Rangitane.*

**Remuera** (New Zealand Shipping Company)
Built by Harland & Wolff Limited, Belfast, Northern Ireland, 1948. 13,619 gross tons; 531 feet long; 70 feet wide. Steam turbines, twin screw. Service speed 18 knots. 350 one-class passengers.

**Rhodesia Castle** (Union-Castle Line) – see *Braemar Castle.*

**Rio de la Plata** (Argentine State Line)
Built by the Ansaldo Shipyard, Genoa, Italy, 1950. 11,317 gross tons; 550 feet long; 66 feet wide. Fiat diesels, twin screw. Service speed 18 knots. 116 first class.

**Rio Jachal** (Argentine State Line) – see *Rio de la Plata.*

**Rio Tunuyan** (Argentine State Line) – see *Rio de la Plata*

**Rossini** (Italian Line)
13,225 gross tons – otherwise see *Donizetti.*

**Ruahine** (New Zealand Shipping Company)
Built by John Brown & Company Limited, Clydebank, Scotland, 1951. 17,851 gross tons; 584 feet long; 75 feet wide.

Doxford diesels, twin screw. Service speed 16½ knots. 267 one-class passengers.

**Ruys** (Royal Interocean Lines)
Built by by De Schelde Shipyards, Flushing, Holland, 1937. 14,304 gross tons – otherwise see *Boissevain.*

**S. A. Oranje** (Union-Castle Line) – see *Pretoria Castle.*

**S. A. Vaal** (Union-Castle Line)
Built by John Brown & Company Limited, Clydebank, Scotland, 1961. 32,697 gross tons; 760 feet long; 90 feet wide. Steam turbines, twin screw. Service speed 22½ knots. 763 'hotel class' passengers.

**St Helena** (Curnow Shipping Limited)
Built by Burrard Drydock Comany, Vancouver, British Columbia, Canada, 1963. 3150 gross tons; 321 feet long, 46 feet wide. Diesel, single screw. Service speed 16½ knots. 88 one-class passengers.

**Sangola** (British India Line)
Built by Barclay Curle & Company Limited, Glasgow, Scotland, 1947. 8647 gross tons; 479 feet long; 63 feet wide. Doxford diesels, twin screw. Service speed 14½ knots. 1415 passengers (21 first class, 34 second class A, 30 second class B, 335 bunked class, 995 deck class).

**Santhia** (British India Line)
Built by Barclay Curle & Company Limited, Glasgow, Scotland, 1950. 8908 gross tons; 479 feet long; 63 feet wide. Doxford diesels, twin screw. Service speed 14½ knots. 1193 passengers (25 first class, 70 second class, 68 intermediate, 268 bunked class, 762 deck class).

**Schwabenstein** (North German Lloyd)
8955 gross tons – otherwise see *Bayernstein.*

**Sirdhana** (British India Line)
Built by Swan, Hunter & Wigham Richardson Limited,

Newcastle-upon-Tyne, England, 1947. 8608 gross tons; 479 feet long; 63 feet wide. Doxford diesels, twin screw. Service speed 14½ knots. 1403 passengers (21 first class, 32 second class A, 30 second class B, 333 bunked class, 987 deck class).

## Southern Cross (Shaw Savill Line)

Built by Harland & Wolff Limited, Belfast, Northern Ireland, 1955. 20,204 gross tons; 604 feet long; 78 feet wide. Steam turbines, twin screw. Service speed 20 knots. 1100 tourist class passengers.

## Stirling Castle (Union-Castle Line)

25,554 gross tons – otherwise see *Athlone Castle.*

## Straat Banka (Royal Interocean Lines)

Built by P Smit Jr, Rotterdam, Holland, 1952. 9138 gross tons; 472 feet long; 64 feet wide. B&W diesel, single screw. Service speed 16 knots. 46 first class passengers.

## Strathaird (P&O-Orient Lines)

Built by Vickers-Armstrongs Shipbuilders Limited, Barrow-in-Furness, England, 1932. 22,568 gross tons; 664 feet long; 80 feet wide. Steam turbo-electric, twin screw. Service speed 17½ knots. 1242 tourist class passengers.

## Stratheden (P&O-Orient Lines)

Built by Vickers-Armstrongs Shipbuilders Limited, Barrow-in-Furness, England, 1937. 23,372 gross tons; 664 feet long; 82 feet wide. Steam turbines, twin screw. Service speed 19 knots. 1200 all-tourist class passengers.

## Strathmore (P&O-Orient Lines)

Built by Vickers-Armstrongs Shipbuilders Limited, Barrow-in-Furness, England, 1935. 23,580 gross tons; 665 feet long; 82 feet wide. Steam turbines, twin screw. Service speed 19 knots. 1080 tourist class passengers.

## Strathnaver (P&O-Orient Lines)

Built by Vickers-Armstrongs Shipbuilders Limited, Barrow-in-Furness, England, 1931. 22,270 gross tons; 664 feet long; 80 feet wide. Steam turbo-electric, twin screw. Service speed 17½ knots. 1,252 tourist class passengers.

## Tahitien (Messageries Maritimes)

Built by the Brest Naval Dockyard, Brest, France, 1953. 12,614 gross tons – otherwise see *Caledonien.*

## Tegelberg (Royal Interocean Lines)

Built by Netherlands Shipbuilding Company, Amsterdam, Holland, 1937. 14,300 gross tons – otherwise see *Boissevain.*

## Thysville (Compagnie Maritime Belge)

10,946 gross tons – otherwise see *Albertville.*

## Tjiluwah (Royal Interocean Lines)

Built by the van der Giessen Shipyard, Krimpen, Holland, 1951. 8679 gross tons; 479 feet long; 63 feet wide. Werkspor diesels, twin screw. Service speed 16 knots. 222 passengers (104 first class, 118 tourist class).

## Tjinegara (Royal Interocean Lines)

9067 gross tons – otherwise see *Straat Banka.*

## Tjitjalengka (Royal Interocean Lines)

Built by Netherlands Shipbuilding Company, Amsterdam, Holland, 1939. 10,972 gross tons; 476 feet long; 65 feet wide. Stork diesel, single screw. Service speed 14 knots. 629 passengers in several classes.

*One of the Blue Star Line's postwar quartet of ships, the* Uruguay Star, *shown in June 1948 soon after her completion.*

*Tjiwangi* (Royal Interocean Lines)
8765 gross tons – otherwise see *Tjiluwah*.

*Transvaal Castle* (Union-Castle Line) – see *S. A. Vaal*.

*Uganda* (British India Line)
Built by Barclay Curle & Company Limited, Glasgow,
Scotland, 1952. 14,430 gross tons; 540 feet long; 71 feet wide.
Steam turbines, twin screw. Service speed 16 knots. 300
passengers (167 first class, 133 tourist class).

*Uige* (Companhia Colonial)
Built by John Cockerill S/A, Hoboken, Belgium, 1955.
10,001 gross tons; 477 feet long; 63 feet wide. Burmeister &
Wain diesel, single screw. Service speed 16 knots. 571
passengers (78 first class, 493 third class).

*Uruguay* (ELMA Lines)
12,627 gross tons – otherwise see *Libertad*.

*Uruguay Star* (Blue Star Line)
10,722 gross tons – otherwise see *Argentina Star*.

*Vera Cruz* (Companhia Colonial)
Built by John Cockerill S/A, Hoboken, Belgium, 1952.
21,765 gross tons; 610 feet long; 76 feet wide. Steam turbines,
twin screw. Service speed 20 knots. 1296 passengers (150 first
class, 250 cabin class, 232 third class, 664 dormitory third
class).

*Verdi* (Italian Line) – see *Donizetti*.

*Victoria* (Lloyd Triestino)
11,695 gross tons – otherwise see *Asia*.

*Viet-Nam* (Messageries Maritimes)
13,162 gross tons – otherwise see *Cambodge*.

*Warwickshire* (Bibby Line)
8917 gross tons – otherwise see *Leicestershire*.

*Willemstad* (Royal Netherlands Steamship Company)
5088 gross tons – otherwise see *Oranjestad*.

*Winchester Castle* (Union-Castle Line)
Built by Harland & Wolff Limited, Belfast, Northern Ireland,
1930. 20,001 gross tons; 657 feet long; 75 feet wide.
Burweister & Wain diesels, twin screw. Service speed 20
knots. 587 passengers (189 first class, 398 tourist class).

*Windsor Castle* (Union-Castle Line)
Built by Cammell Laird & Company Limited, Birkenhead,
England, 1960. 37,640 gross tons; 783 feet long; 92 feet wide.
Steam turbines, twin screw. Service speed 23 knots. 822
passengers (237 first class, 585 tourist class).

*Worcestershire* (Bibby Line)
Built by Fairfield Shipbuilding & Engineering Company,
Glasgow, Scotland, 1931. 10,329 gross tons; 501 feet long; 64
feet wide. Sulzer diesels, twin screw. Service speed 14½
knots. 115 first class passengers.

*A stern view of Messageries Maritimes'* Viet-Nam. *She
was one of the all-white trio built for the colonial
Indo-Chinese service.*

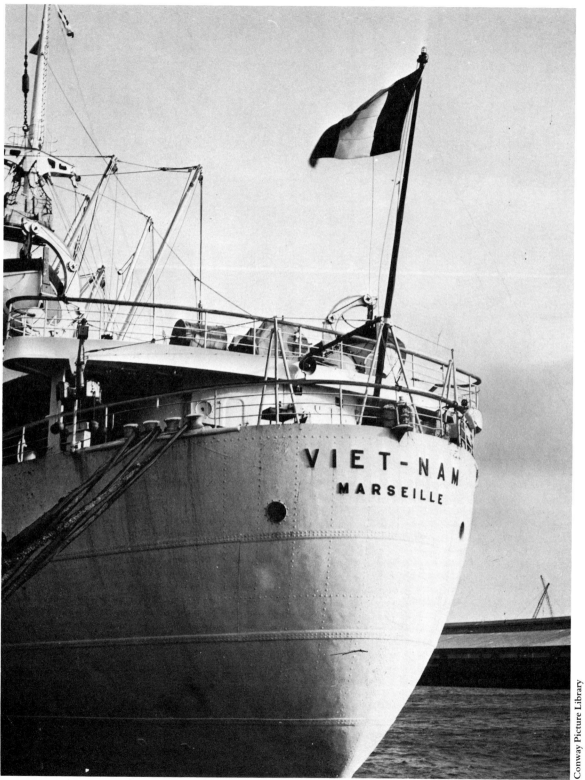

# BIBLIOGRAPHY

Crowdy, Michael (editor). *Marine News* (1964–85). Kendal, Cumbria: World Ship Society.

Dunn, Laurence. *Passenger Liners*. Southampton: Adlard Coles Ltd, 1961.

Dunn, Laurence. *Passenger Liners* (revised edition). Southampton: Adlard Coles Ltd, 1965.

Eisele, Peter (editor). *Steamboat Bill* (Journal, 1966–85). New York: Steamship Historical Society of America Inc.

Kludas, Arnold. *Great Passenger Ships of the World, Volumes 1–5*. Cambridge: Patrick Stephens Ltd, 1972–76.

Kludas, Arnold. *The Great Passenger Ships & Cruise Liners of the World*. Herford, West Germany: Koehlers Verlagsgesellschaft MBH, 1983.

Mitchell, W.H. & Sawyer, L.A. *The Cape Run*. Lavenham, Suffolk: Terence Dalton Ltd, 1984.

Morris, Charles F. *Origins, Orient & Oriana*. New York: McCartan & Root, 1980.

Padfield, Peter. *Beneath the Houseflag of the P&O*. London: Hutchinson & Co Ltd, 1981.

Sawyer, L.A. & Mitchell, W.H. *From America to United States*, Volumes 1–3. Kendal, Cumbria: World Ship Society, 1979–1984.

Williams, David L. & de Kerbrech, Richard P. *Damned by Destiny*. Brighton, Sussex: Teredo Books Ltd, 1982.

# INDEX

Entries in *italics* refer to illustrations